Educational Policy
and National Character

Educational Policy and National Character

Africa, Japan, the United States, and the Soviet Union

Dickson A. Mungazi

Westport, Connecticut
London

Library of Congress Cataloging-in-Publication Data

Mungazi, Dickson A.
    Educational policy and national character : Africa, Japan, the
United States, and the Soviet Union / Dickson A. Mungazi.
        p. cm.
    Includes bibliographical references and index.
    ISBN 0-275-94423-9 (alk. paper)
    1. Education—Aims and objectives—Cross-cultural studies.
2. Education and state—Cross-cultural studies. 3. Education—
Social aspects—Cross-cultural studies. 4. History—Study and
teaching—Cross-cultural studies.   I. Title.
LB41.M967 1993
379—dc20   92-31842

British Library Cataloguing in Publication Data is available.

Library of Congress Catalog Card Number: 92-31842
ISBN: 0-275-94423-9

First published in 1993

Praeger Publishers, 88 Post Road West, Westport, CT 06881
An imprint of Greenwood Publishing Group, Inc.

Printed in the United States of America

The paper used in this book complies with the
Permanent Paper Standard issued by the National
Information Standards Organization (Z39.48-1984).

10 9 8 7 6 5 4 3 2 1

To Buddy and Marcia Aalbers, friends,
humanitarians, and ambassadors of goodwill
whose lives have been a blessing to many

Enlighten the people and the tyranny and oppression of both body and mind will vanish like evil spirits at the dawn of day.

Thomas Jefferson, 1816

Without education as the chief spiritual mainstay of our existence democracy cannot be firmly established.

Mikhail Gorbachev, 1989

Contents

Preface

THE PURPOSE OF THE STUDY

The purpose of this book is to take an integrated approach to a comparative study of the problems of education in Africa, Japan, the United States, and the former Soviet Union. The Soviet Union was selected to represent socialist systems, the United States to represent Western democracies, Africa to represent Third World nations, and Japan to represent emerging nations. The assumption is that a detailed study of these four will give the reader a clear picture of the problems of education in the world. The fact that as of January 1992, the Soviet Union no longer existed as a nation as it had since 1917 offers a unique opportunity to discuss the main characteristics of its education as a major component of its national character compared to the other three examples.

In this approach the book focuses on seven specific areas of critical importance. These are: the condition of education in the world at the conclusion of the Second World War in 1945; the importance of history; theoretical considerations; educational objectives and how their implementation determines the character of education and their effectiveness to serve national purpose; the curriculum; administrative structures; and current problems.

THE APPROACH

The study begins by examining some reasons why there has been a global crisis in education. This examination suggests reasons why, at the conclusion of the Second World War several nations made a concerted effort to collectively diagnose the causes of the outbreak of the war in 1939 and to set an agenda to avoid such conflict in the future. In this regard, the San Francisco conference, at which the UN was inaugurated, played a critical role. The action that the San Francisco conference took, the objectives it set, and their results are discussed in this study.

The study then goes on to discuss the influence of history on contemporary educational settings and why it is important to have a functional knowledge of the past; to both understand the present and plan the future. It then discusses the importance of theory as the basis for effective education. The problems that education is facing in the four examples are discussed in the context of a response to theory. Some essential theoretical considerations that may make or break education are also presented.

The relationship that exists between society and the individual is the primary focus of education as a product of putting theory into practice. That the former Soviet Union, as the chief spokesman of the socialist ideology, and the United States, as the principal spokesman of the capitalist ideology, differ on this relationship presents an interesting perspective from which to discuss a theory of education.

The study then discusses educational objectives as an outcome of theory. This section first examines how objectives determine the character of education and then discusses the curriculum as an instrument of fulfilling objectives and national purpose. How the curriculum is designed in the countries selected for this study provides a fascinating account of how the nations see themselves in relation to global events.

In using the need for a curriculum to suggest the need for an administrative system of education, the study outlines differences and similarities to determine why the educational systems are what they are. Here the study concludes that the administrative system of education is the vehicle of the educational system itself. It concludes that without an effective system of administration, the educational system becomes a haphazard operation even though it is based on good theory, objectives, and the curriculum. This section presents some suggestions on what it takes to have an effective administrative system.

Finally, the study discusses some problems that all nations encounter in their educational system. No nation is immune to problems. How nations attempt to resolve these problems provides a fascinating account of the struggle for survival. It shows that these problems are detractors from the educational process and that unless they are resolved education will continue to deteriorate and will have a profoundly adverse effect on national endeavors.

SUMMARY, CONCLUSIONS, AND IMPLICATIONS

The last chapter presents summaries of the preceding main features and arguments. It also draws some conclusions and discusses some implications. Some of these conclusions are the following: (1) all four examples are experiencing some serious problems, ranging from an increase in illiteracy to the lack of financial resources, from violence in schools to contradictions between rural and urban schools; (2) the Soviet Union under Mikhail Gorbachev initiated a radical approach to efforts to reform its education under *glasnost* and *perestroika* to reform society itself;

(3) in its efforts to maintain technological superiority in a competitive world, Japan has strengthened its system of examinations to the detriment of the real educational interests of the students; (4) African nations have found the problems of educational innovation so difficult that they have stopped trying; the demand in 1990 by the African masses for political and educational reform underscores the seriousness of the problems; (5) the educational reform package announced by President George Bush in April 1991 received mixed response because many thought it fell short of providing a clear direction for development. This contributed to his defeat by Governor Bill Clinton in the Presidential election held on November 3, 1992.

Unless these nations make new and concerted efforts to find solutions to the problems, the deterioration in education will have a negative effect on the societies themselves. This grim reality was recognized in 1983 by the U. S. National Commission on Excellence in Education. To find solutions to these problems, nations need to remember that no nation has sufficient resources to go it alone; they need to coordinate their efforts and to cooperate because these problems have global implications. Nations can overcome their ideological differences and the impact of their different levels of development to find a common ground on which to cooperate in launching a new *safari* to educational development as a means to national development and international peace.

Acknowledgments

In the process of writing a book that covers several critical areas of three nations and the whole of Africa, one must rely on the materials supplied by the countries concerned, as well as, of course, on other sources. For this reason, the author wishes to thank the embassies of the former Soviet Union, Japan, and several countries of Africa in Washington, D. C., for sending the materials he requested and needed to produce this study.

The author also wishes to thank several colleagues at Northern Arizona University for the support and encouragement they have given him. Among these are Robert Holloway, Linda Shadiow, Sam Minner, Margaret Hatcher, Ardeth Cropper, and David Williams. He is also grateful to members of the National Social Science Association, the Association of Third World Studies, and the Comparative and International Studies Society for the encouragement given while he was presenting papers at professional conferences from 1986 to 1991. The idea of this manuscript came from those papers.

The author also thanks Betty Russell, Ed Belunski, Susan Antonucci, and Jeanette Weatherby in the Center for Excellence in Education at Northern Arizona University for programming the computer to produce the manuscript more efficiently. Special gratitude goes to Jill Talley, Jennifer Covert, Deborah Vandivort, Amanda Coy, Marcella Olivera, Binny Patel, Tammy Thieme, Tammy Albin and Becky Steed, all students in the Faculty Services Office in the Center for Excellence in Education, for sharing the responsibility of typing parts of the manuscript; to Carla Duran, also of Northern Arizona University, typographer, and to Linda Gregonis, indexer, and Candace Baker, proofreader. The author wishes to express his special gratitude to Dr. Eugene M. Hughes, President of Northern Arizona University, and Dr. Patsy B. Reed, Vice-President for Academic Affairs, also at Northern Arizona University, for their constant support and encouragement.

Finally, the author wishes to thank the members of his family--wife, Della, daughter Marcia; and sons, Alan and Gaylord--for their support and encouragement, without which the study would not have been completed.

Introduction

THE PURPOSE OF THE STUDY

The signing of the nuclear arms reduction treaty by President George Bush of the United States and President Mikhail Gorbachev of the Soviet Union in Moscow on July 31, 1991, ushered in a new era of relationships between the two superpowers and members of the international community. This event suggested the changing character of relationships between and among nations. The purpose of this study is to discuss the role that education plays in shaping the character of three nations--Japan, the United States, and, until January 1992, the Soviet Union--and Africa without focusing on a specific country in order to allow a complete discussion of the extent of the continent's problems.

The approach made in this study is quite different from the conventional approach to comparative educational studies in some important respects. Instead of discussing education in each country by itself, this study attempts an integrated approach in which specific educational features in the four selected examples are discussed in the same chapter in a comparative manner. This approach enables the author to develop a coherent argument and enables the reader to see and follow the critical nature of the influence of education on national development.

The fact that in 1992 the Soviet Union, as it had been known since the Bolshevik Revolution of 1917, went out of existence and was substituted by the federation of independent republics, does not negate the reality that for seven decades the country operated under a socialist system. This study helps put the major developments that took place during that time into the context of their significance to the dramatic events that began to unfold in 1990.

RATIONALE AND ORGANIZATION

The four areas were selected for this study for an important reason. The development of the world falls into four basic categories: Western democracies, socialist nations, emerging nations, and Third World nations. In this study, therefore, Africa represents Third World nations, Japan represents emerging nations, the United States represents Western democracies, and the former Soviet Union represents socialist nations. A discussion of these four areas will give the reader a clear picture of the problems the world is facing.

Because, since the end of the Second World War, each of these areas has been facing enormous problems in its education, a question must be asked: Are there some things that each could learn from the other three to find solutions to the problems of its own education and national development? This is the question the reader is invited to answer.

The attempted coup in the Soviet Union August 19 - 21, 1991, and its implications are discussed in Chapter 8. The economic decline in all four areas had reached alarming proportions by 1992 and cast a long shadow of doubt on the ability of political leaders to shape the future character of their countries. Moving away from the conventional approach of discussing problems of education in a specific country in Africa, the study makes a continental approach in order to see the role of education on the problems of national development in Africa from their proper perspective.

Indeed, the world of 1991 and 1992 was experiencing enormous problems that seemed to defy solution. The rapidly increasing population-- estimated at 5.3 billion people with an annual growth rate of 1.8 percent. and with per capita income of $3,470--has compounded the problems of poverty and declining resources. The inability of nations to find solutions to national and international conflict has accentuated the age-old myth that military power ensures national security.

This is the reason national priorities have been influenced by huge military spending that has robbed the people of their legitimate access to national resources to ensure the best form of national development and security. The end of the cold war means that national priorities have to be set. That, by the beginning of 1992, this had not been done created an international climate that raised questions about the nature of relationships among nations.

THE ILLUSION OF MILITARY POWER

There are two disturbing aspects of military power as the ultimate cause of the illusion of national security. The first is that it gives politicians a false sense of security and an intransigence that makes them arrogant and refuse to see issues of international relationships from their proper perspective. The world witnessed this tragedy in the crisis in the Persian Gulf caused by Iraq's invasion of Kuwait on August 2, 1990. The level of destruction that is always evident in wars does not seem to influence the thinking or the action of national leaders; all they think of is the political gain they make in pursuit of their own political agenda and purpose.

Quite often, as the world saw in 1991 when hostilities mounted between Iraq and the Western coalition forces, national leaders whose own political positions were weak took advantage of the conflict to improve their standing with the people. In this way an opportunity is lost to put in place elements that are needed to find genuine solutions to the problems of international conflict.

To achieve their own political objectives, many national leaders deny their people the opportunity to utilize national resources to ensure development. Instead, they use resources to bolster their own political positions. For example, in the United States, it was widely reported in 1991 that the White House Chief of Staff, John Sununu, had used tax payers' money to make frequent trips of a personal nature. This is not to suggest that there was wrongdoing in this practice, but to indicate that public officials are constantly faced with the problem of trust when it comes to using national resources.

It really does not make any difference whether national leaders are democratically elected or whether they impose themselves on their people their political behavior is quite often identical. They claim that the pursuit of military objectives is in the national interest. They portray the party with whom they are in conflict as the aggressor. They convince the military establishment that theirs is a mission to save the world, or, as President Woodrow Wilson of the U.S. put it in 1917, their objective is to make the world safe for democracy.

While the action taken by the UN on December 3, 1992, to send a multinational military force to Somalia to enable relief agents to distribute food to the starving masses seems plausible, it must be recognized that it also carried a serious potential for greater conflict than was acknowledged. The UN did not consider the question of what would happen to Somalia if the force left before solutions to political problems were found. This suggests that the UN's efforts would have been better directed in bringing much needed education to the parties in conflict and the country as a whole.

If the UN wanted to help Somalia, then it should have given it the educational assistance it desperately needed when it was struggling for development. The action also shows the ultimate illusion of using the military to resolve political and socioeconomic problems. Further, if the UN wants to adopt this strategy of dealing with national and international problems, then it must be consistently applied in all cases, such as seeking an end to the tragedy of the civil conflict in the former Yugoslavia and the continuing oppression of apartheid in South Africa.

One must regret the military action taken on January 13, 1993, by Western coalition forces against Iraq for what President Bush said was "Saddam Hussein's failure to comply with the UN resolution forbidding his forces to violate the no-fly zone" which was imposed in southern Iraq following the conclusion of hostilities that broke out two years earlier. One is led to the conclusion that in this action the Western leaders who were part of the coalition against Iraq neglected some important considerations; among them that military action often robs leaders of the ability to utilize human reason to resolve conflict. How did the coalition forces hope to create a climate of peace through dialogue under conditions that made Iraq an occupied country?

EDUCATION AND THE ESSENCE OF POLITICAL BEHAVIOR

The fact of the matter is that whether or not national leaders are democratically elected, they institute legislation and take action as instruments for carrying out their own political agenda. The sad part of all this is that the people often regard national leaders who take them into war as heroes. This is why President Bush's popularity rose sharply at the conclusion of hostilities in the Persian Gulf in 1991. The people tend to believe anything their national leader says and give him the support he says he needs to carry out a national policy he claims to be in the interest of the people.

Any action that may question the policy of such a leader is considered unpatriotic. These are characteristic features found in all national leaders but they do not contribute positively to national purpose. In January 1992, for instance, the economy of the United States was weakened by a combination of powerful factors that included the aftermath of the war in the Persian Gulf. This contributed to President Bush's defeat by Bill Clinton, his Democratic opponent, in the elections held on November 3, 1992.

The second disturbing aspect of the illusion of military power is that because national leaders are not able to see their own errors, they operate on the assumption that the party with which they are in conflict is always wrong and that they are always right. This is the environment in which President Saddam Hussein convinced his followers to see President George Bush as the ultimate threat to the world of Islam. This is also the same environment that President Bush utilized to convince his fellow Americans to believe that Hussein was the embodiment of Moslem extremism that must be stopped to deny him an opportunity to become another Adolf Hitler.

The frequent use of such terms as "the Great Satan" and "the Infidel" to characterize Western leadership, "the brutal dictator" to characterize Saddam Hussein, and "the evil empire" to characterize the Soviet Union contributed nothing to the creation of a climate of real knowledge of the issues that caused conflict between nations and the need to initiate dialogue to resolve problems. To refrain from using extreme language would have enabled the parties to understand and appreciate the concerns of the other. The process of understanding and appreciation requires education. Indeed, the conflict in the Persian Gulf underscores the importance of education for leaders to understand the essence and the art of diplomacy.

Another critical factor that stood in the way of seeking a peaceful resolution to the crisis in the Persian Gulf was the enormous ego manifested in the attitudes and actions of both President Hussein and President Bush. This problem was caused primarily by previous international events whose impact they sought to turn into an advantage. On the one hand, having come out of the six-year war with Iran, Hussein, seeking to fill the regional leadership void left by the death of Anwar Sadat, wanted to assert himself as the undisputed leader of the Arab world. On the other hand, the United States having endured the humiliation of the war in Vietnam and the tragic drama of the hostages held in Iran and Lebanon in 1979, Bush sought to assert his own country's leadership role in the Western world.

Indeed, the personality of both men left no room for dialogue or accommodation. Instead, they acted in ways that accentuated rhetoric that was partly carried out by the media. This is why, at the conclusion of the war with Iraq in 1991, Bush proudly proclaimed that the Vietnam syndrome was finally over, suggesting that he used the war with Iraq to eliminate the residual effect of the demise the United States had endured in that conflict.

President Bush's proudest moment was his claim that the Patriot missiles had elevated the American spirit to a new level of national pride and self-confidence. He appeared to neglect the importance of developing the ability to reason things out, rather than to utilize military power to seek solutions to international problems. Indeed, it is quite clear that both men needed a new level of education to help them understand that humility and self-restraint are distinct qualities of national leaders and that they do not diminish the power of leadership and the office they hold simply because they seek to understand the concerns of their potential adversary as a condition of dialogue. This suggests that education is the essence of political behavior and action. To neglect its development in favor of building the military is to undercut the very essence of national endeavors.

THE ROLE OF EDUCATION IN A CONTEMPORARY WORLD SETTING

The situation discussed above is a reality that delegates in San Francisco took into account in their deliberations. But by 1992 too many leaders had already forgotten this basic principle. The world of 1991 showed much that could be related to events of earlier times. The change of leadership in Britain from Margaret Thatcher to John Major, the continuing saga of apartheid in South Africa, the conflict between Mikhail Gorbachev and the Baltic states, the political crisis in eastern European countries, and the end of the Soviet Union--all were manifestations of conditions that could easily lead to a major global conflict unless nations learn what they must to bring about a lasting peace.

The sad part of the tragedy in the Persian Gulf is that in this kind of environment the real causes of the conflict were not addressed. On the one hand, Hussein, claiming to be the guardian of the Palestinian cause, wanted linkage to that cause interpreted in his invasion of Kuwait. On the other hand Bush, believing that he was the guardian of Western democratic values, rejected the idea of linkage and argued that the invasion was nothing less than naked aggression that must not be allowed to stand.

Failure to resolve this difference through dialogue is what caused the war in the Persian Gulf in 1991. Must one assume that differences of opinion on issues of international relationships and human existence could be resolved only by military means and not by applying reason? It would be a sad day for the international community to be forced to accept such thinking. Yet, in 1991 this kind of thinking became the norm of international relationships when the UN itself voted to authorize military use to force Iraq out of Kuwait. Then, on January 12, the U.S. Senate voted 52 to 49 and the House of Representatives 250 to 183 to authorize President Bush to use military means to force Iraq out of Kuwait. While this action yielded considerable political support, it had its dark side, a lingering and devastating effect that would last for years. Victorious in military action, the United States entered a new phase of economic decline that forced Bush to undertake a mission to Japan in January 1992 in an effort to revive the economy.

In examining the role that education must play in helping nations seek an improvement in the human condition and international relations, one must remind oneself of the diagnostic approach that the world community made at the conclusion of the war in 1945. This is the place and time that this study begins. Painful as this exercise was, the delegates to the San Francisco conference concluded that rather than blame the Axis powers for causing the war, all nations must share the responsibility for its outbreak. If they had come to this conclusion in 1939, the war would have been avoided in the first place. And if nations had come to this realization in 1991, the devastation caused by the war in the Persian Gulf would have been avoided and the billions of dollars used to wage the war could have been directed toward the much needed social services that not all countries have been able to extend to their people.

Neither the U.S. Senate nor the House of Representatives predicted the setting on fire of oil fields in Kuwait and the displacement of the Kurds as outcomes of the war. If the restoration of Kuwait was accomplished at the price of the displacement of the Kurds and the destruction of natural recourses in Kuwait, then one must conclude that the victory that allied coalition forces thought they scored against Saddam Hussein must be considered a disaster. This means that using military means to force Iraq out of Kuwait had a much darker side in form of human cost that could not be measured.

There is another cost to this tragedy: prospects for peace in the Middle East, which Western nations thought would become possible with the defeat of Iraq, have remained as distant as ever. The shuttle diplomacy that Secretary of State James Baker initiated at the conclusion of hostilities did not yield any tangible results. Indeed, Baker's efforts amounted to a reincarnation of Henry Kissinger's shuttle diplomacy but with its weak side. As the Presidential campaign got underway in August 1992, President Bush removed Baker from the State Department and appointed him manager of his reelection efforts. This created more doubt than confidence in the minds of Americans about his ability to design a good foreign policy.

The fears that Israel and its Arab neighbors had about the intention of one other even intensified as both sides hardened their respective positions, refusing to see the critical issues they faced from the other's perspective. With Baker out of the negotiations the crisis in the Middle East took a dramatic turn for the worse. As of January 20, 1993, President Bill Clinton inherited from the Bush administration a critical foreign issue complicated by Israel's decision to expel a hundred Palestinians from occupied land in December 1992. The continuing crisis between Saddam Hussein and George Bush added a perilous twist to an already difficult situation.

THE CONSEQUENCES OF MILITARY ACTION

There is yet another disturbing aspect of the war in the Persian Gulf that the Western forces had not anticipated. As it progressed and allied forces were reported to be within striking distance of victory, social and economic conditions in the United States began to deteriorate rapidly. In his PBS television program on June 2, 1991, Bill Moyers gave the following facts as an outcome of the war: Nearly a million Americans were lining up for welfare benefits that were not there. The recession was having a devastating impact on education as nearly 54 percent of the programs were being cut. Hospital care and other services were being reduced. The scourge of homelessness was rapidly increasing and the plight of the less fortunate was deteriorating. In New Jersey the Office of Social Services was advising those 55 years and older to seek economic and financial help from their children in order to survive.

Many American servicemen returned home from the Gulf to find their families in a state of economic ruin. Some experienced family trauma that they had not anticipated, such as divorce. Even conservative journalist George Will argued in June 1991 that the war with Iraq had left behind "broken homes, broken hopes, and broken hearts" in both Iraq and the United States. Tom Foley, the Speaker of the U.S. House of Representatives, added on June 16 that the preoccupation with the war in the Persian Gulf had created an array of problems at home that the nation was now finding hard to resolve. On August 2, ABC published the results of a poll that indicated that those Americans who had supported going to war with Iraq now questioned the decision to do so by a margin of 54 to 46 percent. While this was happening, controversy between the president and the Democrats in Congress over the civil rights bill of 1991 was having a paralyzing effect on the political process.

Can one conclude that all these adverse effects justified going to war with Iraq over Kuwait? Why was it not possible to utilize human reason to resolve the problem of Iraq's invasion of Kuwait? Yes, the Bush administration argued that it had tried to resolve the problem through dialogue, but the conditions Bush specified for such dialogue undercut the very essence of its universal meaning.

This is the reason why on May 16, 1991, Baker returned to the United States to report to President Bush that he had accomplished nothing with his shuttle diplomacy. On May 18, during a television broadcast, Bruce Morton of CBS concluded that the comprehensive peace that the United States had hoped would result from the defeat of Iraq remained as distant as ever, and suggested that what may be needed to find solutions to the problems of the Middle East was a new strategy --education.

The tragedy in the Middle East shows that there is always a price to pay for conflict as long as nations refuse to learn about the concerns of other nations and as long as they see issues exclusively from their own point of view. To reach this realization and alter their thought processes all nations require an education that creates a climate of understanding so that problems can be resolved. The truth of the matter is that conflict exists in human existence only because people do not know what it takes to avoid it. In May 1991 Bush came close to recognizing this reality when he addressed another unexpected fallout of the war with Iraq.

Speaking to the graduating class of the U.S. Air Force Academy on May 24, 1991, President Bush decried what he saw as the proliferation of weapons of massive destruction in the Middle East, and indicated that his administration would do everything in its power to stop it. However, Bush's decision to continue supplying weapons to what he called "our friends in the Middle East" manifested a classic example of the kind of behavior that has always been one of the major causes of conflict between nations. He failed to emphasize the importance of understanding and dialogue as principal pillars that sustain the edifice of lasting international peace.

The sad part of this unfortunate development is that neither Bush nor any other world leader could do anything to stop it. Although Bush outlined his plan to eliminate weapons of massive destruction in the Middle East, he fell short of explaining the need to initiate an international approach to the development of an educational system as a strategy to enable all people to understand the importance of the mutuality of trust through utilization of knowledge. In stating,"We are committed to stopping the proliferation of weapons of massive destruction in the Middle East," Bush neglected to put all relevant aspects into proper perspective.

The tragic death of Rajiv Gandhi in May 1991 demonstrates the equally tragic outcome of resorting to violence or military action to resolve human and international problems. Bush must have been frightened by the extent of the destruction he saw during the war with Iraq, and he must have pondered what the future held if nations did nothing to learn to resolve problems through dialogue.

THE RELEVANCE OF EDUCATION
TO THE HUMAN CONDITION

The knowledge that before the war in 1939 educational opportunity was a privilege of a few individuals, the reality that economic development was not possible without adequate education, the reality that poverty and urban decay were a product of the Industrial Revolution, the knowledge that political and economic power was an inherited right of a few--all these factors combined to create an international climate that, by 1939, made conflict on a global scale inevitable.

In 1992 this conflict took a perilous twist when a multinational military force was sent to Somalia to protect UN agents who were distributing food to starving masses. It did not occur to the UN that the best course of action would have been to help Somalians develop an educational system that would have helped them achieve a national character compatible with their aspirations.

The balanced and objective approach the delegates to the San Francisco conference took to seek solutions for the world was also evident in other areas of their endeavors. They concluded that the environment of conflict was created because people of the world did not know each other and because they were not sufficiently educated to understand the causes of human conflict. That they placed the responsibility for this situation squarely on the shoulders of national leaders substantiates the conclusion that leaders design policies that, while seeming to serve the interests of their nations, actually serve their own political interests.

However, one must not negate the reality that the delegates to the San Francisco conference took into account in concluding that educational development was the best means of resolving conflict, both international and national. As it lay in ruins, Japan realized in 1945 that before the war it had had a fully developed industry which it gambled away in military adventure. Now, it was time to start all over again.

In this context it is interesting to note that the delegates to the San Francisco conference saw a definite relationship between the effort to create ideal national conditions and international peace and security. They readily recognized that when people of any nation had the right to education, economic security, political participation, and basic civil liberties that include freedom of speech, self-expression, and association, they provide a stable environment that eliminates national conflict. This environment translates into the creation of one of international peace and security. The delegates emphasized that the journey to this international destination must begin with a single educational step and underscored their belief in the value of education as a relevant factor of the human condition.

In spite of the enthusiasm of the delegates to the San Francisco conference to utilize education to create a brave new world order in which the position of the individual would supersede the political interests of the national leaders, there were enormous problems that they did not anticipate. The rapid increase in population translated into a rapid increase in school enrollment. The poor facilities then in existence combined with poor resources to limit the effectiveness of the new thrust in seeking improvement in education.

The new level of enthusiasm among parents to provide their children with an opportunity for education as a preparation for the future accentuated the hope among the dispossessed that the route to a better future lay in their pursuit of education. Decline in economic programs also combined with rising inflation and declining national resources to severely impinge on the efforts nations were making individually and collectively to plan a future different from the past.

CREATING A BRAVE NEW WORLD: SETTING NEW OBJECTIVES

In spite of recognizing these problems, the delegates to the San Francisco conference established an impressive set of objectives to guide their actions. They set 1960 as a target date for all nations to achieve 100 percent literacy. They decreed that every child in every country must be allowed to attend school. They passed a resolution calling on all nations to establish adult literacy programs to combat illiteracy on all fronts. They called on all nations to cooperate in building the economy and national institutions in order to meet the varying dimensions of human need and to serve the educational purpose of their people.

That the participants at the San Francisco conference also called on all nations to reform their political systems so that they would become more representative in their operations in order to sustain democracy was a condition demanded by the times. They reminded national leaders that they held office as a public trust, and that if they violated that trust they must be removed from office. They called on national leaders to observe at all times that sacred democratic principle: governments are instituted with the express consent of the governed. They created UNESCO as an agent to coordinate scientific, cultural, and educational programs throughout the world to bring about improvement in the human condition.

ORGANIZATION OF THE STUDY IN PERSPECTIVE

The organization of this study takes these varied aspects of education into account to present a lucid picture of educational systems in disarray and to provide new insights into where systems are similar and where they are different, as well as where they are weak. To accomplish this objective, the study begins with a discussion of conditions surrounding education at the conclusion of the Second World War in 1945. This is the context in which Chapter 1 examines the ideals, the aspirations, the crises, and the strategies to resolve the problems of education. This helps set the stage on which a discussion of other aspects of education is based. It also examines the human condition as a product of the war.

Chapter 2 examines the influence of history. Although, in human experience, history teaches us that people do not always learn from history, nations cannot realistically endeavor to initiate national programs without taking lessons from the past into account. Those who ignore the lessons of history are condemned to repeat errors of the past. The importance of history has a different effect on the four areas selected for this study. For example, in an effort to avoid mistakes that Nicholas II had made prior to 1917, the Bolsheviks initiated a program of education in the Soviet Union that moved from one extreme to the other. The problem is that the Bolsheviks did not realize that their own extreme was as detrimental to educational development as that of Nicholas. In a different way, the action of African nations to adopt the policies pursued by the colonial governments has had as retarding an effect as that of the colonial systems. The question is: What do nations need to know about their past to avoid the errors that surround it?

Chapter 3 examines some theoretical considerations that nations must take into account in designing their system of education. It is a universal practice that every educational system, whether considered "primitive" or "modern," is based on some theoretical precepts central to the educational norms. Without theory, education has no direction. Here the question is: What does a nation need to have or to know to develop a theory around which to structure its educational system? This chapter attempts to furnish some answers to this question.

In a similar fashion, Chapter 4 discusses educational objectives as a critical factor that shapes the character of education. It will be seen that while theory is important to the structure of education in general, objectives determine the character of the curriculum. This is why Chapter 5 presents a discussion of the curriculum as an instrument of fulfilling educational objectives and national purpose.

Chapter 6 discusses administrative character as a vehicle of the educational process. It is important for nations to realize that, without an effective system of administration, the educational process has neither character nor direction. But it is equally important for them to recognize that the administrative system can cause problems if it is not properly structured. This chapter also discusses differences and similarities that are present in this aspect of education. The three levels of administration-- national, regional (or state, as is the case in the United States), and local-- share the responsibility for administration under an arrangement that more often than not causes confusion that in turn disrupts the educational process.

Chapter 7 discusses some problems that these four examples encounter in their education. These problems range from a lack of adequate financial resources to a lack of reform, from irrelevant curricula to the disruption caused by the drug culture, from placing emphasis on the political process to apathy, from apportioning blame when things go wrong to failure to recognize areas of potential problems. The only exception in realizing a need for reform was the Soviet Union under Mikhail Gorbachev, who recognized soon after assuming office in 1984 that *glasnost* (openness) and *perestroika* (reconstruction) are factors critical for reform. Gorbachev also readily recognized that reconstruction of the social and political system cannot be undertaken in a shroud of secrecy. The nuclear disaster at Chernobyl in 1986 convinced him that it was no longer possible for the Soviet Union to conduct national programs under the veil of secrecy behind the iron curtain. Once Gorbachev reached this conclusion he was not going back to the days of the Bolsheviks.

In 1990 Gorbachev was part of the move to end the cold war. It was the beginning of the new era for the Soviet Union. However, the sad part of the end of the cold war is that neither the former Soviet Union nor the U.S. put in place a national program to reverse the course of development by drastically reducing military spending so that adequate resources could be directed toward social programs. Even the disbanding of the Soviet Union in January 1992 did not persuade the United Sates to reduce its military budget, setting in position events that deepened the recession.

Chapter 8 offers a summary of the essential features of education, the problems that nations face, and some implications they pose. Two critical events occurred on September 2, 1991, that had a profound impact on Gorbachev's reform program. They cast the Soviet Union into a shadow of confusion between the past and the future and so spelled its own demise. The first was that President Bush, following the example of other Western leaders, officially recognized the independence of the Baltic republics of Latvia, Estonia, and Lithuania. The second was that Gorbachev proposed a radical reform that would give the ten republics that decided to remain part of the Soviet Union total independence in carrying out programs, including defense. Beginning on December 13, 1991, the Soviet Union would no longer exist as the republics decided to become independent and form a loosely structured confederation.

Finally, this last chapter offers some interpretive comparative insights that are critical to a national approach to education. The fundamental consideration is: What do nations, not just the four examples in this study, need to do to design educational systems that adequately respond to the needs of their people as a condition of meeting those of the nation? Some answers are in this study.

In approaching the topic in the manner that he has the author hopes that this study provides some important insights into differences and similarities that existed in the educational systems of the four areas selected and how in turn they shaped their national characters.

Summary of Focus of the Study

Area	Objectives	Theory	Curriculum	Administration	Problems
Africa	1. Increase national development 2. Promote literacy 3. Enrich culture 4. Develop national resources 5. Facilitate international understanding	1. Promote national values 2. Show relevance for survival 3. Protect environment 4. Promote national development 5. Facilitate social change 6. Promote culture	1. The 3 Rs 2. Academic and vocational 3. National syllabus 4. Geared toward passing public exams 5. Emphasis on agriculture, industry, national economy, national development	1. National 　(a) policy 　(b) finances 2. Provincial 　(a) supports national level 　(b) coordinates provincial activity 3. Local 　(a) principal 　(b) teachers	1. Urban/rural conflict 2. Cultural: women still have lower social status 3. Ethnic differences 4. Poverty 5. Lack of motivation 6. High illiteracy 7. Lack of educational priorities 8. Lack of planning
Japan	1. Develop character 2. Promote language 3. Enrich culture 4. Promote international understanding 5. Promote technology	1. Develop ethics 2. Teach moral values 3. Offer diverse courses. 4. Education is continuous 5. Promote vocation and intellect	1. Diverse 2. Emphasis on passing exams 3. *Juku* is part of curriculum 4. International studies 5. Study of technology 6. Language skills	1. National 　(a) policy 　(b) finances 2. Provincial 　(a) provincial coordination 3. Local 　(a) principal	1. Too much emphasis on exams 2. Higher education is elitist 3. Emotional trauma 4. Exams too rigid 5. Too much emphasis on needs of state
United States	1. Promote individuality 2. Seek self-fulfillment 3. Prepare for role in society 4. Teach the 3 Rs	1. Provide individual development and that of society) 2. Students learn better in age groups 3. Using teaching aids is essential	1. The 3 Rs 2. Curriculum reflects local needs 3. Language skills 4. Science, math 5. Social studies 6. Foreign languages	1. National (HEW) 　(a) informational 2. State 　(a) enacting legislation 3. Local 　(a) defining policy	1. Decline in SAT scores 2. Subtle inequality 3. Increase in illiteracy 4. Conflict in policy 5. Disparity in facilities 6. Violence in schools
Soviet Union	1. Promote all-round education 2. Eliminate capitalism 3. Provide diverse education 4. Develop technology 5. Serve the state	1. Student-teacher relationship 2. Learning related to human stimuli 3. Meet the needs of society to meet those of the individual	1. Language skills 2. Ten-year plan 3. Science, math, social studies 4. International studies 5. Space technology 6. Research since 1972 7. Foreign languages	1. National 　(a) national policy 2. Provincial regional coordination 3. Local headmaster, teachers, parents	1. Lack of choice 2. Seeks to protect state 3. Few incentives 4. Too much emphasis on needs of state 5. Exams too rigid

Educational Policy
and National Character

1

Crisis in Education after the Second World War

Enlighten the people and the tyranny and oppression of both body and mind will vanish like evil spirits at the dawn of day.

Thomas Jefferson, 1816

THE SETTING

The conclusion of the Second World War in 1945 transformed the way people all over the world thought about their nations and the way nations thought about the world. The use of the atomic bomb to end the war ushered in a new perspective from which people began to view themselves in relationship to technology. While the bomb ended the war, it created an entirely new environment in military power was seen as the only viable solution to the problems of human and international relationships.

The bitterness that both the victorious Allies and the vanquished Axis powers felt transformed man's mental and intellectual ability into a notion that might is right. For the first time in history, people came face to face with a dilemma: Which is more important, the utilization of human reason to resolve problems or the utilization of military power to sustain the notion of peace?[1]

Although the United States had tested the atomic bomb in New Mexico on July 16, 1945, American scientists underestimated the extent of the damage that the actual bombs dropped on Japan caused. When the first bomb was dropped on Hiroshima on August 6, 1945, it killed 70,000 people and injured many more. It also left a radioactive effect that lasted for years. Three days later, on August 9, the second bomb was dropped on

---

[1]Donald K. Grayson, "Human Life vs. Science," in Thomas Weaver (ed.), *To See Ourselves: Anthropology and Modern Social Issues* (Glenview, Ill.: Scott, Foresman, 1973), p. 32.

Nagasaki and killed 36,000 people. The total damage caused by the two bombs was of such huge proportions that it surprised even the best scientists. That the world had now entered the nuclear age also transformed people's perceptions of both themselves and their society in ways that had not been done before.

One question appears obvious, but is pertinent to this study: What did the introduction of atomic military power mean to human relations and international relationships? There is no question that nations saw this enormous power as the only modus operandi. The implications of this new situation were incalculable for the world as a whole. It meant, among other things, that the stronger nations became militarily, the more they exerted undue influence and pressure on the nature of the relationships between themselves and other nations.

Now, nations were prepared to go to any length to ensure their military power as the only form of their security. Many national programs, such as social services, were either neglected or relegated to the process of building military might. The formation of the Warsaw Pact in May 1955, in response to the formation of NATO in April 1949, created a new global system of alliance in which the cold war grew to powerful and dangerous dimensions.

The promotion of socialism by the Warsaw Pact members as a new political ideology and the determination of NATO members to foil it also created a new environment in which global relations were seen as an ideological conflict between between nations. The reality that came out of this ideological conflict is that nations, even those that could not afford it, were forced to align themselves with either one or the other of these military organizations to ensure their own security.

The system of alliance that had been the major cause of conflict in Europe before the outbreak of the First World War was being played out once more. While this was happening, nations continued to neglect the real issues of national and global security, such as social services, education, political reform, and economic development. This meant that although the war had ended, the decision to introduce new ways of thinking about military power in the nuclear age posed problems for humanity that had not existed before.

THE PURPOSE OF THE STUDY

The notion of military power as the only way to international peace was not only eroding away the application of human reason to resolve problems but was also slowly transforming the atomic age into the age of nuclear military technology. The frightening reality of this situation was that instead of limiting membership in the nuclear club to Warsaw Pact countries and NATO countries, nuclear capability was steadily being acquired by nations of the Third World. How realistic was it, therefore, to expect that nuclear power would ensure the security of the world? Since the end of the war in 1945, nations have been increasingly thinking in terms of returning to human reasoning to find solutions to international problems.[2]

To take this approach to the problems of human existence, nations began to believe that the development of worldwide education, quite different from what it had been prior to the outbreak of the war in 1939, must become a major commitment of all nations. The purpose of this study, therefore, is to discuss some features of educational development that nations believed in 1945 should form part of the thrust for the construction of a new world order[3] based on the application of human reason, understanding, and cooperation. It examines how the major features of education influence the thrust for national character and development in Africa,[4] Japan, the United States, and the former Soviet Union.

THE FOUNDING OF THE UNITED NATIONS AND IMPLICATIONS FOR A NEW GLOBAL ORDER

The outbreak of the war in 1939 was an event that not only changed the thinking process among the people of the world but also demanded a appraisal of old values cast in a new international setting. What was at stake was not that the Axis powers sought to rule the world, but how human relations would be determined and how social institutions would operate in the future. Indeed, the outbreak of the war was, in a sense, a conflict between old and new values. The use of the atomic bomb created new problems in human and international relationships.

The confusion and the fear of atomic destruction were combined with the concern of the victorious Allies, posing new questions about the extent to which nations were prepared to use this awesome power to protect national interests. The fact of the matter is that the existing world had been altered by questionable perceptions about the future. Instead of ensuring world peace and security, the use of the atomic bomb compounded old problems and created new ones. The world of 1945 was no more secure than that of 1939. Into what directions was the world moving?

Before nations endeavored to reshape the fabric of a new order in the presence of this immensely destructive power, they decided to engage in a collective effort to examine the past in order to understand the present and plan the future. As the war came to an end, both the victorious and the vanquished nations decided to form an organization known as the United Nations (UN). But the formation of the UN must be seen in the context of

---

[2]Ibid., p. 33.

[3]Indeed, on January 16, 1991, during an address to the nation, President George Bush argued that the reason the United States had launched an attack on Iraq for invading Kuwait on August 2, 1990, was to create a new world order.

[4]While there are differences in the educational process among African nations, there are essential similarities that will become the focus of this study. The study does not focus on any one country in Africa, rather it discusses concepts that African countries have in common to give the reader a perspective of the problems the continent as a whole faces.

several events that began to unfold between 1941 and 1944. Among them are two that deserve mention and a brief discussion.

The first event was the Atlantic Charter of August 14, 1941, in which President Franklin Roosevelt and Prime Minister Winston Churchill of Britain declared: "We respect the right of all peoples to choose the form of government under which they will live, and we wish to see sovereign rights and self-government restored to those who have been forcibly deprived of them."[5] The second event was the Dumbarton Oaks Conference of October 1944. This conference produced the international climate that was needed for the formation of the UN.

Following discussions that had been started in August, representatives from the Soviet Union, Great Britain, China, and the United States agreed on conditions for the founding of the UN. Meeting at Yalta in February 1945, Churchill, Roosevelt, and Joseph Stalin went further to define the structure of the UN itself. They agreed to convene a conference in San Francisco to begin on April 25, 1945, to prepare a charter for the UN, mindful of the enormous consequences of the demise of the League of Nations in 1920.

Exhausted by the war and unsure of the future, these four nations agreed to invite forty-one other nations to the San Francisco conference. By the time the UN Charter came into being on June 26, 1945, delegates representing fifty nations had signed it. With its ratification in October, the UN Charter was poised to alter the character of the relationships between nations. In 1946, John D. Rockefeller, Jr., believing in the cause for world peace, gave $8.5 million to the UN to buy the site it was built on in New York City. Construction of the building began in 1949 and, when it was completed in 1952, had cost $67 million. The cooperation, the enthusiasm, and the support that came from all over the world suggest that the international community was now ready to accept the challenge of constructing a new world order.

The preamble of the UN[6]--its drafters seemingly quite sensitive of its implications for world peace and security--was meant to ensure that all members of the UN understood and accepted their responsibility in this collective endeavor, saying:

> We the people of the United Nations, determined to save succeeding generations from the scourge of war, which twice in our life-time, has brought untold sorrow to mankind, and to reaffirm our faith in fundamental human rights, in the dignity and worth of the human person, in equal rights of man and women, and of nations, large and small, and to establish conditions under which justice and respect for the obligation arising from treaties and other sources of international law, and to promote social progress and better standards of life in larger freedom, wish to practice tolerance and live together in peace with one another as good neighbors and employ international machinery for the promotion of the economic and social

---

[5]President Franklin Roosevelt and Prime Minister Winston Churchill, *The Atlantic Charter*, August 14, 1941.

[6]Ironically, Jan Christiaan Smuts, the prime minister of South Africa, a country that would soon become notorious for its racial policy of apartheid, is credited with drafting the preamble.

advancement of all people. Accordingly our respective governments have agreed to the present Charter of the United Nations and hereby establish an international organization to be known as the United Nations.[7]

The euphoria and the excitement that characterized the response of nations throughout the world can be understood in the context of the hope expressed for a lasting world peace. For many this was a new day of hope that their people would not be subjected to political domination that was their lot in the past. They felt that the possibility of ensuring a future different from the past was within their grasp, and a new collective effort would yield the results that would translate into a new world order in which the role of nations would not be viewed in terms of military might, but in terms of mutual respect, because that was the goal to which the UN was committing itself.

But nations, big and small, powerful and weak, were not aware that the task of bringing this reality about was not an easy one. There were still lingering doubts that embracing the principles that the UN was now asking all nations to accept would ensure their security. There were still nagging questions that this collective endeavor had not been fully resolved. Would all nations rise to the occasion and identify themselves fully with the objectives and principles that the UN had enunciated? Would the victorious Allies give up their military dominance to embrace the concept of sovereignty of nations and the operative principle of equality between nations? Would weak nations struggling for self give up their quest for military power as a means of ensuring their security to the protection of the values and principles of the UN?

RENDEZVOUS WITH THE PAST: CAUSES OF THE WAR

The excitement with which nations supported the inauguration of the UN and the hope that characterized their activity to map out a better future were tempered by the nagging feeling that in spite of the claimed commitment by nations to embrace its principles, global conflict was likely to break out again in the future. For this reason, the delegates assembled in San Francisco decided that, before they asked nations to embark on the collective task of reshaping the future, they needed to take a journey into the past to examine developments that had brought the world to the brink of self-destruction twice in the century. The belief that one must study the past to understand the present and plan the future was a central component of their strategy. Painful as this exercise was, they felt it had to be undertaken in order to take all relevant dimensions into account in planning that future.

The first step toward this encounter with the past was to make an assessment of what had caused the war in 1939. Beyond accepting the popular view that the war had been caused by the reckless policies of the Axis powers, the delegates to the San Francisco conference went much

---

[7]Preamble to the UN Charter, June 26, 1945.

further to look for a broader field from which to understand human behavior in order to deal with all relevant aspects of their efforts to plan for the future in a more realistic and comprehensive manner. To do this they reached three basic conclusions regarding what they identified as causes of the war. The first conclusion was that the war had been caused by ignorance, poverty, and greed.

The delegates concluded that these three pillars of the negative monument of human weakness had often combined to create a climate of conflict, both national and international. Ignorance of the needs and feelings of other people, of what it takes to build a peaceful and happy society, and of the conditions that control the universal person often becomes a prime factor in selfish behavior. Selfish behavior itself leads to greed. Once one has the power, one can use greed to exploit those who are in a vulnerable position in society.

The delegates also recognized that exploitation then leads to the poverty of those who are exploited. Exploitation breeds resentment, and resentment eventually leads to conflict. The recognition of these three factors as causes of human conflict means that mankind must assume the responsibility of eliminating them in order to create a new climate of peace. It is ironic that coming out of the Industrial Revolution of the nineteenth century, ignorance, poverty, and greed were the very negative features of society that technological advancement was expected to eliminate; on the contrary, they intensified in contemporary global settings.

The recognition by the delegates to the San Francisco conference that these negative features of human existence had been a major cause of the war meant that a new effort had to be made to eliminate them if the future was to be different and more meaningful than the past. But the delegates fully recognized that they needed to employ new strategies to achieve this objective.

The second conclusion was that nations and their people prior to 1939 failed to understand each other because neither their leaders nor their citizens were educated sufficiently to grasp human issues fully and the conditions that controlled relationships between them. Remembering that up to 1939 educational opportunity was a privilege of a few, this led to the conclusion that if nations were to avoid conflict in the future, a new collective effort had to be made to educate people, both national leaders and citizens alike, to help them understand their respective responsibilities in developing democratic societies. This endeavor required rethinking the objectives and content of education itself. Educational practices of the past had to give way to educational programs based on new theoretical considerations.

This self-appraisal led to the recognition that one basic objective of education in the postwar era was to produce more rational human beings whose thought processes and behavioral patterns would be influenced by reason and rationality, rather than by emotion. This line of thinking was influenced by the ideals arising from the Age of Reason, or the Enlightenment, and was based on the belief that educated individuals become controlled by a rational thought process and are therefore less likely to do anything wrong because their sense of what is right and what is wrong is much sharper than those who are not as well educated.

Among the prominent spokesmen of the Enlightenment was Thomas Jefferson, president of the United States from 1801 to 1809. A well-educated man, Jefferson saw human behavior as a product of education, and he argued that society had a duty to provide education to elevate people to a higher plane of reason and rationality and so reduce their tendency to make behavioral errors. Indeed, Jefferson so believed in the value of education in promoting people's ability to exercise proper reason and rationality that he felt it would liberate everyone from the timeless oppression of irrationality. He thought that with education humankind was poised to scale down oppressive forces and rise up for the benefit of society itself. In a letter dated April 24, 1816, addressed to P. S. Du Pont de Nemours, Jefferson left his mark on the importance of education when he argued the following: "Enlighten the people and the tyranny and oppression of both body and mind will vanish like evil spirits at the dawn of day."[8]

This was, indeed, a testimony of a founding father of a nation struggling for self and a man and leader whose own experience had shown him that without proper education man and his society were always victims of oppression and tyranny, and that to educate people is to liberate them from the scourge that undermined their potential for greatness. Having experienced the devastation of the war, it is not surprising that the delegates to the San Francisco conference embraced this line of thinking in their efforts to ensure future world peace and security.

The third conclusion was that discrimination and prejudice based on race, gender, and religion had always been a scourge that marred relationships between nations and their people. While they recognized that the Nazi efforts to exterminate the Jews were the ultimate manifestation of racial hatred and prejudice, this negative aspect of human behavior was found among all nations, although it was more pronounced in some than in others. It was not until the 1950s, however, with increasingly painful evidence of discrimination, that the international community concluded that society needed to make a new thrust to eliminate it. Nations such as Great Britain and the United States, which had often been considered citadels of democracy and beacons of freedom, suddenly found themselves at the center of controversy generated by various forms of discrimination and prejudice. In 1944, Gunnar Myrdal, the Swedish sociologist and researcher, appropriately called the situation in the United States an American dilemma.

The delegates to the San Francisco conference took these realities into consideration in concluding that discrimination of some people, whether it was based on race, religion, or gender was repugnant to the principles of national development and that it had be eliminated by making efforts to provide equality of educational opportunity. Such programs as affirmative

---

[8]Quoted in William van Til, *Education: A Beginning* (Boston: Houghton Mufflin Company, 1974), p. 141.

action and positive discrimination have been demonstrated efforts to eliminate this scourge in human experience.

But the fact that discrimination has continued to exist in all nations underscores the importance of finding solutions to it, so that nations can put it behind them as they endeavor to chart a new course in their search for human fulfillment. This is the only viable means to national development and international peace and security. The recognition that discrimination and prejudice were the prime cause of inequality in society led to the conclusion that they were the basic cause of conflict both among people of the same country and among nations.

Indeed, in this collective self-examination, delegates to the San Francisco conference also recognized that there are other adverse effects of discrimination and prejudice which they identified as contributing causes of conflict in the world. They concluded that the practice that nations had been pursuing in regarding some people and their nations as less important than others implied that equality as a basic operative principle of social justice was reserved for a special class of people, and that those who were excluded from it were less than human.

The fact is that those who practiced discrimination and prejudice neglected one important consideration--that is, discrimination and prejudice combined to form cancer cells that often destroyed the vital tissue of national life and depleted the most important resources that any nation needs to ensure its own development. Indeed, discrimination and prejudice have always been a manifestation of a sick and degenerate society. It is not surprising that delegates to the San Francisco conference concluded that extending equal educational opportunity in all nations was essential for global peace and security.

While the delegates to the San Francisco conference readily recognized that discrimination and prejudice have always been two features of human existence that have persistently retarded efforts toward national development and often cause untold misery, they did not have a formula to eliminate them. The horrors caused by the Nazi perpetration of discrimination and prejudice are only a small part of the evidence showing that a society based on these two adverse conditions, created by man himself, robs itself of the opportunity to build a progressive social system that enables its people to recognize the vitality and dignity of every person in it. Idealistic as they were in engaging in this painful rendezvous with the past in order to plan the future, the delegates were not aware that problems of discrimination and prejudice would continue to ravage the beauty and glory of the human person far into the future.

One graphic description shows the cruelty of discrimination and prejudice as late as 1990 toward a young couple belonging to the untouchables in India at the hands of the upper class. After suffering from brutality and humiliation because of her social class, Kuchchi, 24, told her husband, Dhanraj, 26, that she was no longer willing to endure the indignities and cruelties that members of her social class had suffered for many years. Arjun Singh, a member of the upper class and also a local political lord, ordered the elimination of Dhanraj because he protested the humiliating treatment that his wife had received.[9]

The fact that this tragedy occurred in Utter Pradesh, the constituency of the prime minister of India, V. P. Singh, underscored the grim reality that discrimination and prejudice are well and alive forty-five years after the decision of the San Francisco conference that they must be eliminated. That Dhanraj's tragic death did not invoke public outrage suggests the extent to which people accepted discrimination and prejudice as a way of life. This undercut the hope of a new start in collective efforts to build a new world order along the lines that the San Francisco conference had defined. It is equally disturbing that the UN itself failed to use these tragedies to reaffirm the principles that it so eloquently defined in 1945.

The vote this world body took in November 1990 to sanction the use of force to compel Iraq to withdraw from Kuwait was itself a tragic action and a violation of its sacred principle never to resort to force to resolve conflict. Does this suggest that the UN is now reversing itself in suggesting that principles were good only during the years following the conclusion of the Second World War? Can nations assume that they are at liberty to resort to military force to resolve international problems?

Perhaps the UN needs to reevaluate itself and its goals. Perhaps it has outlived its usefulness. Perhaps it needs to redraw its charter to remove the overwhelming power that permanent nations in the Security Council have in exercising vetoes. What that veto power clearly shows is that some nations are more important than others. Nothing is more dangerous to relationships between nations than the belief in this notion.

Further, there are two frightening realities that one must understand about discrimination and prejudice. The first is that they can deliver a deadly blow against those they select for victimization. The second is that India is not the only country in the late twentieth century to endure this scourge. The resurgence of KKK activity in the United States, ethnic violence in the Baltic states of the former Soviet Union, the continuing tragedy of apartheid in South Africa, and the surge of racial violence in France and Great Britain are all examples of the pervasiveness of discrimination and prejudice in the world today. Indeed, conflicts between ethnic groups and between whites and blacks in South Africa are a direct result of the application of the policy of apartheid.

Elsewhere in Africa the situation is no better, as corruption by government officials, nepotism, and other irregularities have become the order of things. In a letter dated March 14, 1991, addressed to this author, a bright, hardworking, and ambitious student in Sierra Leone expressed the problems that he and other students in similar situations are facing: "You see, sir, in Sierra Leone education has become a matter of privilege, not of right for the citizens. Scholarships are only awarded to the children and relatives of top government officials or civil servants. A system of nepotism and corruption has taken over the operations of the government. Because I do not have a relative working for the government I have no means of continuing my education beyond what I have done. God only

---

[9]*Time*, May 28, 1990, p. 37.

knows if I will ever have the opportunity I desperately need. The government has abandoned its responsibility to its own people, and we are paying the price. Sir, I need your help!"[10]

In a similar manner the conclusion of the San Francisco conference that discrimination and prejudice were major causes of social conflict is evinced by the effects of apartheid and the inability of whites to see the need to end it and to recognize that while they might derive short-term political benefits from it, they are placing their own long-term interests and those of the country in jeopardy. The effect of apartheid on the people of South Africa is quite consistent with the conclusion of the San Francisco conference that discrimination and prejudice in any nation pose a threat to international peace and security.

Since its official introduction in 1948, the policy of apartheid has victimized both its perpetrators and its victims. The tragedy of this infamous racial policy is that those who designed it were unable to see the devastating consequences that it posed, not only for South Africa but also for the world as a whole.

THE TASK OF DEFINING NEW OBJECTIVES

The conclusion of the San Francisco conference that the development of education throughout the world was the only viable means to end national inequality and, thus, international conflict led to the hope that a thrust for educational development would help eliminate the problems that society faced--poverty, ignorance, prejudice and discrimination, and political oppression. For the first time in history the universal human being began to place hope in the realization that ending inequality of educational opportunity was possible and that the future carried prospects for self-fulfillment. This hope also meant that origin of birth, class, and other considerations that had perpetuated inequality in society would no longer be used to determine who received an opportunity for educational development. The belief that a little black girl of humble origin in a remote rural area and a little white boy in an exclusive suburban neighborhood stood on the same and equal plane to launch their educational *safari* led to new endeavors to realize national goals.

To make this hope a reality, nations began to make plans, especially in three essential areas. The first was that because existing systems and programs were insufficient to meet the projected needs of a changing society, educational expansion must become a national commitment and a high priority; the reason for this strategy was that educational development is essential to all other forms of national development. The second was that economic development was needed during the critical stage of the new thrust for educational development to invest in it, but that at some point in the future economic development and educational development would have a symbiotic relationship. The third was that educational opportunity was essential to seeking an improvement in the quality of life of all the people

---

[10]Letter addressed to the author from a student in Sierra Leone, Africa, March 14, 1991.

and that it would enable them to play a dynamic and constructive role in the political process.[11]

The thinking that popular participation in the political process was essential to political stability as a condition of social development led to the conclusion that this participation was not possible without adequate education. Without political stability a climate of national development would not be created. This was how educational development made the practice of democracy possible. The idea of political elites who had controlled and exploited the dispossessed and oppressed masses had to give way to a new thinking that political stability was possible only within a national environment of popular participation under the principle of freedom of expression. This made educational expansion an imperative of the hope for the future.

The delegates to the San Francisco conference also concluded that this rendezvous with the past, as an expression of hope for the future, would have little meaning unless all nations took specific action in setting goals and making concerted efforts to fulfill them. Among these goals we must cite and briefly discuss six.

The first objective was that nations must invest in educational development with specific reference to seeking an improvement in the curriculum and making it comprehensive enough to allow students to learn about other people in the world. It was believed that knowledge of other people was essential to global peace and security.[12]

The second objective was for all nations to set 1960 as a target date for achieving 100 percent literacy. The reason for this objective was that basic literacy was the only viable basis for the development of the individual as an essential component of national development. The development of the individual manifested itself in a variety of ways that would constitute elements of national development. They include economic well-being, freedom of political expression, and participation in national affairs so that no group of individuals has a monopoly on political power at the expense of other groups.

Indeed, nations of the post war period began to realize the grim reality that the oppression that illiteracy imposed on the individual would soon translate into an oppression of the nation itself. Simply stated, this means that no nation can ensure its own development if its people are still in the grip of illiteracy. The generation of new ideas, the creative activity of the human mind, the ability to become an essential and viable element of society all emanate from an ability to envisage oneself. Literacy has been recognized as the touchstone of self-actualization. Without literacy any activity, mental or physical, has little meaning to the development of a people and their nation. This was the reason for setting 1960 as the year of eliminating discrimination in all its forms, especially based on race, gender, and religion, throughout the world.

---

[11]Philip Coombs, *World Crisis in Education: The View from the Eighties* (New York: Oxford University Press, 1985), p. 31.

[12]Ibid. p. 32.

The third objective was to develop adequate educational facilities, such as classrooms, improved teacher-training programs, and the adequate educational equipment. Prior to the outbreak of the war in 1939, these facilities were totally inadequate or seriously wanting. The training of teachers was considered especially essential to providing adequate educational facilities. Moreover, teachers understood the purpose of education better than perhaps any other group, and they inspired their students with confidence for the future. They understood the problems of human understanding in general and the nature of relationships that were intended to improve the human condition. They sharpened their students' perceptions of both themselves and their world. Teachers in the post war era were therefore expected to demonstrate unquestionable competency in discharging their responsibility to their students and to show a clear understanding of the importance of human relationships beyond the local level.

In order to fulfill their duties well, teachers need tools that enable their students to function effectively, not only within the limits of an educational environment, but within society itself. As of 1945 teachers were expected to see the value of education beyond the classroom and to impart it to their students and to the larger community in a way that was understood for what it was, beneficial to society.

It was quite clear to the members of the international community that the tools that the teachers needed to enable them to do a good job were facilities. The responsibility for providing these facilities was not that of teachers, but of nations. This means that all nations were called on to do nothing less than their best in providing facilities so that teachers could discharge their responsibility fully.

The fourth objective was to extend educational opportunity to both men and women, boys and girls, equally. The reality that, due to cultural traditions, some nations had a bias for educational opportunity in favor of men and boys had to be discouraged because, as the argument went, a nation with only educated men was like a cake baked on one side. The thinking that society needed both men and women to progress suggested the need to end all forms of bias against the educational advancement of women. It also suggested that bias that had to be eliminated in society itself.

The fundamental consideration relative to the need to end all forms of bias against the educational development of women was that, as long as this bias continued, schools would be unable to discharge their proper responsibility to their students. Besides, it would inhibit the ability of women to do their best and would psychologically condition them to believe less of themselves and their potential. Society has always paid a price for this negative traditional approach to the question of education. Now, the conditions of the postwar era demanded change.

The fifth objective was to encourage families to do their best to enable their children to go to school. In many countries of the world, it had been the practice before the outbreak of the war for parents to depend on their children to contribute to the family's economic well-being. It was stressed that parents must adopt the attitude that encouraging children to go to school was the best way of preparing for the future. Parents actively enabling their children to go to school, combined with the commitment of national leaders to stress education, made it possible to plan for a future quite different from the past. Parents who had missed an opportunity for education now began to see its value for the future of their children in an entirely different way.

The dramatic change in attitude toward the importance of education was the ultimate manifestation of the critical assessment or appraisal of the meaning of the past to the present in order to plan the future. In Africa, this dramatic change in attitude towards education was fully recognized by the colonial governments. In colonial Zimbabwe (known as the British colony of Southern Rhodesia from 1895 to 1964), for example, a high-ranking colonial official acknowledged in 1961: "The rather apathetic prewar outlook of the African masses toward education was rapidly being transformed into a general and urgent realization that education was the essential tool for gaining a foothold in a competitive civilized world."[13]

For Africans, tragic as it was, the war had transformed their thinking from accepting the colonial condition as inevitable into questioning its assumed values. They now began to see colonial system, not as something that they had to accept in order to ensure their survival, but as institutions with negative features designed to engulf their existence and which they felt had to be eliminated in order to plan the future. This realization created a new environment in which they saw themselves not as mere caricatures of human beings that the colonial condition had made them believe to be, but as people with a potential and resources that had not been tapped for the good of all. This new level of awakening was the beginning of the rise of African nationalism. Indeed, the world of 1945 was poised for an unprecedented quest for new meaning through educational endeavors.

The sixth objective was that all nations must initiate carefully planned campaigns to provide adult literacy programs. The conclusion that adult education was important was a result of the view that those who had missed the opportunity for education earlier in their life must make a contribution to national development without waiting to complete their education in the way regular students were expected to do. The approach to the question of adult literacy was also an outcome of the belief that those who had missed an opportunity for education earlier must not endure the perpetual life sentence of illiteracy because every adult has a critical contribution to make to the development of society.

The idea that adult education was an integral component of the thrust for national development had a special appeal to the participants of the San Francisco conference in their efforts to pass a set of resolutions that would guide nations as they engaged in this collective task of planning the future. While the enthusiasm for this endeavor was embraced by individual nations, especially those struggling for development, its success lay in a collective effort to identify problem areas and to make plans to resolve

---

[13]Southern Rhodesia, *The Report of the Commission of Inquiry into Discontent in the Mangwende Reserve*, James Brown, chairman (Salisbury: Government Printers, 1961), p. 77.

them. The reality was that no single nation had sufficient national resources to launch the campaign alone.

THE CONSEQUENCES OF A NEW HOPE

To suggest that nations of the world recognized the importance of a new thrust for educational development is to conclude that they went beyond the level of raising hopes for its role in shaping the future. They envisaged a global system of social justice based on the belief that equality of educational opportunity was the touchstone of a peaceful and secure world. But a number of things happened as a result of considering education as a panacea for all social evils. The very fact that nations placed their total confidence in education as the chief instrument of resolving all human problems posed risks that they did not foresee.

If education succeeded in this endeavor, then it would indeed become a panacea of all the ills of society and human experience and existence. But if it failed, it would dash the aspirations that nations were trying to promote as the ultimate solution to all problems. In planning this undertaking, nations were not willing to consider the real possibility that they would encounter problems they did not anticipate. But for the moment, considering these problems was not something that they had to take into account, because the excitement of a new era was too strong for the enthusiasm that was at the base of their thinking and action to be offset.

Parents began to encourage their children to go to school in the hope that education would offer them what was not possible in the past. By 1960, the year nations collectively set as a target date for achieving 100 percent literacy, enrollment, especially in the urban areas, had doubled. But still there were as many children who were denied admission because there were not enough room and facilities.

It is ironic that the first sign of a new global crisis in education came as a result of the action of the nations themselves in raising a hope for a changed world. Along with the dramatic increase in enrollment came a dramatic increase in population itself. This put severe limitations on financial resources needed to support the development of education. The following table shows literacy in relationship to total population as of 1990:

Area	Population	Literacy
Africa	470,600,000	41%
Japan	123,230,000	99%
U.S.	247,498,000	95%
Soviet Union	287,015,000	98%

Source: *World Almanac and Book of Facts*, 1991.

One major problem that nations encountered is that, in spite of the efforts they made to eliminate illiteracy, this scourge continued to handicap national development which they had planned as the only viable means to a world of peace and security. That no country has succeeded in eliminating illiteracy together helps explain how difficult the problem was, and still is. In 1990 there was serious concern that illiteracy throughout the world was steadily increasing, even in Western nations,[14] for a number of reasons, such as rising population, declining economy, inflation, instability in global trade, political strife, a lack of adequate strategies to eliminate it, and continuing conflict in national priorities.

There was yet another consequence of this hope for the future through education. Inequality, that dark spot on the trail of human endeavor, had persisted in various forms. In Western countries inequality based on race and gender showed no signs of abating. The efforts of the U.S. Supreme Court to end this form of inequality came first in the postwar period in 1954 in the famous *Brown* decision. That racial inequality has persisted in the United States, a nation that espouses the philosophy of equal opportunity for all people as a central tenet of its social system, suggests the critical nature of this problem. That in recent years problems of racial inequality have resurfaced in Europe, especially in Britain and France, demonstrates the inability of nations to resolve one of the fundamental issues delegates to the San Francisco conference identified as essential to mapping out a strategy for the future.

Indeed, one of the most notorious examples of racial inequality in the world is the system of apartheid in South Africa. Since its introduction unofficially in 1652[15] and officially in 1948, the policy of apartheid has caused a level and extent of bitterness rarely known in the history of mankind. The enactment of the Bantu Education Act in 1953 has caused so much pain among Africans that their education has lost the meaning for which it was created. On this dimension of apartheid, Leo Marquard wrote:

> Such acts of parliament as the Group Areas Act, the Population Registration Act, the Immigration Act, the Mixed Marriages Act, the Extension of University Education Act, and the Industrial Conciliation Act, all discriminate between different racial groups in South Africa. While some provisions of these acts entail serious economic hardships, their main purpose is to achieve as much social and racial separation as possible.[16]

In 1953, Hendrik Verwoerd (1901-1966), prime minister of South Africa from 1958 until his tragic death in 1966, argued as the Minister of Bantu Affairs, which had responsibility for education of the Africans: "Native education should be controlled in such a way that it should be in

---

[14]PBS, *A Chance to Learn,* documentary film presentation, 1989.

[15]For evidence to support this conclusion, see Dickson A. Mungazi, *The Struggle for Social Change in Southern Africa: Visions of Liberty* (New York: Taylor and Francis, 1989), p. 74.

[16]Leo Marquard, *The Peoples and Policies of South Africa* (London: Oxford University Press, 1969), p. 129.

accord with the policy of the state. If the Natives are being taught to expect that they will live their adult life under a policy of equal rights with whites, they are making a big mistake. The Natives who attend school must know that they will be the laborers in the country."[17] By the time of the Soweto uprising in June 1976, apartheid had become a religion that was to guide the whites and the government of South Africa into a total and absolute belief in their assumed superiority and the inferiority of black Africans.

Indeed, apartheid has reduced the black South Africans to the level of bare existence, presumed incapable of showing any positive attributes of being human. In spite of the stated intention of the San Francisco conference to end all forms of racial inequality in society, including education, this dark side of human existence has continued to cast a long shadow over the endeavors of the world community to plan the future in a way that is different from the past.

By the beginning of 1993 the perils of apartheid posed threat to the very existence of South Africa. The international community stood and watched helplessly as South Africa used the weapon of apartheid to destroy its own future. Where had the spirit of the San Francisco conference gone? What had happened to its resolution that race must never be used as a criterion to determine a person's worth and place in society? What had happened to its determination that equality of opportunity must be extended to all people as a prerequisite of national development?

It is not surprising that South Africa has been paying the price of underdevelopment in more painful ways than other nations. Until it has succeeded in removing this national scourge, South Africa will continue to slide on the perilous road of uncertainty and conflict, denying itself an opportunity to tap the priceless human resources it needs in order to make national progress possible.

Inequality in educational opportunity based on gender had been as pervasive as that based on race. Differences in ways societies have treated men and women have been the practice for thousands of years. From biblical times and the Greek and Roman cultures, through the Thirteen Colonies of North America, to modern societies, men and women have often been treated differently both in education and society simply because of sex.[18] At all levels of education women have not been afforded equal opportunity. The following figures show that women have received less educational opportunity than men.

---

[17]Alex La Guma (ed.), *Apartheid: A Collection of Writings of South Africa by South Africans* (New York: International Publishers, 1971), p. 46.

[18]Coombs, *World Crisis in Education*, p. 224.

Percentage of Women in Total Enrollment, 1965-1960

Region	Primary		Secondary		Higher	
	1965	1980	1965	1980	1965	1980
Developed	49	49	50	51	38	47
Developing	41	43	32	39	27	34

Source: UNESCO, *Statistical Yearbook*, 1982, cited in Coombs, *World Crisis in Education*, p. 225.

The reasons given for inequality in education due to gender vary. Among them are that women are weaker physically than men, that they are less intelligent and less creative than men, that their real place is in the kitchen. It is true to say that educational inequality based on gender is more acute in developing countries than in developed nations. However, the problems of overall inequality are as acute in developed nations as they are in developing nations. For example, the United States has had to resort to such controversial programs as affirmative action to end that inequality. In 1990, women in the United States, on the average, earned 65 percent of what men earned; this shows that the United States still has a long way to go to eliminate this negative feature of its society. If there is an aspect of life in which all nations need to cooperate in order to find lasting solutions, it is in making an effort to end inequality based on gender.

In many Third World nations, such as those in Latin America, Africa, and the Middle East, differences in the treatment of men and women are part of cultural traditions and therefore hard to eliminate. The presence of allied troops in Saudi Arabia in 1990 made it possible for Westerners to observe the extent of inequality that exists between men and women there. They learned, for example, that women are not allowed to drive cars.

That, in their enthusiasm to plan the future, the delegates to the San Francisco conference attempted to develop strategies of dealing with inequality shows how idealistic they were in seeking ways of eliminating a climate of conflict. It was obvious by 1965 that disappointment was the consequence of the new hope. While the delegates recognized the pervasive nature of inequality in both society and education, their inability to find a workable solution reduced the confidence of both the delegates and the nations they represented in dealing with one of the most serious problems in human existence.

However, the failure to find a solution to this problem did not mean they would stop trying; it simply meant that efforts to find an answer be continued. The reality of the problems that all nations faced is that they were rooted in cultural traditions that they felt could not be altered without threatening the fundamental basis of society itself. This is why many of the problems that nations identified in San Francisco have still not been solved.

THE WILLIAMSBURG CONFERENCE:
MAKING A FRESH START

By 1967, nations felt that no tangible progress had been made in solving the problems that the delegates to the San Francisco conference had identified and the objectives that they had set. They therefore decided to convene another conference at Williamsburg, Virginia, to review the situation and to establish new goals and strategies for their implementation. Unlike the San Francisco conference, which included mainly government officials, this conference included politicians, civic leaders, educators, economists, and interested individuals.

All assembled at Williamsburg in October 1967 to assess the condition of education throughout the world and to decide what action should be taken to solve the many problems all nations faced. They did not think they should begin where the San Francisco conference left off, they wanted a fresh start.

The Williamsburg conference was different from the San Francisco and other preceding conferences in one important respect. It was not run on issues raised by conflicting positions, but on a single working document that had been sent to participants before they arrived. The document centered on two basic issues: how to eliminate illiteracy and how to end inequality in both education and society. The conference approached these two issues from a practical standpoint.

With respect to the first issue, participants concluded that illiteracy had not been eliminated because nations failed to convince their people of the practical value of equality in both education and society. The feeling that granting equality of these two critical aspects of society would erode a system of social values and cultural practices that had been in place for so long was a major problem that the Williamsburg conference faced, just as the San Francisco conference had.

The participants of the Williamsburg conference also recognized that nations had not made a concerted effort to solve the problems they were facing. This is why they recommended that nations intensify their efforts to demonstrate that extending equality and eliminating illiteracy were both essential to national progress. One method of seeking to accomplish this fundamental objective was to turn over the responsibility of education to local communities where everyone was encouraged to contribute ideas for improvement. The logistical matters of running programs were also believed to be best handled at the local level.

In this seemingly innovative approach to these critical issues of national development, the participants to the Williamsburg conference appear to have neglected a critical factor for their success, financial outlay, and local communities were not in a position to discharge this responsibility. However, these local communities would be asked to keep records of all activities. As local businessmen and farmers, for example, would need to know how to keep records, they would demonstrate the practical value of literacy and so help combat illiteracy.

The Williamsburg conference also recognized that demographic changes, the migration of people from rural settings to urban areas in search of employment opportunity, made it necessary to acquire basic literacy in order to function in a new socioeconomic environment. This meant an initiative had to be taken to provide facilities so that local communities could pool their resources to combat illiteracy.

The participants at the Williamsburg conference concluded that nations must increase their budgets toward education in general and literacy in particular because they were essential to other forms of national development. In addition to placing emphasis on formal education, nations were encouraged to initiate new adult literacy programs to ensure that no segment of the community was neglected. To make this investment would require a commitment to the new start. Nations were therefore urged to make the economy stronger than it had been in the past.

The Williamsburg conference concluded that educators alone must not be expected to assume the responsibility for improvements in education, but that all segments of society should share the responsibility for providing adequate facilities so that education could serve the purpose for which it was intended. Industry, religious organizations, financial institutions, and private organizations must all cooperate in a national effort to fight illiteracy and inequality. The conference also recognized the need to resolve another growing problem--that is, the inability of nations to adopt national programs to new conditions. Changes in technology, politics, institutional structures, and industrial development all demanded fundamental revamping of educational systems.

To seek solutions to an increasing number of problems, the Williamsburg conference made other suggestions. The following are among them: Nations must cooperate more closely in the future than they had in the past. Developed nations must offer their assistance to developing nations because it is in their own interests to do so. Nations must place education higher on the national agenda and allocate more money for it than they had in the past.

Nations must recognize the importance of initiating innovation in an educational system because, "if it clings to conventional practices merely because there are traditions that cannot be changed, that system is a satire of education itself. From the standpoint of society, the resources invested in perpetuating such a system are misused resources because a higher proportion of students will emerge ill-fitted to serve well either themselves or their society."[19]

The Williamsburg conference warned developing nations not to import educational systems from developed countries without making necessary adjustments to suit local conditions. Its members must have recognized that in their enthusiasm to initiate national developmental programs, developing nations erroneously equated the educational systems in developed countries with development itself. They neglected the reality that due to many years of neglect, all nations had to make new efforts in planning the future by taking other important considerations into account. These considerations included establishing informal education and eliminating rural-urban conflict, a major cause of underdevelopment in many developing nations.

---

[19]Williamsburg conference, 1967, in Coombs, *World Crisis in Education*, p. 6.

In realizing that the thrust for educational development must not be removed from the thrust for economic development, the Williamsburg conference fully acknowledged that manpower development was a critical component of this strategy.

The importance of the Williamsburg conference is not in its accomplishments but in its representative character and its ability to articulate elements of a new start in the endless quest for educational improvement. Its participants did not try to discredit the efforts of the San Francisco conference to come to grips with a very serious situation that the entire world faced. But, while it recognized the critical nature of this situation, the Williamsburg conference also failed to produce a magic formula to solve the problems that were being compounded by a combination of forces that the San Francisco conference did not envisage.

But one must not conclude that the Williamsburg conference was a failure, because it was not. To attract people from all walks of life, to pinpoint the nature of the problem, to lay out the prerequisites of finding solutions--all these combined to enable the conference to make an indelible imprint on the crisis that mankind was facing in the struggle for self. Indeed, the Williamsburg conference represents a fresh start in the human drama of survival.

In all their efforts and endeavor, nations had to resolve a critical question, and that was: What exactly had they learned about past educational practices that could now shed some light on programs of the future? If they were able to provide an answer to this question, both individually and collectively, then they would place themselves in a better position to face the problems of building a new national character necessary in order to make the future better than the past.

SUMMARY AND CONCLUSION

In spite of the enthusiasm that characterized the approach of nations to education following the conclusion of the war in 1945, there were a number of problems that had to be resolved in order to encourage national development as a prerequisite to world peace and security. The conclusion that the delegates to the San Francisco conference reached--that world security and peace were only possible if nations endeavored to give their people a viable education--signified the beginning of a strategy to--seek new solutions to age-old problems of human conflict. While this strategy had a real potential, the inability of nations to make education what it should be translated into an inability to find solutions to problems of human conflict.

The exercise in self-appraisal that nations engaged in at San Francisco, painful as it was, was a gallant effort to put that thrust into proper perspective in order to ensure a future better than the past. Tragic as it was, the war itself had been an eye-opener to the grim reality that nations faced a greater danger of conflict in the future than they had experienced in the past unless they utilized education to seek a better understanding of each other. The outbreak of hostilities in the Persian Gulf in August 1990 and January 1993 was a grim reminder of this reality. But, in order for nations to understand each other, they have to make sure that they design educational programs that bring this about. Without resolving the problems that this chapter has discussed, it is not quite possible to eliminate the possibility of that conflict.

The crisis in education since the conclusion of the war in 1945 suggests that, in spite of the efforts that nations have made to solve them, problems of national development and international relationships have continued to intensify. With Iraq's invasion of Kuwait in August 1990, there was nothing to suggest that nations had learned the lessons of war. Chapter 2 discusses some historical developments that helped shape the educational policy and national character of African nations, Japan, the United States, and the former Soviet Union.

2

The Influence of History: The Importance of Knowledge of the Past

Knowledge of past achievement of science and education is critical to our development.

Mikhail Gorbachev, 1989

THE IMPORTANCE OF HISTORY
TO HUMAN EVENTS

Of the six areas selected for the focus of this study--history, theory, objectives, the curriculum, administration, and current problems--historical perspective puts the other five in a context that makes it possible to examine all the relevant features. Although some say of human experience that the only thing we learn from history is that we do not learn from it, one can also conclude that we cannot ignore the significance of history to human events. The old saying "study the past to understand the present in order to plan the future" must form an important component of human effort to resolve problems of development.

Indeed, major human developments and efforts to structure the future to serve human needs are a result of lessons from the past. It is not easy for man to understand the present and plan the future without an effective knowledge of the past. The astronomer who explains how the universe operates does so from a historical perspective. The biologist who studies how a species can become endangered also does so from a knowledge of the past. The economist who warns nations of the consequences of inflation or makes economic projections also does so from an understanding of similar situations that existed in the past. This is why the delegates to the San Francisco conference attempted to discover a formula for global peace and security by stressing the importance of education from a historical perspective. In doing so, they were becoming sensitive to the influence of history in their collective endeavor to plan the future.

Another factor to consider in any human enterprise is that mankind is a product of history. The anthropologist tells us that the study of man's past yields important information about the present and the future. The paleontologist informs us that the study of fossils reveals important information about species in general to tell us about the present and possible future development. The archaeologist advises us that the study of material remains of the past shows how people used to live. This information helps in making decisions about how we must plan the future. The fact of the matter is that whether it is in economic issues, political action, religious innovation, or educational endeavors, human institutions are a product of history. We must now examine how history has influenced the development of educational policy and how it has in turn shaped the national character of Africa, Japan, the United States, and the former Soviet Union.

AFRICA: THE LEGACY OF THE COLONIAL PERIOD

The conclusion of the Berlin conference on the partition of Africa by European nations in February 1885 ushered in the colonization of the continent. The social, cultural, and educational systems that had operated in Africa for many years were substituted by those of European origin in order for the colonial governments to suit their own purposes, and not to ensure the advancement of the Africans.[1] The introduction of Western education to Africa by Christian missionaries was effected because the governments believed that the Africans would have better relationships with them than with the colonial officials themselves. It is a sobering reality that by the very nature of colonialism the effect of Western education on the Africans was to condition them to accept the colonial governments as a new order of things, and that any resistance was regarded as uncivilized behavior.

An interesting phenomenon occurred at the conclusion of the Berlin conference: Each colonizing nation began to develop a program of action in Africa consistent with its own policy. Although European nations pursued individual educational policies suited to the conditions of their particular colonies, they had three features in common: The educational programs were operated by missionaries to reduce the likelihood of the Africans rejecting the kind of education they were receiving; the educational process was intended to convert the Africans to Christianity,

---

[1]David Scanlon, *Traditions of African Education* (New York: Teachers College Press, 1964), p. 4.

which was considered essential to African acceptance of Western culture, and the educational process was practical in content because the Africans were considered incapable of engaging in any form of academic education.[2] In pursuing these elements in a uniform way, the colonial governments developed a well-coordinated strategy to make sure that the Africans in one colonial system would not compare the conditions that controlled them with those of another.

Beyond the primary objective of persuading Africans to accept Christianity as the first step toward accepting Western culture and colonialism itself as a civilizing act, a central purpose of missionary education was "to bring up a new generation of Africans that will have accepted the new civilization and train men and women who will eventually become leaders of their people."[3] If this was a hidden agenda in the missionary objectives of education for Africans, it was not shared by the colonial governments. Many colonial officials agreed with Ethel Tawse Jollie, one of the first women to sit in a colonial legislature in colonial Zimbabwe, who as late as 1927, during a debate on the question of African advancement through education, said: "We do not intend to admit the Natives to the same social or political position that we ourselves enjoy. Let us therefore make no pretense of educating them in the same way we educate whites."[4]

The difference of opinion between the colonial officials and the missionaries about the purpose of education for Africans would later help set the stage for a major conflict to emerge when conditions were right. Nevertheless, while this cooperation lasted, both the missionaries and the colonial governments wanted to utilize it to bolster their own position and take maximum advantage of it. By the end of the nineteenth century it was clear that behind the difference of opinion between the missionary view; that offering education that entailed more than instruction in Christianity would bring about change in the life-style of the Africans for the good of the colonial societies themselves, and the view of the colonial governments, that education must not include anything more than instruction in manual labor, lay elements of institutional conflict that alerted Africans to dangers to come.[5]

The missionaries, mindful of the universal application of the principles of human brotherhood, wanted to include the Africans into the family of believers as equal members. The colonial governments wanted to structure a society based on a vertical, rather than a horizontal, system. This would mean that the Africans would always occupy an inferior position in society, just as Jollie argued. The superiority of the white man would be

---

[2]Ibid., p. 5.

[3]Martin Schlunk, *Des Hamburgischen Kolonialinstitutes*, vol. 18 (Hamburg: L. Friederichsen, 1914), p. xx.

[4] Ethel Tawse Jollie in *Rhodesia: Parliamentary Debates* (Salisbury: Government Printer, 1927), p. 20.

[5]Dickson A. Mungazi, *Education and Government Control in Zimbabwe: A Study of the Commissions of Inquiry, 1908-1974* (New York: Praeger, 1990), p. 13.

sustained by placing black Africans in an inferior position. That the Africans noted this difference later became a crucial factor in their struggle for self-government.

Beyond the conflict between political ideology and theological precepts, the missionaries and the colonial governments created a socioeconomic and political environment in which the Africans had to decide which of these two Western institutions to believe and trust. David Scanlon argues that while the thrust for African education was the responsibility of the missionaries, the colonial governments made sure that the education they actually provided was a result of the policy they designed.[6] This is the environment that led black Africans to question both the purpose and the content of the education they received.

If the missionaries were able to impart to the Africans a clear understanding of the need for education, then they could rightly claim that their mission was a success. But the continuing struggle between them and the colonial governments meant that the Africans were placed in a situation that forced them to reject Western education until after the First World War. How did the missionaries react to the Africans' rejection of the education they were trying to offer them, knowing that it was intended to bring them into the Christian fold and the circle of the human family? They did not take it well.

The advent of the Industrial Revolution compelled even the most ardent missionaries to adjust their policy from the pursuit of religious ideals as a viable basis of African development to the pursuit of European commercial goals and entrepreneurial adventure in Africa. This is what David Livingstone (1813-1873), one of the most revered missionaries to Africa, argued during an address at Oxford University in 1864:

> Sending the Gospel to the heathens of Africa must include much more than is implied in the usual practice of a missionary, namely, a man going about with a Bible under his arm. The promotion of commerce ought to be specially attended to as this, more than any thing else, makes the heathens of Africa depend on commercial intercourse among civilized nations. I go back to open a new path to commerce in Africa, do you carry on the work I have started?[7]

It sounds ironic from what Livingstone said that the missionaries readily acknowledged that promoting European commercial interests was a more important objective in Africa than promoting the development of Africans and yet still expected the Africans to accept their message. When, in 1912, one British colonial official argued, "I do not consider it right that we should educate the Native in any way that will unfit him for service. The Native is and should always be the hewer of wood and the drawer of water for his white master,"[8] the missionaries did not register any protest

---

[6] Scanlon, *Traditions of African Education*, p. 4.

[7] David Livingstone,"Missionary Travels in Southern Africa, 1857-70," in the Zimbabwe National Archives.

[8] Letter to *The Rhodesia Herald*, June 28, 1912.

against an official policy that was clearly detrimental to the developmental interests of Africans, a group of people they were in Africa to serve.

The position of the colonial officials that "It is cheap labor that we need out of Natives, and it has yet to be proved that the Native who can read and write turns out to be a good laborer,"[9] and the view of another colonial official that "The Native in his ignorance almost invariably abuses a purely bookish education, utilizing it only as a means of defying authority. A purely literary education for Natives should not be considered for many years to come,"[10] reduced the education of Africans to a level where it was nothing more than a meaningless drill on manual labor and conditioning them to Western culture. It is equally strange that by the outbreak of the Second World War in 1939, colonial officials were still thinking in terms of these Victorian views of the Africans.

Tragic as it was, the war created an entirely new set of conditions for the Africans. Following the *blitz* of 1941, the Allied nations that had colonies in Africa launched a campaign to recruit Africans into their military forces by trying to convince them that if the Axis powers won the war, they would reintroduce slavery, as if to suggest that existing conditions governing African life were any better. However, while not believing that the Allied nations were better than the Axis powers, the Africans still joined the ranks of Allied forces--not to serve the interests of the colonial systems, but to demonstrate that they had a potential to be counted and to reassure themselves of their role during a period of global crisis. As the brutality of the war dragged on, the Africans faced the danger of instant death with a clear knowledge of the significance of their role.

The impact the war had on the Africans was profound. It made it possible for them to see how colonial governments designed policies to promote their political and socioeconomic positions. It also made it possible for them to see how institutions in Europe were being run. They saw how democracy, or a lack of it operated. But by making it possible for Africans to see the weaknesses inherent in the colonial systems, the Allied nations also made it possible for Africans to question what they had previously thought were infallible institutions. They began to have a new vision of their future.

The Africans began to see themselves as people with a potential that the colonial systems either ignored or did not consider important to develop. The Africans then concluded that, as they existed, colonial systems were inadequate and therefore unable to serve their needs, and that they needed fundamental change. But, more important still, they concluded that the colonial systems were vulnerable to concerted efforts to change their central structure, even though colonial officials did not want their institutions tampered with.

The Africans who fought in the war were made to believe that they were fighting for equal opportunity, yet they returned home to endure new

[9]Southern Rhodesia, *Annual Report of the Chief Native Commissioner*, 1905, in the Zimbabwe National Archives.

[10]Southern Rhodesia, *Annual Report of the Chief Native Commissioner*, 1904, in the Zimbabwe National Archives.

forms of inequality. They thought they were fighting for the liberation of the universal human being, yet they returned home to encounter new forms of colonial oppression. They were made to believe that they were fighting for the advancement of all people, yet they returned home to face new and more powerful restrictions. They were made to believe they were fighting for justice and fairness in society, yet they returned home to endure new forms of injustice. Unable to make any sense out of this contradictory situation, the Africans responded to the end of the war in the way that the colonial governments did not anticipate: they became aware of themselves as a people.

These are the conditions that the Africans recognized as a product of colonialism and which they felt had to be eliminated to create conditions for their own advancement. Robert July summed up the effect of colonialism on the Africans after their participation in the war:

> Colonialism contained the germ of its own destruction. By conquering the Africans, it aroused in them a desire to be free. By exploiting them, it produced a rising resistance to tyranny. By introducing Africa to the modern world, it generated visions of a better life consummated in liberty. By educating the Africans to function as cheap labor, the colonial governments taught them the skills of self-directed activity and purpose.[11]

This realization was an environment from which the rise of African nationalism became inevitable. The return of Kwame Nkrumah (1901-1972) from his educational *safari* in Europe and the United States in 1947 ushered in a new era in the Africans' perception of themselves as a people cast in a colonial setting. They began to direct their efforts toward seeking a better life within the colonial systems. When they found that the colonial governments were not willing to accommodate their aspirations, they changed their strategy from seeking advancement within the colonial structures to seeking an end to colonial governments themselves. Once the Africans reached the conclusion that as long as colonial governments continued they would inhibit their ability to make progress, they became determined to put their quest for development on hold until the colonial systems were brought to an end.

In championing the cause of political independence for the Africans, Nkrumah convinced his fellow Africans that their search for development had to be initiated from a position of political independence as a prior condition. He argued that their search for education to make other forms of development possible was handicapped by the deliberate policies of the colonial governments to foil their efforts. Paraphrasing the scriptures, Nkrumah urged the Africans to "seek ye the political kingdom first and all

---

[11]Robert July, *A History of the African People* (New York: Scribner, 1974), p. 581. See also Dickson A. Mungazi's review of Robert July, *A History of the African People*, 4th Edition, in *The International Journal of African Historical Studies* 26 (1993:1B.

other things shall be added unto you."[12]   On the first anniversary of Ghana's independence in 1958, Nkrumah outlined the goals that he believed his administration must pursue both to fulfill his own mission and to chart a new course of development in Africa. Among these goals was that Africans must achieve political independence as a prerequisite to other forms of development.

From this point on, the course of events in Africa was changed permanently. The Africans understood Nkrumah to say that their destiny was in their own hands. But in seeking an end to colonialism, the Africans came face to face with the formidable problems of national development, which they did not anticipate. Among these problems was educational development. Were the Africans equal to the task of building nations in which educational development played a major role? The answer provides a fascinating account of the struggle of a people under colonial domination.

JAPAN: FROM THE MEIJI TO THE OCCUPATION

To understand the importance of the historical background of Japan, one must understand the philosophy of Buddha, or Siddhartha Gautama (563-483 B.C.), the great teacher and founder of a religious movement that stressed the acquisition of knowledge as a basis of true human essence. Although the facts of his life are not fully known, Buddha exerted as great an influence as any other great religious leader in history. As a young man, Buddha became deeply troubled by the suffering he saw in his society and concluded that the acquisition of knowledge, not only about humanity in general, but also about the process of finding solutions to problems, would enhance the quality of life. Out of this thinking came an emphasis on education as a means of elevating man to a higher level of life.

Although Buddha gave the Japanese a religious belief that has remained a distinctive feature of their cultural strength to this day, it was the Chinese philosopher Confucius (551-479 B.C.) who had the most profound influence on the Japanese understanding of education as a means to shape a new national identity. The influence that Confucius left behind is most powerful in his philosophy that the secret of good government lies in intelligently selecting honest and educated leaders.

Although leaders of modern Japan are as vulnerable to corruption as those in other societies, the influence of both Buddha and Confucius is a constant reminder of how greatness can be achieved for the benefit of all. Because both men considered human life the most important component of national life, they argued that everything possible must be done to elevate individual life to a level where all people are happy, and that the happiness of all people in any society is what is needed to build a utopian system. For this to happen society must endeavor to educate all its people well.

Beginning about A.D. 750 the Japanese were persuaded to accept many Chinese institutional structures, including form of government, literature, and the arts. However, by the twelfth century, Japan began to

---

[12]David Hapgood, *Africa in Today's World Focus* (New York: Gunn and Co., 1971), p. 85; see also Matthew 6:35 and Luke 12:30.

develop its own culture to minimize the Chinese influence. Displeased with the changes that were taking place in the eighteenth century, Shogun Tokugawa reintroduced the Confucian concept of society. Under Tokugawa subjects were expected to demonstrate their absolute loyalty to the emperor by their unquestionable dedication to learning. Academic excellence was now considered a duty to both the emperor and to one's family. Failure in the pursuit of learning was considered a disgrace to both oneself and to society. Ronald Anderson observed on this aspect of Japanese education: "The solid imbedding of education in its value system helps to explain the importance placed on education in Japan today. The didactic moral training in the feudal school helps us understand the current insistence of modern Japanese parents on systematic moral instruction in schools."[13]

The restoration of the Meiji the dynasty of Emperor Mutsuhito, whose reign began in 1868, spelled the demise of the feudal system as the new leaders began to design programs that would bring Japan into modern times. Among the goals they set were to inculcate a new nationalism, to train technicians needed to operate national institutions, and to develop a centralized system of education under the supervision of a national department. The creation of the Fundamental Code of Education in 1872 assisted in dividing the country into eight academic districts, each with one university, thirty secondary schools, and two hundred primary schools.[14]

The Fundamental Code of Education decreed that there must be no illiteracy, underscoring the importance that the Japanese placed on education as part of a national purpose. For Japan a new national purpose was not possible without education. Education thus became a rallying point of any national endeavor toward development.

An important highlight in the historical background of Japan is that during the reign of Emperor Mutsuhito (1867-1912) Japan moved from a feudal state into an industrial and military power. In 1890, at the advice of his Confucian tutor, Mutsuhito decreed a new national policy known as the Imperial Rescript on Education. This policy brought into being the Shinto practice of worshiping the emperor under the Confucian principles of absolute loyalty and obedience. At the end of Mutsuhito's reign Japan was about to embark upon a new period of development.

Mutsuhito stressed the importance of educational development as a condition of national development. Instituting unqualified reverence of the emperor was his way of emphasizing to his subjects his belief that a nation without adequate education remains in a state of underdevelopment. This is why the rescript required that students demonstrate the ability to learn from anyone in a position to impart knowledge. He wanted his subjects to understand that success in education was a national duty.

The inclusion of the rescript into the core curriculum was intended to help all students understand that success in learning formed the fabric of

---

[13]Ronald Anderson, "Japanese Education," in Edward Ignas and Raymond Corsini (eds.), *Comparative Educational Systems* (Itasca, Ill.: F. E. Peacock Co.,1981), p. 237.

[14]Ibid., p. 238.

moral values which essential to shaping a new national character. It was also intended to teach students to recognize the danger of accepting Western values by reminding them of the importance of remaining loyal to their own cultural heritage.[15] Whereas the rescript warned against the dangers of accepting foreign cultural and social values, its influence was felt most in the Japanese search for a new national direction within an environment of global peace, understanding, and cooperation.

The rescript offered an opportunity to schools to teach the importance of basing national life on democratic principles in which the student and the teacher entered into a learning partnership based on mutual respect along the lines that John Dewey developed in his writings.[16] The rescript was also intended to impart to students the reality that when education makes it possible to bring people together in an atmosphere of mutual respect and trust, then it becomes an instrument of creating a happy society along the lines that Confucius taught.

Military Adventure

But this road to national development was short-lived as Japan's relations with other nations began to deteriorate. The rivalry for influence in Manchuria and Korea that developed between Japan and Russia beginning in 1901 led to increasing tensions. Britain, fearing that Russia's rising military power would upset the balance of power, supported Japan in 1902 by helping Japan become more aggressive toward its rival. In 1904 Japan declared war on Russia, derailing the progress that the rescript had initiated on the domestic front.

The educational innovation that the emperor had introduced was suspended as national efforts were directed toward winning the war with Russia. In 1905 President Theodore Roosevelt succeeded in persuading the warring sides to sign a peace treaty. The treaty of Portsmouth required Russia to recognize Japanese interests in Korea, putting an end to its own intention to extend its influence.

Having come out militarily stronger from this confrontation with Russia, Japan now adapted an aggressive foreign policy, which put in abeyance its relations with other nations through diplomacy and education. When World War I started, Japan, as an ally of Britain, declared war on Germany. Although Japan was one of the original members of the League of Nations when it was formed in 1920, it did not abandon its policy of aggression toward other nations in the Pacific. On September 18, 1931, for example, Japanese forces invaded Manchuria. Although the League of Nations passed a resolution condemning the invasion and asking Japan to withdraw, the resolution had little effect on Japanese behavior. Already disabled by the refusal of the U.S. Senate to ratify the treaty by which the

---

[15]Ibid., p. 239.

[16]For example, in *Experience and Education* (New York: Collins, 1938), Dewey argues that for any education to be considered progressive, it must serve the needs of students. This demands they have the respect of their teachers and the freedom to think critically on their own.

league would have been strengthened, the league was in no position to enforce its resolution. The failure of the league made it possible for Italy to invade Ethiopia in 1935.

When Japan signed the anti-Communist treaties with Adolf Hitler in 1936 and 1937, it felt that its military forces could now turn against the United States. This is why, in December 1937, Japanese planes bombed and sank the U.S. gunboat *Panay* in the Yangtze River. Although Japan later apologized and agreed to pay the United States $2 million in damages, relations between the two countries were permanently damaged. To make matters worse for Japan, Hitler and Joseph Stalin signed a non-aggression treaty in 1939, forcing Japan to sign a neutrality pact with Russia. This meant that relations among Japan, Russia, and Germany were formalized in order to adopt a well-coordinated hostile policy toward the rest of the world.

On the home front things did not work out well for Japan. The fall of the government of Fumimoro Konoye (1899-1945) on October 17, 1941, allowed General Hedeki Tojo (1884-1948) to become prime minister. Thus, the military had full control of the country and a new national policy came into being. Japan's hostility toward the United States dramatically increased within weeks of Tojo's assumption of office. On December 7, 1941, a day that President Franklin Roosevelt said would live in infamy, Japanese bombers attacked U.S. military bases at Pearl Harbor in Hawaii, forcing the United States to enter the war, with the consequent drop of the atomic bombs on Hiroshima and Nagasaki in August 1945. Japan's military policy finally came to an end, and it once more had an opportunity to redirect its efforts toward the development of education.

The Occupation: The Period of Reform

From 1945 to 1952, Allied forces under General Douglas MacArthur of the United States occupied Japan. Among MacArthur's first actions were the reopening of schools and a vast program of innovation based on democratic principles. That MacArthur and his aides considered schools an essential component of orienting Japan toward a new role in world politics suggests how much conditions had changed. MacArthur also wanted Japan to change its attitude from thinking about producing war materials to producing goods needed to improve the standard of living of its people. Also among the first things that MacArthur did was to draw up a new constitution for Japan with a clause renouncing war and introducing democratic principles and land reforms. Little did MacArthur realize that in less than forty years Japan would rise from the ashes of atomic destruction to pose an economic threat to the United States itself.

The visit of the U.S. Education Committee to Japan soon after the war ended, consisting of distinguished leaders and scholars, helped form the basis of the new thrust for reform. As a result of the visit, the Japanese Education Reform Council was formed under the general supervision of the Ministry of Education and was charged with the responsibility of overseeing the reform process. The U.S. Education Committee assisted the

Japanese Education Reform Council in identifying three changes that would form the thrust for educational reform in Japan.

The first was to decentralize the administration system to make it comparable with that of the United States. This was done in the belief that decentralization would respond to the needs of students better than the system under the old bureaucracy. The second was to define a new national educational policy to replace the one formulated in 1890 under the Rescript of Education. It would eliminate worshiping the emperor so that students could direct their energy toward creating a new society that was consistent with the realization that nations of the world must endeavor to put global security above provincial and national interests. Therefore, the reform council considered restructuring the curriculum to reflect this line of thinking. The third was to reorganize the entire school system onto a single track so that educational programs would be coordinated better, finances would be more equitably distributed, and facilities and personnel be more evenly divided.

Although the purpose of these reforms was to lessen the power of the central government and reduce bureaucratic red tape, subsequent developments in education produced contrary results. The desire of the Japanese to rebuild their society and to regain their national independence and the new wave of nationalism inspired by Emperor Hirohito combined to establish a set of national goals and objectives. Central to this national endeavor was the conviction that education must be utilized to promote a new national purpose. Indeed, the occupation of Japan proved to be a blessing in disguise. It allowed its forces to ensure Japan's defense and security while it directed its efforts toward rebuilding the country's economy and elevating itself to new heights of power and influence among nations.

By 1992 the strength of the Japanese economy posed serious implications for the United States, the nation that had controlled it during the occupation.[17] Would it be fair for the United States to complain in 1992 that Japan was practicing unfair economic and trade policies when its own policy had been part of the system that Japan had been using to rebuild its national character? The end of the occupation in 1952 accelerated the pace toward reconstruction to erase both the legacy of the occupation to erase both the negative effects of the occupation and the psychological, the physical, and the economic devastation caused by the atomic bomb. Japan was now ready to chart a new course of national development.

THE UNITED STATES: THE JACKSONIAN ERA AND THE BEGINNINGS OF MODERN EDUCATION

A discussion of major developments in American education must begin with the election of Andrew Jackson[18] as president of the United

---

[17]PBS, "Inside Japan," a documentary film, November 22, 1992.

[18]Andrew Jackson (1767-1845) served as president of the United States from 1829 to 1837.

States in 1828. That Jackson took pride in being the first president to be born in a log cabin symbolized a new direction that he would chart for the development of his nation. It is not surprising that his term of office, from 1829 to 1837, left a legacy that has become known as the Jacksonian era, or, as it is known to history, the age of the common man.

Jackson's social reform rightly earned him a place in history as the leader of Jacksonian democracy. His legal training under Spruce Macey, a wealthy attorney, helped him understand the social implications of the office he held. During the War of 1812, Jackson served with distinction. Tragic as this war was, it gave Jackson an opportunity to understand the need for social reform to serve the needs of the people. He utilized his defeat by John Quincy Adams in the presidential election of 1824 as a form of education that he felt he needed to plan efficiently for the election of 1828, in which he defeated Adams.

Because of his background as the first president born in a log cabin, Jackson fully identified himself with the aspirations of the common man. Therefore, his social reforms permanently transformed the United States from an aristocratic society into a nation in which the concept of democratic values and principles had a practical meaning to the struggling masses. His administration was based on his conviction that educational development based on equality would ensure national development. Five basic reasons explain Jackson's thrust: (1) education improves social institutions and their functions so that they serve the needs of the people, (2) education is an instrument with which to sharpen individual perceptions of self and of society, (3) education creates a social environment and conditions in which individuals see themselves within a larger context of collective principles and values, (4) education helps develop talent to serve the needs of society, and (5) education makes democratic values more viable.

In an effort to implement these principles, Jackson operated on the basic belief that equality of educational opportunity is the hub around which social justice, stability, and development revolve. He also believed that in a society in which slavery and other social inequalities were the order of the day, this line of thinking had a special appeal to the masses of deprived people who were struggling for improvement of the conditions that controlled their lives. By demonstrating sensitivity to the plight of the masses, Jackson charted a new course in the development of the United States. A critical component of his philosophy of education was his view that in order to implement democratic values the educational system must be reformed. The development of society is ensured when its people participate in its operations.

The Legacy of the Reform Movement

The legacy of the Jacksonian era is that it created a national consciousness that suggested some glaring weaknesses in the American system, both social and educational. Political and economic power were still the privilege of a few. This inhibited the thinking that democracy was at its best when the largest number of people possible participated in the political and economic systems. The exclusivity of the political process generated fears that America was becoming an aristocratic society as existed in Europe. With the increase in population from 5,308,000 in 1800 to 12,866,000 in 1830, poverty and other social ills were on the rise, putting the value of social institutions into doubt.[19]

These are some of the realities that made the reform movement imperative beginning in 1837, the year that Jackson completed his second term of office. But the question is: What type of reform was envisaged for education? From that time to the end of the nineteenth century American education was based on three basic philosophical assumptions. The first assumption was that education must be the duty of the state and the right of all people. Even though the U.S. Constitution delegated education as a local responsibility, it was evident that the federal government had an important role to play in its development. The second assumption was that because exclusive private schools embodied elements of an aristocratic society, there was a need to complement them with public schools. The third assumption was that there must be a better way of financing education than was the case at the time.

These three assumptions also brought individuals like Henry Barnard (1811-1900) and Horace Mann (1796-1859) into the arena of educational reform to chart a new course for its development. Mann so believed in educational reform that he gave up his law practice to become secretary of the Massachusetts Board of Education. In thirteen years, from 1835 to 1848, Mann championed the cause of educational reform in a way that reflected the ideas of Andrew Jackson for the improvement of American society through educational development. The success of Mann's efforts must be seen within the context of the strategy he followed to accomplish the objectives he had identified.

First, he persuaded the business community to become involved in reforms in education because he convinced them that better-educated workers were more productive. Edmund Dwight, a leading industrialist who had nominated Mann for the position of secretary of the Massachusetts Board of Education, played a leading role in raising the consciousness of members of the business community about the need to support the reform movement. Mann also persuaded workers to support the concept of common schools because they would generate a new awareness of equality, not only in education but also in society as a whole.[20] But Mann's and Barnard's influence was felt more in the structure of the school system they advocated than in philosophical arguments for reform. Major revision of the curriculum, introducing common schools, training of teachers, tax support of education, and better administrative systems all combined to form a central element of the thrust for educational reform that is evident in the American educational system today.

---

[19]David Nasaw, *Schooled to Order: A Social History of Public Schooling in the United States* (New York: Oxford University Press, 1979), p. 29.

[20]Ibid., p. 481.

That the mass migration of the Irish to the United States beginning in 1837 that coincided with the beginning of the reform movement further enabled Americans to see the need to transform their society through transforming the school system. Enactment of the Land Grant Act in 1861, forming the state university system, underscored the federal role in the development of education.

By the time that Grover Cleveland (1837-1908) began his second term as president in 1893,[21] American society had been transformed by technological and industrial development--achieved through education. Cleveland's dedication of the Statue of Liberty in October 1896 and Henry Ford's first car in the same year marked the end of the nineteenth century with the hope that the twentieth century would be even better.

THE SOVIET UNION: THE EFFECT
OF THE BOLSHEVIK REVOLUTION

In December 1992, *Time*, writing on the impact of history on critical developments that were unfolding in the former Soviet Union, observed, "The 20th century has dealt harshly with Russia: revolutions, three wars, sixty million dead, a people enslaved by a 70-year experiment in failed ideology. Now Russia is at a critical juncture in its struggle to be reborn as a democracy. Even as Bill Clinton turns his attention to domestic issues, he has both moral and selfish reasons to care about Russia's success. Global security depends on it, and by providing U.S. help, Clinton can make it more likely that he will remain free to tend to the urgent business at home."[22] One must examine events that were taking place in the nineteenth century to understand why this was happening.

The Bolshevik Revolution of 1917 was a climax of events that had begun to unfold before 1894, the year that Czar Nicholas II ascended the Russian throne. The restoration of the Meiji in Japan in 1868 created an environment that by 1894 brought Russia and Japan into a state of conflict because each nation wanted to promote and protect its national interests in the Pacific. Nicholas, conscious of the fact that Russia and Japan viewed international relationships from conflicting positions, did everything possible to ensure his own position and the security of his country. In this strategy, Nicholas became less sensitive to the needs of his people, relying on a few close advisers to carry out a national agenda and implement his policy. He became increasingly intolerant of opposing views on how the country should be run. This did not sit well with the masses. Great Britain's support of Japan in 1902 and Japan's declaration of war on Russia in 1904 set the stage for increased disillusionment with Nicholas as a national leader. The signing of the Treaty of Portsmouth in 1905, requiring Russia to recognize Japanese interests and influence in Korea, spelled trouble for Nicholas.

---

[21]Cleveland had been defeated in seeking in 1888 by Benjamin Harrison, whom he in turn defeated in 1892.

[22]*Time*, December 7, 1992, p. 32.

Among the nineteenth-century Russian educational thinkers who were opposed to the excessive power that the czar exercised were N. I. Pigorov (1810-1881), K. D. Ushinsky (1824-1870), and L. N. Tolstoy (1828-1919). All three shared one fundamental philosophy of education: that educational reform was necessary for reforming society. They also believed that reforming society was necessary to promote human development and advancement. This meant, among other things, that the right of the people to be masters of their own destiny must be recognized. This would happen only when the power of the czar was reduced in order to allow the people more involvement in government's structure and functions, a position that Nicholas rejected.[23]

The seeds of the revolution germinated in January 1905, when thousands of unarmed workers marched to Nicholas's winter palace in St. Petersburg to demand improvement of the conditions of their lives and better education for their children. Things came to a head when troops fired on the demonstrators, killing many and wounding many more. Nicholas thought he had found an answer to his problems, totally unaware that he had compounded them. In 1917, taking advantage of the weakened position that Nicholas found himself in as a result of World War I, Vladimir I. Ulyanov, better known as Lenin (1870-1924), and Leon Trotsky (1879-1940) provided the leadership needed to successfully launch the revolution. This time military troops joined the crowds who were demanding the end of the oppressive rule of the czar. The Bolshevik Revolution lasted until the death of Joseph Stalin in March 1953.

Educational Reform: From Lenin to Gorbachev

As soon as it was evident that the revolution had been successful, Lenin assumed the leadership role to direct its course and development. At the top of his political agenda was reconstruction of the educational system. He appointed his wife, N. K. Krupskaya (1869-1939), commissar for education to ensure that his policy and programs were carried out as he had outlined them. The centerpiece of his educational policy was his belief that all-round education was an absolute necessity for all students in order to eliminate what he saw as the capitalist legacy of the czarist regime and create a socialist state.[24] Lenin's view that capitalism had no place in the educational environment of a socialist state shows his dedication to the transformation of Russian society through fundamental educational reform.

One must consider Lenin's efforts to reform education from a larger social perspective. In 1919, consistent with basic socialist ideology, Lenin ordered the schools to serve as a training ground for workers to reorganize their position in a socialist state. To achieve this objective he demanded that socialist literature be used in all schools. Lenin considered

---

[23]Gennadi Lisichkin, *Socialism: An Appraisal of Prospects* (Moscow: Novosti Press, 1989), p. 18.

[24]N. Kuzin and M. Kondokov, *Education in the U.S.S.R.* (Moscow: Progress Press, 1977), p. 7.

both teaching and learning crucial to building a socialist state. This is why he argued: "Teaching is an important part of education. Without teaching there is no knowledge, without knowledge there is no socialism, without socialism society degenerates into a capitalistic decay."[25] Lenin's approach to education was the result of his observation in 1913 that "Russia is the exception. There is no other country so barbarous and in which the masses are robbed of their right to education and knowledge."[26]

When Lenin died in 1924, there was a bitter struggle to succeed him for the next four years. Joseph Stalin (1879-1953) emerged as victor in 1928, when the Bolsheviks ignored Lenin's warning against allowing Stalin to assume the position of power. As soon as he took over, Stalin introduced the first of his five-year developmental plans, during which he forced the formation of collective agricultural communities in which education was to play a leading role along the lines that Lenin had established. Stalin did this not because he believed it was the right thing to do for the country, but because he thought that by showing some respect for Lenin's ideas he would have the support of the people he needed for the success of his own programs. His desire to promote industrial development motivated him to try raising the literacy rate from 8 percent in 1928 to 40 percent by the time of his death in 1953.

Under Stalin's slogan "a culture national in form but socialist in content,"[27] the educational reform movement now entered a new phase. Stalin himself rejected John Dewey's idea that education be child-centered and offered instead an educational program intended to promote development of the country to a higher economic level and increased industrial productivity. By requiring that the schools to help increase productivity he hoped to strengthen the socialist political system. This is also why in 1935 Stalin imposed a strict national system of examinations and demanded a higher level of performance by both teachers and students. Both were made to understand that success in their educational efforts paved the road to national development, and that they must regard personal failure as the failure of the nation. Under Stalin it was made clear to everyone that failure carried serious penalties .

Because Stalin was not willing to compromise his views of both education and society, he instituted, also in 1935, the purge. Millions of people were executed or sent to forced labor camps either for failing to meet the standards he had set or for becoming disloyal to his programs. The old Bolsheviks, all of them associates of Lenin, were eliminated. Stalin's decision to cooperate with Adolf Hitler in 1939 created a national social and political climate that had the effect of reducing the pace of the educational reform that he thought he had initiated. Terror and fear among the people derailed most of his national programs, including education and collective agricultural operations.

25Ibid., p. 8.

26Ibid., p. 12.

27Nigel Grant, *Soviet Education* (London: Penguin, 1979), p. 78.

Stalin's aggressive policies toward the Western nations helped push the latter to form NATO in 1949 because they saw him as someone who could trigger a new international crisis by globally pursuing such policies as he was implementing at home. In this context Stalin was feared both by his own people and the international community. His efforts to reform the educational system were made in order to sustain his own position of power and not to ensure the development of the country. This is why he introduced the purge to eliminate those who disagreed with him.

Stalin's death, in March 1953, was followed by another struggle for power. This time the main contenders were Lavrenti Beria (1899-1953), chief of the secret police, Georgi Malenkov, Vycheslav Molotov, and Nikita Khrushchev (1894-1972). As soon as Khrushchev emerged the winner in March 1958, he introduced a new element into the educational reform process that had started with Lenin. He decreed that success in education was a national duty for all students and teachers.

Khrushchev's approach was Stalin reincarnate. He wanted education to help increase both awareness of the values of socialism and the level of industrial and agricultural productivity. He wanted to strike a working balance between academic education and vocational and technical training. In 1959 he introduced a ten-year schooling system, shown in the table on the following page and increased part-time university education. Khrushchev took advantage of the launching of Sputnik in October 1957 to stress the importance of teaching science and space technology in institutions of higher learning. He also tried to attract students from countries that he thought were struggling for independence, especially those in Africa. He ordered the University of Moscow to be renamed renamed Patrice Lumumba University in 1961 in honor of the Congolese leader who was considered to have adopted a socialist ideology for his country, renamed Zaire in 1970 by Joseph Mobuto Sese Seko. At that time there was considerable competition between Western nations and the Soviet Union for influence in the course of development of newly independent countries in Africa, Khrushchev felt that the emerging nations could be persuaded to follow a socialist line because they had inherited enormous political and socioeconomic problems from colonial governments.

These seem to be remarkable achievements for the leader of a country that was struggling for development and to rediscover itself. That Khrushchev did not utilize the methods that Stalin had to carry out his programs suggests an attempt to avoid practices of the past.

In October 1964 Khrushchev fell from power and was replaced by Leonid Brezhnev (1905-1982), a political technocrat whose views of socialism were similar. Among the reasons that the presidium used to take this action against Khrushchev were the following: his behavior at the UN in 1959 when he threatened to bury the West; his handling of the Cuban missile crisis in 1962; his failure to relate education to the development of industry and agriculture; and his adopting a policy that sought to balance academic education and technological education at the expense of meeting the social and economic needs of the people. Many saw these failures as a threat to the Soviet Union as the undisputed leader of the socialist movement in the world not withstanding Red China.[28]

Ten-Year Curriculum

Hours per week in class

Subject Grade	1	2	3	4	5	6	7	8	9	10
Russian language	12	12	11	10	6	6	3	3	2	-
Literature	-	-	-	2	2	2	2	3	4	3
Mathematics	6	6	6	6	6	6	6	6	5	5
History	-	-	-	2	2	2	2	3	4	3
Geography	-	-	-	-	2	3	2	2	2	-
Biology	-	-	-	-	2	2	2	2	1	2
Physics	-	-	-	-	-	2	2	3	4	5
Astronomy	-	-	-	-	-	-	-	-	-	1
Chemistry	-	-	-	-	-	-	2	2	3	3
Foreign language	-	-	-	-	4	3	3	2	2	2
Physical education	2	2	2	2	2	2	2	2	2	2
Labor training	2	2	2	2	2	2	2	2	2	2
Pre-military education	-	-	-	-	-	-	-	-	2	2
Total	22	22	21	24	28	30	28	30	33	30

Source: Grant, *Soviet Education*, p. 91.

Brezhnev embarked on an ambitious educational program. He mandated university students to study more science and foreign languages, especially English. He demanded that students at all levels excel in all educational endeavors and ordered Khrushchev's ten-year plan be improved to make it more effective. He demanded that students excel in athletic competition as an important part of the educational process and as a means of strengthening the competitive edge of the nation in international relations. He ordered a major revision of the curriculum at the primary and secondary levels to include more courses in mathematics and science in order to meet national goals.

Brezhnev saw the development of socialism in the world as the direction that most nations would take, and he wanted the Soviet Union to play a major role in influencing its course. This is why he required that research be part of higher education and demanded all students to demonstrate a sense of patriotism in order to promote socialist doctrine against the challenges of a capitalist world. By 1975 schools in the Soviet Union had a total enrollment of forty-nine million students compared to less than ten million at the time of the revolution.[29]

During an address to the twenty-fourth Communist Party Congress, Brezhnev took pride in his accomplishments when he boasted: "A new historical community of people, the Soviet people, took shape in our country during these years of socialist reconstruction. The people of the

---

[28]Kuzin and Kondokov, *Education in the U.S.S.R.*, p. 14.
[29]Ibid., p. 15.

U.S.S.R. are united by common vital interests, the development of education to promote communism."[30]

Following his death in 1982, Brezhnev was succeeded by Yuri Andropov, the KGB chief. But Andropov died a few months later and was succeeded by Konstantine Chernyenko, who also died in 1984. The central committee of the Communist Party decided that a younger man was needed to give stability and direction. They selected Mikhail Gorbachev. Two years later the world added two words to its vocabulary from the Soviet Union. *Glasnost* (openness) and *perestroika* (reconstruction) were synonymous with Gorbachev's approach to national problems.

Gorbachev felt that these two elements could not be separated from efforts toward national development. Under their influence Gorbachev became aware that if socialism were to serve its intended purpose, meeting the needs of all people, instead of those of the state as had been the practice in the past, then it had to be reformed in ways that had not been done in the past. He decided that these two elements were basic to the national strategy for improvement.[31] Thus, the Soviet Union, as the world had known it since 1917, was poised for transformation.

Gorbachev wanted his fellow citizens to understand that education has an important role to play in social, political, and economic reconstruction. This is why he argued that: "The development of education, enlightenment, and culture and the encouragement of competitive ideas, talent, and intellect are essential to harnessing new conditions of our society as a product of history."[32] These are the factors that, from 1986 to 1991, Gorbachev took into consideration in initiating a new social reform under *glasnost* and *perestroika*. That Gorbachev was the first Soviet leader to recognize that his nation needed basic reform in all major areas places him in a category of his own. With these two words, *glasnost* and *perestroika,* Gorbachev launched a reform campaign for democracy unequaled in any other period in the history of the Soviet Union.

In launching the *glasnost* campaign Gorbachev was motivated by a number of important factors, among them that: (1) open society makes it possible for all citizens to see themselves as they really are; (2) openness allows all people to offer new ideas in order to serve the needs of society; (3) openness makes it possible for segments of the community to evaluate national programs and offer new suggestions for improvement; (4) openness is an important step toward creating a free society, and (5) openness provides the lifeblood of a nation's livelihood--a definition of national character.

In a similar manner, Gorbachev believed that *perestroika* was fundamental to national development because it makes it possible to help people direct their activity toward those things that serve their needs. It

---

[30]Ibid., p. 14.

[31]Mikhail Gorbachev, *Towards a Humane and Democratic Socialist Society,* address to the 28th Congress of the Communist Party, February 5, 1990 (Moscow: Novosti Press, 1990), p. 25.

[32]Ibid., p. 26.

also gives all citizens an opportunity to examine national programs for needed improvement. It promotes change in political, economic, and social systems.

Using this line of thinking Gorbachev appointed an education commission. He believed that the development of education is directly related to other forms of national development. He argued that the purpose of educational reform under *glasnost* and *perestroika* was to improve the socialist system, not to abandon it.[33] However, Gorbachev was different from previous Soviet leaders in that he believed that education must serve the needs of the individual so that he in turn can serve the needs of society. While he believed that socialism must remain the framework of national development, he argued that it must incorporate some democratic principles if *glasnost* and *perestroika* were to build a new society. The fact that in 1990 Gorbachev was facing increasing criticism from hard-line Soviets about his experiment in democracy suggests the critical nature of all this.

Just when he thought things were going according to his plan, Gorbachev began to encounter problems he had not anticipated. The resignation of his foreign minister and close friend, Eduard Shevardnadze, in 1990, combined with the demands of the Baltic states for political independence, posed an unexpected threat to the experiment he was carrying out in social reform and to Gorbachev himself. The people of the Soviet Union were perhaps unaware that if Gorbachev and his programs failed, they would only have themselves to blame for a possible return to conditions similar to those that existed under Joseph Stalin, or for disintegration of the country. Although the results of the national referendum held in March 1991 to determine the fate of the Soviet Union as a united nation were an encouragement to Gorbachev, his problems were by no means over. The bitter rivalry between him and Boris Yeltsin also had an adverse effect on his reform programs.

By 1992 the Soviet Union ceased to exist as a unified nation and gave way to the concept of independent republics. Gorbachev retired from national politics unsure of how history would judge his efforts and programs. An attempt is made in this study to assess their impact .

SUMMARY AND CONCLUSION

The discussion in this chapter leads to two conclusions. The first is that history is the foundation on which the development of any thriving nation is built. A knowledge of history provides the essence of self-assessment-- an opportunity to pause and reflect, to plan new directions, to pose relevant and searching questions so that mistakes of the past are avoided and its positive attributes are strengthened. This suggests that while knowledge of history makes it possible for nations to see themselves as they are in order to plan programs and ensure development.

The second conclusion is that because the development of education is critical to other forms of national development, nations have become increasingly aware of the reality that taking historical factors into

---

[33]Ibid., p. 29.

consideration in planning the future may not ensure success, but it does minimize the likelihood of failure. This is the line of thinking that Gorbachev took into consideration when he argued in November 1989 that "Knowledge of past achievement of science and education is critical to our development. It is important that over the last several decades less attention has been devoted to them. Was this not the reason why production started lagging behind?"[34] This is the line of thinking that Alfred North Whitehead took into consideration, saying, "In the conditions of modern life the rule is absolute, the race which does not value trained intelligence based upon history is doomed. Not all heroism, not all social charm, not all wit, not all victories on land or at sea, can move back the finger of fate. Today we maintain ourselves. Tomorrow science will have moved forward yet one more step because history is on the march and there will be no appeal from the judgment which will then be pronounced on the uneducated."[35]

Arnold Toynbee, a leading British historian of the twentieth century, captured the impact of history on future generations in saying, "Our age will be remembered chiefly for having been the first age since the dawn of civilization in which people dared to think it practicable to make the benefits of civilization available to the whole human race."[36] In his *Study of History* (1934) and *Civilization on Trial* (1948) Toynbee concluded that man must acquire a working knowledge of history to avoid man-made catastrophe. H. G. Wells saw the importance of education in this regard, saying, "Human history becomes more and more a race between education and catastrophe."[37]

If the Western nations that formed a coalition in 1990 and 1993 against Iraq had taken history into account, their action may have been different. If Iraq had understood this reality also, it would not have invaded Kuwait in the first place. Neither Iraq's action nor the coalition's response contributed anything positive to the development of civilization as Toynbee defined it. Both sides needed to learn from history to initiate behavior appropriate to conditions of the modern world.

In January 1993, following the Western coalition military attack on Iraq, a professor of international studies at Northern Arizona University remarked, "There is no question that in launching this latest attack on Iraq, two days before he left office, George Bush wanted to make sure that Saddam Hussein went with him into retirement. He did his best in trying to take attention away from Clinton's inauguration. A study of history would suggest that Bush failed to realize that solutions to problems of international conflict are always found in education. It is hoped that Clinton

---

[34]Mikhail Gorbachev, *Channel the Energy of Youth into Perestroika*, speech given to the All-Union Student Forum, November 15, 1989, (Moscow: Novosti Press, 1989), p. 5.

[35]Quoted in William Van Til, *Education: A Beginning* (Boston: Houghton Mifflin Company, 1974), p. 421.

[36]Ibid., p. 420.

[37]Ibid., p. 6.

will study this history to initiate a new approach because the Willie Horton psychology did not work for Bush."[38]

In becoming conscious of the importance of history to future national endeavor, Gorbachev demonstrated a sensitivity to that old saying: "Those who forget the past are condemned to repeat its errors." Nations must take this wisdom into account in planning their educational development. Without taking historical developments into account, any efforts that any nation makes in planning the future are likely to yield only peripheral results.

---

[38]Conversation with the author in Flagstaff, Arizona, January 17, 1993.

3

Theoretical Considerations: The Basis of Effective Education

The individual cannot find educational fulfillment without freedom to choose his own course of study.

Conference of Catholic Bishops, Zimbabwe, 1987

Education today is more than the key to climbing the ladder of opportunity. In today's global economy, it is an imperative for our nation. Government fails when schools fail.

Bill Clinton, U.S. presidential candidate, 1992

THE IMPERATIVE OF THEORY

One fundamental question that dominated the deliberations of the San Francisco conference in 1945 was how to prevent the outbreak of another world war. Since the participants concluded that a new thrust for education would help resolve problems of human conflict, education directed at meeting this objective demanded taking theoretical considerations into account. What complicated the discussion about education to increase human understanding and so reduce the likelihood of conflict was that developing a new theory of education had to be based on the needs of individual nations. One country's needs were not necessarily the same as those of other nations. Identifying needs that all nations could use education to meet was the real challenge that the delegates faced.

Contemporary society places great importance on human interaction and mutual understanding as ways to avoid conflict. National character is built on understanding. It is also important to understand that human conflict is caused primarily by political, cultural, and socioeconomic factors. Therefore, it is important for all nations to understand that the character of society itself is determined by how individuals in it function. How individuals function is determined by the level of their understanding of the effect of the above factors and how they respond to them.

This is how theory of education plays an important role in shaping the kind of education society offers and how education in turn shapes the character of society. It is equally important to understand that the character of an individual society has a profound effect on shaping the character of the world. Because the world has become a global village, a theory of education that takes into account the importance of historical, sociological, cultural, political, and economic realities of total human existence can shape the character of the world.

These are the considerations that the participants at the San Francisco conference, in their enthusiasm to build a new world order in which conflict would be avoided, took into account in emphasizing the importance of education. In doing so they seemed to imply that seeking solutions to the problems that individual nations were facing should extend to seeking solutions to international conflict, rather than seeking solutions to problems of international conflict to resolve national problems.

If this approach had been observed, the likelihood of conflict between Iraq and allied Western nations in August 1990 could have been minimized. This suggests that the search for a new theory of education is a more difficult exercise than the participants at the San Francisco conference had anticipated. Nonetheless, it was an exercise that had to be carried out.

The reality that each country faced enormous social, economic, and political problems combined with the fact that nations had to make concerted efforts to find a common educational ground on which to build international understanding and cooperation. This is the line of thinking that John D. Pulliman took into consideration to conclude: "In a world marked by war, inflation, population explosion, pollution, social strife, and anxiety about the future, education and schooling cannot be taken for granted."[1] One critical factor has remained consistent since 1945, and that is: Conditions that determine theoretical considerations also determine the character and quality of education.

When these conditions are not met, the educational process they are intended to serve becomes haphazard and loses its proper direction. This leads inevitably to disillusionment, first at the national level and then at the international level. Once this has happened, nations and their people lose their sense of the future and so create a climate that leads to a lack of confidence in international efforts to build a global system for lasting peace. To prevent this from happening, nations must focus on the need to educate the individual as a starting point to any larger objective, national or international. The Soviet educational thinker Yuri Azarov took this line of thinking a step further when he argued in favor of developing a theory that is designed to serve the needs of individual students in order to serve those of the nation as a means of building bridges to global understanding. Azarov argued: "Education can be effective only when it is intended to help solve problems of the learner and is not divorced from social

---

[1]John D. Pulliman, *History of Education in America* (New York: Macmillan, 1991), p. 1.

conditions that have implications for national development and international understanding and cooperation."[2]

Azarov suggested that this kind of education does not just happen it is a result of carefully considered and formulated theory that all nations must undertake to ensure an effective educational system. Azarov went on to argue that any nation that fails to articulate an effective theory of education has no understanding of the responsibility that it is being called on to fulfill, because the educational process has become so complicated that it demands clear knowledge of the theory on which it is based.[3] Coming from an individual who was trying to operate under conditions of *glasnost* and *perestroika*, Azarov's theoretical ideas must be taken seriously.

THE NEED FOR A NEW THEORETICAL PERSPECTIVE

The San Francisco conference was hardly an appropriate setting for the world to examine broad theoretical concepts relative to the education of a new era. This is why what came out of it was a narrow perception of theoretical considerations of education required to suit the demands of the changing situation they expected. There were some critical points that the conference did not consider carefully. One is "men and women are essentially unfree and so inhabit a world rife with contradictions."[4]

The world since 1945 has witnessed unfree people as a result of actions that man has taken in an action to serve his own interests. For example, the number of millionaires has rapidly increased among those who are in positions of political power. At the same time, the number of poor has dramatically increased. This has not happened by chance but by design.

The "asymmetries of power and privileges"[5] that author Peter McLaren concluded to be the major cause of conflict in the world have accentuated the differences in which educational opportunity is extended to some people of a nation at the expense of the others and have created a situation that translates into a dire need for a new theory of education. Failure to recognize the imperative of a dialectical theory of education has created problems for the global society that are broader than limiting individuals to an environment that renders them inefficient to function in a larger order. The reality of the resulting situation is that neither the individual nor the society in which he or she lives can have a determining influence on the character of the other. To initiate a program with specific objectives to serve the educational interests of all students is the only viable means of serving the interests of a nation. This is a critical element of global peace and security.

---

[2]Yuri Azarov, *Teaching: Calling and Skills* (Moscow: Progress Press, 1988), p. 30.

[3]Ibid., p. 31.

[4]Peter McLaren, *Life in Schools: An Introduction to Critical Pedagogy*, in *the Foundations of Education* (New York: Longman, 1989), p. 166.

[5]Ibid., p. 166.

Peter McLaren also concluded that utilizing a dialectical theory of education makes it possible for society to see the school not only as a place where instruction and socialization take place but also as a basis of the revitalization needed to understand the essence of the universal human being. This line of thinking suggests that a theory of education that emanates from this sociocultural perspective becomes a viable channel of embracing the essential elements of what it means to be alive in the age of the search for global understanding.

McLaren also suggested that without taking these critical elements of education into consideration, the education that emerges loses the real purpose for which it exists.[6] The thinking that national interests must come before those of the world is a result of an educational system that is not based on a theory of the need to embrace broader human values from an inclusive perspective. The failure of nations to take this perspective into account means that it is difficult, even impossible, to restructure human relationships on a level different from the past, because the process of formulating an education to sustain national interests, rather than global peace, results in a culture "intimately connected with the structure of social relationships within class, gender and age formations that produce forms of oppression and dependency."[7] One has only to look at the results of the war between Iraq and allied forces in 1991 to understand the importance of embracing a broader theory of education than is the current practice.

The concept of cultural diversity, though recent as an area of study, demands not only tolerance of differences but also acceptance of divergent viewpoints that emanate from them. This is how theory brings into focus the shared international values that only education can offer to all people as a route to change. This is the perspective that Robert Manners took into account when he argued in favor of a theory of education that must be designed to initiate social innovation: "If you introduce change in any part of society, contingent changes of varying intensity will make themselves felt throughout the venture. The very change that may be welcomed by the group in power as a desirable innovation may be resented by those who feel oppressed by society because they feel that such change has been introduced to strengthen the status quo."[8]

Immanuel Kant (1724-1804) added in his *Critique of Pure Reason* (1781) that one major function of the state is to make people happy and secure. The best way to do this is to allow them free will so that they can make a viable contribution to society. This approach demands an education based on a dialectical theory . The absence of free will and a theory of education consistent with this create a social climate that generates conflict. The failure of the San Francisco conference to recognize the importance

---

[6]Ibid., p. 167.

[7]Ibid., p. 171.

[8]Robert Manners, "Functionalism, Reliability, and Anthropology in Underdeveloped Areas," in Thomas Weaver (ed.), *To See Ourselves: Anthropology and Modern Social Issues* (Glenview, Ill.: Scott, Foresman Company, 1973), p. 117.

of these considerations has led to the educational crisis that nations have endured since 1945.

What has been emerging as a trend among nations of the world is the notion that to be happy the people have to identify with the objectives, policies, and programs of their government. In turn leaders have built their own popularity on formulating an aggressive foreign policy as the only viable way to ensure national security. In this approach, national leaders forget the lessons of the war that began in 1939. Let us now attempt to discuss the importance of theory as it is related to the four areas selected for this study.

AFRICA: SEEKING AN ALTERNATIVE THEORETICAL BASE

A discussion of theory of education in Africa must, by its very nature, be divided into two sections: theory during the colonial period and theory after it. The important thing to remember about theoretical considerations of the colonial governments is that each formulated a policy it considered suitable to meet its own objectives. From these objectives emerged a set of theories consistent with colonial goals, and these goals were different. For example, Germany formulated a policy known as *Deutsche Kolonialbund*. Portugal initiated a policy of *estado novo* (new state). The Dutch formulated a theory known as apartheid,[9] France and Belgium had a policy of *evalue*, and Britain formulated a policy known as indirect rule.[10]

Why did the colonial governments formulate policies in conflict with those of other governments? Kenneth Knorr argued that in reality these policies were based on theoretical considerations to serve a common objective to "convert the Africans into a commodity or raw materials to be employed in the service of the white man. The Africans were not allowed to decide for their own future because they were considered incapable of doing so. It had therefore to be decided for them to serve the white man as their master."[11] Paulo Freire of Brazil, a leading writer from the Third World, concluded that this is a situation that creates conditions of oppression, and the task of the oppressed is not merely to liberate themselves from the condition of oppression but also to liberate their oppressor.[12]

There is no question that the main objective of the colonial governments was a product of a Victorian theoretical speculation that: "The brain of an adult African looks very much like the brain of a European in

---

[9]Dickson A. Mungazi argues in his study, *The Struggle for Social Change in Southern Africa: Visions of Liberty* (New York: Taylor and Francis, 1989), that apartheid was introduced in 1662, ten years after the Dutch settled at the Cape, not in 1948, as some historians claim..

[10]Ibid., p. 43.

[11]Kenneth Knorr, *British Colonial Theories* (Toronto: Toronto University Press, 1974), p. 378.

[12]Paulo Freire, *Pedagogy of the Oppressed.* (New York: Continuum, 1982), p. 28.

its infant stage. At puberty all development in the brain of the African stops and becomes more ape-like as he grows older."[13] What came out of this perception of the intellectual capability of the Africans is the thinking that, because they were less intelligent than whites, their major function was to serve the white man in every respect. This is also the kind of theory that the colonial governments used to design an education for Africans. This is the line of thinking that a senior colonial official in Southern Rhodesia (Zimbabwe since 1980) took into consideration to argue in 1912: "I do not consider it right that we should educate the Native in any way that will unfit him for service. The Native is and should always be the hewer of wood and the drawer of water for his white master."[14] And this is why James Oldham concluded in his study in 1930 that the colonial governments operated under a theoretical assumption that "the most natural and obvious way of civilizing Natives is to give them employment. This is their best school. The gospel of labor is the most salutary gospel for them because the Negroid people have shown little capacity to establish a fully developed civilization of their own."[15]

It is quite easy to see why in 1927, colonial officials still shared the view expressed by Ethel Tawse Jollie that the Africans must not be educated in the same way the whites were being educated because they would be expected to play a different role. During a debate in the colonial legislature in Southern Rhodesia, Jollie argued: "We do not intend to hand over this country to the Natives or to admit them to the same social and political position that we ourselves enjoy. Let us therefore make no pretense of educating them in the same way we educate whites."[16]

By the end of World War II, it was quite evident to the Africans that the colonial governments were using their theory of education to deny them equal educational opportunity purely for political reasons. But political development was what the Africans wanted to achieve as a result of education. This is precisely why the Africans launched a campaign for political independence at the conclusion of the war. Their demand for better educational opportunity as a means of bettering both their political and social lives ushered in a period of intense struggle for independence.

The Africans did not begin by demanding political independence; they began, instead, by demanding improvement of oppressive conditions within the colonial system. It was only after they realized that the colonial governments were unwilling to consider their demands that they altered their strategy from seeking improvement within the colonial setting to demanding political independence. The victory that the Africans eventually scored in their struggle for political independence then set the stage for a more challenging struggle for national development through education.

---

[13]Charles Lyons, "The Educability of the Africans: British Thought and Action, 1835 - 1965," in V. M. Battle and C. H. Lyons (eds.), *Essays in the History of African Education* (New York: Teachers College Press, 1970), p. 9.

[14]Letter to *The Rhodesia Herald*, June 28, 1912.

[15]James Oldham, *White and Black in Africa* (London: Longman, 1930), p. 11.

[16]*Southern Rhodesia: Legislative Debates*, 1927.

In order to accomplish their newly defined objectives, the nations of Africa found it necessary to formulate entirely new theoretical objectives. In suggesting that the struggle for political independence entailed basic theoretical considerations about the role of education in enhancing the role of the individual in society, Dzingai Mutumbuka, who was soon to become Zimbabwe's first minister of education and culture after independence, argued in 1979: "A new alternative system of education has been developing along a new theoretical perception that education must produce a new man richer in consciousness of humanity. This is the only way a new nation can make life better and more meaningful for all."[17]

The recognition by the Africans that national development is impossible without an education designed to promote development of the individual has led to the formulation of theoretical perspectives to suit the demands of new conditions and times. This endeavor has taken on powerful dimensions, not only in Africa but throughout the Third World. When Paulo Freire of Brazil argued that all human beings, no matter how oppressed, are quite capable of engaging in constructive interaction with other people,[18] he was actually suggesting that education should help define new forms of relationships between the individual and society.

In order to structure these kinds of relationships properly, a theory of education must be evolved in order to shape the direction of national development. Mutumbuka's concept of a person richer in the consciousness of humanity corresponds to Freire's idea of an education designed to promote human interactions intended to shape the emergence of a new social, political, and economic system in which the position of the individual takes precedence over any other considerations.

Increasingly, nations in Africa are beginning to realize that without ensuring the position of the individual in a larger social context, it is virtually impossible to ensure the security of the nation. This is why in 1990 there were demonstrations throughout Africa against one-party or one-man forms of government. The demand for democracy was based on a theoretical assumption that the formation of a new national character depended on the development of the individual. Why the African leaders failed to recognize and operate according to this reality is beyond comprehension. However, they must have at least recognized that sooner or later there would a price to pay.

In 1987 the Conference of Catholic Bishops in Zimbabwe outlined critical theoretical elements that appear to define the relationships between the individual and society, saying: "It is important for Third World nations, especially those of Africa, to recognize that the individual cannot find educational fulfillment without freedom to choose his own course of study. Where there is no clear orientation toward choice in education, educators are like the blind leading the blind. In this kind of setting society itself pays

---

[17]Dzingai Mutumbuka, "Zimbabwe's Educational Challenge," paper presented at the World Universities Services Conference, London, December 1979. In the Zimbabwe National Archives.

[18] Freire, *Pedagogy of the Oppressed*, p. 39.

the ultimate price--underdevelopment."[19] A high school principal in Zimbabwe seemed to agree when he told the author in 1983: "Education must give all students the freedom to choose their own course of study. This means freedom to earn a decent income, to own a home--in essence, self-sufficiency. These are the elements that construct a foundation upon which a good political and socioeconomic system must be built. Without recognizing the freedom of the individual, society remains without a vision for the future and is building its future on quicksand."[20]

One can see that the need felt by African nations for a theory of education to ensure the advancement of the individual as a prerequisite for national development suggests the need to embrace democratic principles, values, and practices. Unless African nations recognize the importance of operating on these values, any definition of national development they may try to utilize in their efforts is bound to have little meaning, and the entire endeavor may fail. The African nations face the enormous task of formulating new theoretical perspectives to ensure their own development. To succeed in their endeavors, African leaders must engage in a rigorous exercise of self-examination in which they put the interests of their nations above their own.

The responsibility of building nations must not be delegated to the political interests of the leaders. Rather, the task demands the total confidence of the people, and the people cannot give their government their total confidence if they have reason to believe that the government is less than sincere in its efforts. The process of formulating a new theory of education must go hand in hand with the process of formulating a new democratic political theory. Many African leaders still have to learn this simple basic principle. Until they do their nations will continue to pay the price of underdevelopment.

JAPAN: NEW THEORETICAL PERCEPTIONS

To understand the development of educational theory in Japan, one needs to understand the philosophy of Confucius, the famous Chinese sage whose influence was felt more profoundly in Japan than in China. Although his father died soon after his birth, Confucius placed himself with the aid of his mother on the road to transforming his society through the power of his ideas. At the age of fifteen he developed an intense interest in the search for knowledge and wisdom as the foundation of a great society. By the time he was twenty-one years old, Confucius attracted the interest of many students through his teaching and ideas. His timeless adage "Do not do to others what you do not wish done to you" was restated by Jesus as the Golden Rule.

Confucius's teaching that a society which does not practice justice and fairness loses the essence of its own existence has become a universal principle of national life. Around the world, nations are struggling against

---

[19]Conference of Catholic Bishops, *Our Mission to Teach: A Pastoral Statement on Education* (Gweru, Zimbabwe: Mambo Press, 1987), p. 6.

[20]Interview with the author, Harare, August 8, 1983.

formidable odds to restructure their societies along the principles of justice and fairness in order to preserve the sacredness of man. Confucius and his followers had no illusions about the enormous importance of this task, and the difficulties that all nations have encountered in this endeavor can be understood within the elusive context of this principle. However, Confucius believed that the educational process would enhance the efforts that any society must make to ensure justice and fairness as two vital elements needed to build a dynamic society.

Confucius forcefully outlined the importance of education to five levels of human relationships that he identified. These are ruler and subject, parent and child, friend and friend, husband and wife, and among siblings.[21] These are still central to Japanese culture and at the very core of the Japanese social system and of values. This is why Confucius stressed the importance of education to create a society in which the position of the people was secure.

Because Confucius was most effective in imparting knowledge on the basis of individualized instruction, he left a legacy to the Japanese theory of education that has embraced the essential elements of his instructional strategy. This is why even today "the elder scholar gathers about himself disciples dedicated to promoting his formula in practice."[22] On this very principle rests the relationship that must develop between teacher and student, whether at the elementary level or at the university level. The theoretical perception that comes out of this tradition is that education of the individual is of paramount importance to sustaining cultural and institutional systems. This perception underscores the belief that learning is best accomplished within an ideal social environment.

This theoretical perception also reflects the thinking that because students learn best at their own rate, they should be placed in groups in order to enable the teacher to discover their individual strengths. Drill and repetition form two basic pillars of the educational process, and the teacher reinforces them with praise. The practice of reinforcing what the teacher thinks to be the student's positive attributes is believed to encourage further learning. In this context class discussions provide a forum in which individuality is encouraged at the early stages of education. That this instructional theoretical practice is employed in all areas of learning underscores its importance. This is why the Japanese practice a theory that success of education must rest upon the principle that both the environment and learning must be nurtured, and that they must never be taken for granted.

The application of this theory appears to have relevance to broader principles of education in several areas. Four of these deserve a brief discussion. The first theoretical perception is that the learning process can start as early as possible as long as an ideal social environment is present. The thinking behind this perception is that because human beings are a

---

[21]Robert Ulich (ed.), *Education and the Idea of Mankind* (Chicago: University of Chicago Press, 1964), p. 4.

[22]Ronald Anderson, "Japanese Education," in Edward Ignas and Raymond Corsini (eds.), *Comparative Educational Systems* (Itasca, Ill.: F. E. Peacock , 1981), p. 243.

product of the environment, society has a responsibility to structure that environment in such a way that learning can take place.[23] Although the responsibility for the success of education rests with the student and his teacher, the responsibility for creating an ideal environment rests with society. Therefore, the Japanese believe that to a certain extent, society shares in the outcome of education for the individual as much it shares in broader educational attainment. This reality creates a situation in which the success or failure of education is shared by the school, the parents, and society itself.

The second theoretical perception that has application to the educational process in Japan is the role of parents. Because parents are expected to understand the individual character and potential of their children better than anyone else, they are also expected to accept the responsibility for providing an environment consistent with their needs and educational endeavors. This is why Japanese parents take special pride in the educational success of their children. This is also why they share the blame when their children fail. In order to minimize the likelihood of failure, parents go to the extent of providing additional private instruction at *jukus*, the famous cram schools, at substantial cost to themselves. Once a student has had this additional instruction, he or she must avoid disgracing the family with unacceptable academic achievement. Japanese culture demands that failure of any kind be avoided, and parents constantly remind their children of the consequences of failure.

The third theoretical perception is that both the teacher and parents must continue to grow to provide a better learning situation for the child.[24] The process of growth involves a number of critical elements, such as elevating oneself to a higher level of intellectual understanding of children, generating a clear perception of the educational needs of students, helping students develop a positive image of themselves, generating self-confidence, and helping students recognize their potential. Because both parents and teachers stand in a position to influence the life of students, they must make a concerted effort to be role models in every way possible. That both teachers and parents take this as a measure of their responsibility to students underscores the importance of this theoretical perception.

The fourth perception is that teachers are more effective when they teach by example and demonstration rather than by mere precept. Teachers must use examples to demonstrate how concepts are comprehended. Demonstration must also relate to the problem-solving process. For this reason, teachers are expected to ask students to become involved in a practical manner to show that they have comprehended what they have been shown. The Japanese believe that once students demonstrate this comprehension the level of their confidence increases and their ability to learn also increases. Therefore, the teacher's ability to arouse self-confidence in their students has a far-reaching impact on their development and on learning skills in general. The essence of this perception is that it

---

[23]Ibid., p. 244.
[24]Ibid., p. 245.

encourages creative thinking, even though creative thinking is not a distinctive feature of the learning process itself because the tendency to memorize is stronger among both teachers and students.

In 1971 the Japanese Ministry of Education tried to introduce a new aspect to the educational theory in order to encourage creative thinking among students. Emphasis on passing public examinations as the only evidence of educational success quickly gave way to new ways of thinking about the theory of education. It was recognized that teaching students to gain new learning skills was essential to success in life after school. This is why the ministry added a fresh theoretical component to the existing one, stating in 1971: "An educational system that encourages creativity must help build the opportunity for students to think creatively. It must also encourage pupils to search freely for solutions to problems with which they are presented."[25] The process of establishing the relationship between the two, however, was neither fully explained nor understood by the people.

The important thing to keep in mind in these four theoretical perceptions is that they help implant elements of creative thinking in students as a product of education and play an important role in an effort to develop their ability to see society from a positive perspective. Creativity as part of the learning process generates originality. Originality provides the vitality of a dynamic society. This is why contemporary Japanese society emphasizes the importance of science, mathematics, and computer technology. Creativity also helps build a sense of individuality, intellectual growth, and personality among students. This is the main reason why, in recent years, the Japanese have recognized that an educational system that promotes this form of human activity makes a viable contribution to the improvement of society itself.

The implications of these theoretical perceptions for the teacher would suggest a method of teaching that is consistent from elementary school to college and in all subjects taught. Ronald Anderson concluded that the teacher "does not shift gears when she moves from subject to subject because the method that works within one subject or child can be used to teach another subject or other children."[26] One sees three advantages to this approach. It minimizes the possibility of confusion on the part of the student about the teaching strategies of his teacher; it provides continuity of progress in the learning process; and it enables the teacher to understand the learning habits of the students and the student to adjust to the teaching method of the teacher.

One should also recognize that this approach can be too rigid to make the adjustments to suit the changing educational conditions and varying needs of students. Recognizing the varying needs of students is not a distinctive characteristic of the Japanese educational system and culture however, because emphasis is placed on homogeneity and sameness. When one remembers that, since the end of the occupation in 1952, the

---

[25]Japanese Ministry of Education, *Basic Guidelines for Reforming Education* (Tokyo, 1971).

[26]Anderson, "Japanese Education," p. 242.

Japanese have made an impressive record of industrial and technological development, then one must accept that the Japanese theory of education has had a profound impact.

In this context, the emerging Japanese theory of education is similar to that of African nations--both are directed at realizing the importance of national development, although the position of the individual in an emerging socioeconomic and political system has yet to be redefined. This situation suggests that the process of formulating theory in Japan, as like in Africa, is a continuous one. In seeking to define the elements of the theory of education, Japan, as in any other country, becomes aware of the fact that it is also in the process of defining the elements of a national character. That character comes into a sharper focus when that theory is implemented for the benefit of the students.

THE UNITED STATES: THE SEARCH FOR A NEW THEORETICAL APPROACH

Discussing the theory of education in the United States is a complex subject because, unlike the other three areas in this study, the heterogeneous character of the country and its historical background place the students and the educational systems in varying environmental settings about which it is difficult to generalize. Among the factors that have impinged heavily on the discussion of the theory of education in the United States are racism, slavery, ethnicity, and social class. The question of whether all Americans, regardless of their racial origin, have equal intellectual potential demands an examination. The question of whether black Americans have the same level of intelligence as whites must also be answered within the context of a discussion of educational theory.

From the time that slavery was introduced into the country in 1609, Americans have been seriously handicapped by a preoccupation with race. It is not surprising therefore that by 1991, the United States and South Africa were the only countries in the world where race was still a major factor in individual development. That American scholars readily disagree about the impact of race on education suggests its strong influence on the thinking process itself.

When it comes to the practice of social precepts, Americans do not seem to share Thomas Jefferson's view that "All men are created equal." Even then, it is generally accepted that Jefferson was actually referring only to white people because how could he include blacks in that statement when he was slave owner? What is important to remember is that in making this statement Jefferson was stating a clear theory of education.

Writing in 1988, Peter McLaren argued that formulating a functional theory of education in the United States has been made harder by the consideration of race, and that racism has hindered the efforts of those who are trying to seek an improvement in the education of all Americans. McLaren stated: "As I write on the anniversary of the slaying of Martin Luther King, Jr., a state holiday rescinded by Governor Evan Mecham of

Arizona,[27] reports of growing racial unrest rattle the airwaves. Images of violence in Howard Beach, New York, and the shrouded specters of Ku Klux Klansmen leading a demonstration in Forsyth County, Georgia, appear ominously across the television screens of America."[28] Logic suggests that race and racism in any society become a major problem in finding a theoretical base from which to seek solutions to problems of national development.

A seemingly simple question such as "Are blacks equal to the whites?" demands a theoretical answer that must relate to the question of equal educational opportunity. While the United States has demonstrated its commitment to this principle because it is a fundamental American ideal, practice of it has been elusive. David Nasaw suggested that a theory of education in the United States began to take shape at the inception of the country. Nasaw concluded that along with the need to develop new religious values consistent with efforts to carve a new nation, early settlers believed that "tenderness, kindness, gentleness must be given a place in the child-rearing regiment as a reward for obedience."[29]

These human qualities, important as they are to any society, were considered critical to the development of character in the young generation of Americans with visions for the future conceived under ideals different from those of the past. It soon became evident that the character of society itself depended on the character of individuals. This is the reason why, during that time, personal character was considered a more important qualification for teachers than academic achievement.

As the United States moved into nineteenth century the emphasis in education began to shift from the development of character to the development of skills needed to function in an industrial society. The regard for education as a measure of an enlightened individual gave way to the search for education to enable the individual to be self-sufficient and so make a viable contribution to the development of society.

John Dewey (1859-1952) took this line of thinking in 1938 when he wrote *Experience and Education*, in which he argued for educational development of the individual as a critical factor in the development of the country. Dewey went on to explain the changing nature of society and how the individual must be educated to play his role effectively: "The political and economic issues which the present generation will be compelled to face demands education. The nature of the issues cannot be understood save as we know how they come about."[30]

---

[27]Mecham rescinded the holiday in 1988, the year he was impeached and removed from office. In 1990 Mecham again led a strong opposition to the King holiday. When voters in the state rejected the holiday, the National Football League rescinded its decision to have the Super Bowl played in Arizona in 1993, costing the state millions of dollars.

[28]Peter McLaren, *Life in School*, p. 2.

[29]David Nasaw, *Schooled to Order: A Social History of Public Schooling in the United States* (New York: Oxford University Press, 1979), p. 18.

[30]John Dewey, *Experience and Education* (New York: Collier Books, 1938), p. 77.

Mortimer Adler saw educational development of the individual in relationship to its role in promoting and maintaining democratic values and the consequences that he said may ensue from the failure to formulate an educational program in response to such a theory, adding: "We are all sufferers from our continued failure to fulfill the educational obligations of democracy. We are all victims of a school system that has only gone halfway along the road to realize the promise of democracy."[31]

What Adler seems to suggest is that formulating a theory of education must entail two critical elements. The first is that education must ensure the development of the individual. This development has a single purpose: to make it possible for a person to function in a larger social order. The second element is that the educational process that ensues from this theory must make it possible for all to endeavor to preserve the principles of democracy. But, here again, while this is a noble social principle, it has not been fully put into practice.

In discussing theory of education as it is understood to apply to the United States one must remember that there are two intrinsic components. These are learning and teaching. With respect to learning, a relatively recent theory has been developing, known as cognitive psychology. This theory suggests that a student is capable of learning in a variety of ways and at different rates and that capability to learn varies from student to student. In the recent history of education in the United States the teachers have endeavored to apply this theory, resulting in a change from individualized instruction to what has become known as cooperative learning.

Although the theory of cognitive psychology has some appeal to a variety of educational settings, Edward Ignas argued that it "has had little positive effect on the schools."[32] This does not suggest that the theory does not work. Rather, it indicates that the conditions of its application are not quite right. For this reason, the search for a theory of education must be related to other critical factors, such as the school and home environment, social conditions, and the level of training of teachers.

Another important element of cognitive psychology is that the educational process must impart to all students a core body of knowledge in order to create a more harmonious society and to prepare students to function in a changing socioeconomic and political environment. The basic theoretical assumption arising out of this theory is that "there exists some body of knowledge that is meant to be passed on to future generations."[33]

There are two problems in connection with this assumption. The first is that it presumes that students have identical educational interests and that a variety of teaching strategies to meet these interests is not necessary. If this assumption were put into operation, it would negate the principle of

---

[31]Mortimer J. Adler (ed.), *The Paideia Proposal: An Educational Manifesto* (New York: Collier Books, 1982), p. 4.

[32]Edward Ignas, "The Traditions of American Education," in Ignas and Corsini, *Comparative Educational Systems*, p. 12.

[33]Ibid., p. 13.

individuality so important to educational success. The second problem is that the teacher is presumed to know better than anyone else what the educational needs of the students are. The danger of accepting this argument is that it becomes a justification for a rigid curriculum that does not accommodate innovation and diversity--two essential principles of national character.

The question of how students learn has not been fully resolved as a theory of education. Since the 1970s a considerable effort has been made to put the Piagetian concept of developmental stages of children into theories to provide a basis for a workable knowledge of how students develop mentally. But the decade of the 1980s witnessed a shift from the Piagetian mode of thinking to the idea that learning how to learn offers a viable starting point for developing learning strategies. Because the assumption that learning to learn is, by its very nature, individual, the process of learning itself is also individual.

If this line of thinking is accepted, then one is persuaded to accept the argument that a collective approach to learning and instruction has no relevance in the educational process. The reality is that nothing concrete has been established as an element of a universally accepted theory of learning. This suggests why there is no agreement about why some students achieve less than their potential and why other students seem to do better than expected. As far as the theory of learning is concerned, the debate continues.

With respect to the theory of teaching, there is a variety of elements that one sees in American educational settings. These range from the inductive to the deductive method. What has been developing in recent years is the concept that the best teacher can do is to provide an environment in which students develop confidence in themselves and their ability to discover answers to educational questions.

Contemporary American educators seem to hold the view that education is far more meaningful when students are allowed to discover for themselves those critical aspects of knowledge associated with the process. Once this process is applied, it accrues benefits to students that they would not secure in any other way. It generates a concept of individuality so critical to American social settings. It helps develop critical thinking. It helps offer students new ways of to interpret old concepts and make them relevant to contemporary conditions.

A theory of teaching that brings out these features of the educational process does not have to have loud pronouncements to be applicable, even though educational thinkers believe that such theories must stand the scrutiny of critics and intellectuals to have universal application. The reality of it all is that teaching, like learning, is essentially a product of individuality. A Marva Collins can be a successful teacher without accepting, or resorting to, the theory of John Dewey or Charles Eliot.

American theoreticians seem to ignore the fact that what determines success in teaching is not so much the kind of theory teachers put into practice, but the goals they establish to ensure that learning takes place. This demands commitment, and clear picture of what teaching is all about. If teachers understand these basic requirements of their responsibility, then one would have to conclude that they have demonstrated understanding of the essential elements of a theory of education.

For most Americans chronological age seems to determine when one does what. This is why, on entering school, students are classified by age. The assumption that children of the same age learn better when they are grouped together seems a violation of the principle of individuality. To accept the thinking that age determines levels of development is to argue that there is little variation among children of the same age. Nothing is more harmful to the educational process than to ignore the different levels of mental development that children of the same age manifest. However, teachers design their materials and instructional methods to suit the age group of their students. One must conclude that while this approach benefits some students it also hinders the educational development of others, because while children may be of the same chronological age they are at the different levels of mental age. In the context of American educational practices, success as a teacher has come to mean success in understanding the behavioral patterns of students as determined by their chronological age.

An interesting phenomenon in the theory of education in the United States is that the legal system has been intimately involved in developing it. The historic ruling of the U.S. Supreme Court in *Brown vs. Board of Education of Topeka* of 1954 gave a new meaning to the quest for a new theory of education. In stating that separate and racially segregated schools were inherently unequal, and so unconstitutional, the Supreme Court was reversing a decision that it had made in 1896 in *Plessy vs. Ferguson,* which affirmed the notion of "separate but equal." It is ironic that the Supreme Court was less concerned with genuine equality than it was with maintaining the status quo. Gerald Gutek observed: "Segregated facilities, especially schools, were not equal. Educational expenditure per pupil was greater for white than for black students. Salaries paid to teachers were generally higher, the school year longer, and physical facilities better for the schools attended by whites than those attended by blacks."[34]

What is important here is not that the Supreme Court knew in 1896 that racially segregated facilities were unequal, but that it had enunciated a theory consistent with the thinking of the time. The thinking of the court that facilities were not inferior as long as the notion of equality was applied was what gave relevance to its theoretical enunciation. It was this same consideration operating in reverse that the court took into account in reversing it in 1954.

It is quite clear that in both 1896 and 1954 the Supreme Court was taking a theoretical position in relation to the Fourteenth Amendment to the U.S. Constitution. Ratified in 1868 soon after the conclusion of the Civil War, this amendment was intended to ensure that the Bill of Rights extended equal protection of the law to all Americans. "No state shall make or enforce any law which shall abridge the privileges or immunities of citizens" was a constitutional condition that the Supreme Court took into

---

[34]Gerald Gutek, *An Historical Introduction to American Education* (Prospect Heights, Ill.; Waveland Press, 1991), p. 284.

consideration in giving the Fourteenth Amendment its appropriate meaning in the life of the people. The Supreme Court of 1986 and that of 1954 espoused different theories on how that objective could be accomplished.

In the course of trying to implement this theory in 1958, President Dwight Eisenhower found himself in serious conflict with Governor Orval Faubus of Arkansas. His successor, John Kennedy, had a similar crisis with Governor George Wallace of Alabama in 1962. In the same way, the U.S. Congress has been intimately involved in formulating a theory of education in the form of legislation. The Civil Rights Act of 1964, for example, makes provision for action against those educational institutions that indirectly or directly attempt to inhibit the concept of equality. Through theory the United States was trying to live up to its principles.

The responsibility for formulating the theory of education in the United States is a collective one. This is why, in 1992, during the presidential election campaign, Bill Clinton articulated a theoretical perspective that might have helped him win, saying, "Education today is more than the key to climbing the ladder of opportunity. In today's global economy, it is an imperative for our nation. Our economic life is on the line. Government fails when our schools fail."[35] There is no doubt that Clinton was suggesting a theory of education that would be utilized in building national character. Nevertheless, controversy surrounding the implications of implementing theory has remained a distinctive feature of American education.

THE SOVIET UNION: SEEKING A THEORY FOR A PERFECT SOCIETY

The development of a theory of education in the Soviet Union has its origins at the conclusion of 1917. It is important to remember that from that time until 1992, the year the Soviet Union ceased to exist as a nation, the formulation of a theory was considered fundamentally important to shaping an educational system to suit socialist ideology that was to direct the course of national development. Therefore, the development of theory was aimed at the development of an educational system that rejected the concept of an elitist society. This meant that from 1917 on, educational opportunity would be available to all on equal basis. In 1977 Mikhail Prokofyev, the Soviet minister of education, attempted to assess the impact of educational theory in terms of comparing the effect of education before and after the revolution.

Prokofyev concluded that implementation of the theory of education under Czar Nicholas II resulted in only 8 percent literacy by the time that Joseph Stalin assumed office in 1928.[36] Prokofyev suggested that the purpose of a theory of education under Nicholas was to sustain the system of serfdom. This was the situation that finally led to the revolution. One

---

[35]Bill Clinton, *Putting People First: A National Economic Strategy for America* (Little Rock, Clinton for President Committee, 1992), p. 13.

[36]Mikhail Prokofyev, "The Rights of Education," in *The Rights and Freedom of Soviet Citizens* (Moscow: Novosti Press, 1977), p. 35.

can see that the educational process under Nicholas had been removed from proper theoretical considerations needed to serve the needs of the students as a way of preparing them to serve the needs of the country.[37] Instead, the system had created a situation that benefited only a small percentage of the population at the expense of the vast majority. Prokofyev concluded that because the educational system had entrenched a system of privileges, it failed in serving the purpose for which good education in any society is designed.[38]

The leaders of the revolution concluded that if a new society had to be created based on socialist ideology, then fundamental change in the theory of education had to be initiated to envisage a future different from the past. This was why Lenin argued, in advancing a new theory, that capitalist education such as existed during the tenure of Nicholas had no place in the socialist society that the Bolsheviks were determined to create.

Speaking to the Young Communist League in 1920, Lenin stressed the importance of adopting a new theoretical perspective, saying, "You can become a Communist only when you enrich your mind with a knowledge of all the treasures created by mankind."[39] Lenin was in fact suggesting that formulating a theory of education to suit the needs of a socialist ideology was an imperative of efforts toward shaping an emerging society. When one considers the conditions of both education and life under Nicholas, one can see how a socialist ideology had a special appeal to the revolutionary leaders.

While Lenin's conclusion that a theory of education was essential to instructional strategy and that the learning process had a universal application, he argued that it had specific relevance to shaping the character of education in the post-revolutionary Soviet Union. In Lenin's thinking a critical element of this new theory was that the educational process must transform old institutions from serving the purposes of a social status quo into new social structures that must embrace socialist values. One of these values is the concept of work in a new social order that eliminated the attitudes that prevailed during the tenure of Nicholas in which serfs were regarded as lacking in intellectual potential. In this new way of thinking about work, Lenin wanted his fellow Russians to understand that because work related to education was fulfilling to the individual, it served a national purpose.[40] In this context, Lenin implanted new attitudes, both in terms of educational values and a sense of belonging to an emerging social order.

Soon after Lenin's death in 1924, the struggle to succeed him embraced the concept of work and study as the core of socialist values that must be utilized to build an emerging society. Joseph Stalin's first five-year development plan was based on this central concept and reflected the

---

[37]Ibid., p. 36.

[38]Ibid., p. 37.

[39]V. I. Lenin, "The Task of the Youth League," in Scientific Socialism Series, *Lenin, Marx, Engels, Marxism* (Moscow: Progress Press, 1970), p. 117.

[40]Ibid., p. 118.

thinking that "a child who has never known the joy of work in the context of his study and who has never experienced pride in overcoming difficulties is a most wretched person."[41]

There is no question that in his enthusiasm to embrace this theoretical perspective as a method of building a new socialist order, Stalin went far beyond the ideals that Lenin had outlined at the beginning of the Bolshevik revolution. The Great Purge was a tragedy that future leaders of the Soviet Union recognized for what it was, as Mikhail Gorbachev put it in 1989: "a distortion of the ideals of socialism that led to the loss of the central idea of the Marxist and Leninist concept of socialism that man is the goal and the highest value of education, not a tool or a cog in the wheel."[42]

Recognizing the mistakes of implementing Stalin's theory of education, not because it was wrong, but because of the manner in which he tried to measure its results, Nikita Khrushchev enunciated a new theory instead. In 1959 Khrushchev added a theoretical dimension that became a distinctive characteristic of his administration when he said: "To arrive at Communism, that most fair and perfect society, we must start right now educating the man of the future."[43] According to Khrushchev, educating the man of the future required a clear understanding of the purpose of education within the context of socialist order he felt he had succeeded Stalin to create.

Khrushchev was not rejecting Stalin's concept of the relationship between education and work. Rather, he was redefining an old theory in relationship to new social and economic conditions. This is why he argued in 1964: "Education as and for work has become the sacred watchword of the Soviet schools. This in no way means a repudiation of production training. Every teacher and worker in education must realize that the new school is a place of labor providing training for all people"[44]--in order to shape the character of a new socialist society at its best.

The essential component of Khrushchev's theory of the relationship between education and the new definition of work is that both help shape human endeavor in a world of change. This, he argued, helps create a national climate from which a high level of human consciousness leads to the emergence of a free people who are uninhibited by the constraints of human shortcomings, provided that the influence of capitalist ideology was eliminated in the educational process. To suggest that these ideals could not properly function under the constraints of socialism is to conclude that this is why Gorbachev took a fundamental approach to both theory and strategy in the form of *glasnost* and *perestroika*. Khrushchev was not aware that trying to integrate his basic ideas into the structure of socialism was the same as trying to mix oil and water.

---

[41]Vasily Sukhomlinsky, *On Education* (Moscow: Progress Press, 1977), p. 164.

[42]Mikhail Gorbachev, *Channel the Energy of Youth into Perestroika*, speech given to the All-Union Student Forum (Moscow: Novosti Press, 1989), p. 9.

[43]Nigel Grant, *Soviet Education* (London: Penguin, 1979), p. 26.

[44]Ibid., p. 116.

In order to implement his theory, Khrushchev made some specific demands education. He required that education be structured to help inculcate a new level of love for learning in general and in specific areas in order to strengthen the socialist values he considered important. He also ordered that education help reshape a new communist world outlook in order to minimize the threat from capitalist ideology. For this reason, Khrushchev saw the role of education in the Soviet Union in a much broader global context than his predecessors. This is why he required that educational output be doubled by 1963, especially vocational, academic, and professional. He increased university enrollment by 40 percent in that year. He stressed the importance of technology and foreign languages at the secondary level. He used the launching of Sputnik to emphasize the importance of research in technology.

When Khrushchev fell from power in October 1964, his successor, Leonid Brezhnev, articulated elements of a new theory that attempted to address the importance of education in efforts to elevate his concept of the universal human being to a higher level of achievement. But Brezhnev soon discovered that this noble universal human value does not function effectively when it is cast in a socialist mold. However, in an address to the twenty-fifth Congress of the Communist Party in 1976, Brezhnev reiterated the importance of putting these elements into practice if the Soviet Union ever hoped to exercise its proper influence in shaping the future of the socialist world. He went on to argue:

> The Soviet man is a man who, having won his freedom, has been able to defend it in the most trying battles. He is a man who has been building the future unsparing of his energy and making every sacrifice. He is a man who, having gone through all trials, has himself changed beyond recognition, combining ideological connections and tremendous vital energy, culture, knowledge, and ability to ease them. This is the man who, while an ardent patriot, has been and will always remain a constant internationalist.[45]

Brezhnev was clear in saying that this new man was a product of the kind of education that he said his philosophy of education helped to effect in order to meet the needs of a new socialist world order.

To implement his theory, Brezhnev strengthened the national ministry of education by giving it more power to formulate educational policy and programs. He required university students to study more science and foreign languages. He demanded that all students excel in all educational efforts including athletic performance. He required general educational programs to produce qualified scientists well versed in the latest advancement in technology and space exploration. He ordered a major revision of both primary and secondary curricula to make them come into line with national goals. He required that research be part of university education. He ordered that institutions of higher learning make a concerted

---

[45]Leonid Brezhnev, *Address to the 25th Congress of the Communist Party* (Moscow: Novosti Press), 1976, p. 6.

effort to bring in students from Third World nations in order to teach them how to fight against capitalist oppression.

Following his death in 1982, Brezhnev was succeeded by Yuri Andropov, former KGB director who died about fifteen months later. Andropov's successor, Konstantine Chernenko, also died about a year later. This unfortunate turn of events temporarily halted development of the theory of education, and the search for a socialist utopia came to a halt while the politburo looked for a new leader. In 1984, the Soviet leadership decided to put into office a younger man, Mikhail Gorbachev. A number of factors, including the decline in the economy; increasing skepticism by the outside world; a lack of tangible results of the basic Communist philosophy of state-run business, and the severity of conditions surrounding the operation of national institutions, convinced Gorbachev that a theory radically different from the past was needed to direct development of the nation in order to bring it into line with international practices.

This is the setting from which Gorbachev gave the world an opportunity to add two new words to its vocabulary and knowledge about the Soviet Union, *glasnost* and *perestroika*. Gorbachev finally removed the veil of secrecy that Winston Churchill called the Iron Curtain to characterize the ideological separation of Europe. Gorbachev believed that the interests of the nation would best be served by openness and reconstruction. These two words underscore critical elements of Gorbachev's theory of both education and society.

Glasnost implies that an open society is essential to helping its citizens see themselves as they really are in relationship to what they could be. Openness makes it possible for ideas to emerge to serve the needs of the people and for all segments of the community to evaluate national programs and offer suggestions for improvement. Because openness makes it possible to take political views into account in designing national programs, it constitutes an important step toward a free society and so provides the needed lifeblood of a national pulse. Gorbachev also recognized that a critical element of an open society is that it makes it possible to construct a foundation of ideas and values freely subscribed to by the people. This is the setting in which he argued that education plays a major role in other forms of national development.

Gorbachev went on to conclude in February 1990: "*Perestroika* is based on a profound understanding of the role of science and the harnessing of its results to achieve equality under new conditions for our society."[46] With this theory Gorbachev launched a revolution in the thought process of the Soviet Union. Although Gorbachev encountered enormous difficulties in his effort to evolve a theory to create a perfect society along the lines that Khrushchev outlined in 1959, his effort must be seen in the context of his desire to redirect the development of society

---

[46]Mikhail Gorbachev, *Towards a Humane and Democratic Socialist Society*, address to the 28th Congress of the Communist Party, February 5, 1990 (Moscow: Novosti Press, 1990), p. 6.

based on the traditional values of his culture. Such an endeavor demands formulating theory.

SUMMARY AND CONCLUSION

The discussion in this chapter leads to two basic conclusions. The first is that a theory of education emanates from a national awareness that, because education is critical to national development, it must be consistent with national purpose. Unless education is based on the combination of theory and national purpose, it is likely to lose its effectiveness, and the educational process that comes out of it will have no proper direction. The important thing that one sees in this chapter is that all four areas selected for this study show that theory is the basis of an effective education. The development of a national character does not come on its own, it is a result of carefully considered theory. That theory is consistent with trends of national development is itself a critical element of national development.

The second conclusion is that the formulation of theory is essential to the formation of the educational process itself. It helps those with the responsibility to articulate objectives, to design the curriculum, to institute administrative structures, to allocate resources, to have priorities, to design strategies for solving problems, and to plan for the future. Without theory, these important aspects of education cannot be undertaken with any degree of success. Therefore, the formulation of theory is not only the basis of an effective system of education, it is also the foundation of a good national system of operations. The formulation of theory must not be regarded as an act that takes place once, but as a principal component of education and national life that demands constant evaluation and review to make it relevant to changing times.

It has been seen in this chapter that from the colonial period to the emergence of independent nations in Africa, from the days of Confucius to modern Japan, from the days of Thomas Jefferson to the period of Bill Clinton in the United States, and from the days of Nicholas II to the era of Mikhail Gorbachev in the Soviet Union, the evolvement of theory has been a deliberate and carefully planned exercise cast within the context of national endeavors. This is how theory helps to give education a distinctive character that, in turn, shapes the character of nations.

4

Objectives: A Means of Constructing the Character of Education

> *Without education as the chief spiritual mainstay of our existence democracy cannot be firmly established.*
>
> Mikhail Gorbachev, 1989

> *To develop education in isolation from national culture means to regard students as people without kith and kin.*
>
> Gennadi Yogodin, 1989

THE UNIVERSALITY OF EDUCATIONAL OBJECTIVES

Writing on the universality of educational objectives, Mortimer Adler, an American educational thinker, outlined three broad objectives of education in any society. The first objective is to ensure personal and individual growth and development.[1] Adler saw this objective as suggesting that students must utilize the school environment to gain experiences that broaden the horizon of their understanding of themselves, values, and the character of their society. Adler added that the educational process must prepare students "to take advantage of every opportunity for personal development that society offers."[2]

The second objective is to prepare every citizen to play an appropriate role in shaping the character of his society--politically, economically, socially, and in any other constructive manner. The third objective is to prepare individuals to learn a vocation or an occupation that will enable them to earn a living. It is in the process of earning a living that individuals find their appropriate place in society. This is also how they make viable contributions to its development. Without belonging, a

---

[1]Mortimer J. Adler (ed.), *The Paideia Proposal: An Educational Manifesto* (New York: Collier Macmillan, 1982), p. 15.

[2]Ibid., p. 16.

person's sense of self is lost and values become confused. This is true of any society, whether it is "civilized" or "primitive." Nations must now operate under the principle that educational objectives ultimately shape the character of society itself.

While these three objectives are important to every educational system and society, they are not the only ones that must become the focus of education. One universal objective that Adler does not discuss is to help students function within their culture. Any education that negates the culture in which it is cast loses the purpose for which it is designed. Gennadi Yogodin, the Soviet educator, took this line of thinking to argue: "To develop education in isolation from national culture means to regard students as people without kith and kin."[3]

Yogodin continued that to set educational objectives within the premises of culture would make it possible for the school to teach students to perceive the importance of mature social and cultural values. These values add a special meaning to students' lives. For the school to inculcate dimensions of culture helps arouse in students diversity and a desire to know more about their world. In this kind of setting learning becomes an enjoyable experience instead of the dread that students often regard it as. This is what makes one want to read or write fiction, to produce drama, and to engage in art, music, and science, for example.

Peter McLaren argued that establishing educational objectives to reflect cultural values constitutes a search for national meaning made possible by the acquisition of knowledge.[4] Because of the imperatives of the twentieth century, leaders of the four areas selected for this study understand that educational objectives that do not reflect cultural values and national identity derail the educational process itself. It may also suggest that education has not succeeded in building a national character. Ethnic conflict in Africa, racial tension in the United States--especially after the Rodney King incident in April 1992--and the Soviet Union, for instance, may persuade us to accept Yogodin's and McLaren's conclusions that education must seek to refine the cultural framework in which it is cast if conflict is to be avoided.

What this conflict, and, for that matter, any form of national conflict, shows is that educational objectives have failed to impart to all students the importance of cultural diversity. Ethnic conflict is a tragic outcome of the inadequacy of education to formulate objectives. That ethnic conflict still exists in many societies in this day and age suggests a dire need to evaluate educational objectives so that the educational process brings a higher meaning to contemporary society than it did in the past. This means that the formulation of educational objectives cannot be taken lightly, because it is an exercise that determines the character of education, and the character of education helps determine the character of society itself.

---

[3]Gennadi Yogodin, *Towards Higher Standards in Education through Its Humanization and Democratization* (Moscow: Novosti Press, 1989), p. 17.

[4]Peter McLaren, *Life in Schools,* in *The Foundations of Education: An Introduction to Critical Pedagogy* (New York: Longman, 1979), p. 168.

In addition to relating education to national culture nations of the world must also recognize other complex national and international problems for which formulating appropriate educational objectives constitutes an essential step toward finding solutions. In this nuclear age, human problems have become far more complex than in the past, and the only viable means of finding solutions to them is through knowledge of human behavior and relationships. In short, educational objectives must be directed toward the development of the individual in shaping a national character. Any other course of action is likely to yield limited results.

Since objectives determine the content of education, it is important to remember that formulating them is a fundamental step toward putting in place national programs to help minimize the possibility of conflict. Resorting to military force to solve problems does not offer a lasting solution. These considerations are essential to the development of any nation. Let us now attempt to discuss how objectives determine the character of education in the four areas selected for this study.

AFRICA: EDUCATIONAL OBJECTIVES AS A STEP TOWARD SELF-DISCOVERY

To understand the importance of educational objectives in Africa, one must appreciate the nature and extent of the problems education must be designed to solve. Of all Third World nations, none is facing problems of development more than African nations. Among the most serious of these problems were the massive demonstrations staged in Lusaka, Zambia, against the political and economic policies of the government of Kenneth Kaunda. Since Kaunda came to power in October 1964, an erosion of basic human rights has combined with the deterioration of the economy .

The political problems that have arisen in Kenya, Zaire, Zimbabwe, Liberia, Mozambique, Ethiopia, Angola, Mali, and South Africa, to name only some examples, have resulted from the desire of those in power to institute a one-party or one-man system of government. There are two basic problems that African nations have encountered as a result of misguided educational objectives. The first is that the inability and unwillingness of African governments to recognize that the one-party or one-man system of government is a major cause of national problems has led to corruption and mismanagement. This has threatened to destroy the vital tissue of national life.[5] It is a particularly sad truth that the African old political guards have themselves become major problems for their nations, and they do not even recognize it. This is not to argue that introducing democracy would provide a panacea for all national problems, but to suggest that it offers an environment conducive to finding solutions better than the existing forms of government.

The second problem has to do with cultural and ethnic conflict. While ethnic conflict existed in Africa before establishment of the colonial system, it was the colonial governments that exploited it in order to entrench the principle of divide and conquer. This is why, for example, in

---

[5] *New York Times,* July 25, 1990.

South Africa the Xhosa and the Zulu were set against each other. In Malawi the Chewa were set against the Nyanja, in Zimbabwe the Nbebele against the Shona, in Zambia the Bemba against the Lozi, in Nigeria the Ibos against the Hausas.

The legacy that this conflict has left behind in Africa is that the brutal civil war in Nigeria has set the pattern for an established practice on the continent. The conflict in Liberia in 1990 and that between the Zulu and the Xhosa in South Africa in 1991, in which the government was known to take sides in supporting the Zulu because Chief Buthelezi has for years been considered more sympathetic toward apartheid than Nelson Mandela, the ANC leader, are a product of the colonial legacy.

Because ethnic conflict leads citizens to regard themselves as members of their ethnic group before they consider themselves members of their nation, it is very difficult for African countries to build an understanding of what a nation is.[6] This is why the first definition of a nation has to start with formulating educational objectives. It is true that members of an ethnic group create an inner circle in which ideas, thought processes, and actions may be considered by the national government as incompatible with national policy. It is also true that a preponderance of ethnic groups creates a situation that demands loyalty to them because they see the national government run on the basis of nepotism and corruption robbing the citizens of their fair share of national resources.

The sad part of it all is that the national government fails to see that it is responsible for creating this unpleasant reality. When these two practices combine, they form a powerful force that runs against the concept of national unity. In this regard, the colonial policy of divide and conquer has manifested itself in Africa in painful and disturbing ways. In this kind of setting, efforts to formulate educational objectives encounter formidable obstacles. The objectives that often come out of this situation amount to what Canaan Banana of Zimbabwe calls the culture of poverty,[7] because the process of implementing them is too weak to bring out the strengths of African culture.

Because formulating educational objectives in independent Africa is a process of trying to eliminate the legacy of the colonial period, one must search for a wider perspective from which to understand the concept of cultural diversity as an objective of education in Africa. When Paulo Freire concluded that efforts of the oppressed to restore their belittled culture constitute an essential step toward self-rediscovery,[8] he was suggesting that the educational process must be divorced from the culture of the oppressor. For nations of Africa this suggests establishing a new set of criteria in which formulating educational objectives can be undertaken with the objective of eliminating the influence of past practices. This will result

---

[6]A. R. Thompson, *Education and Development in Africa* (New York: St. Martin's Press, 1982), p. 4.

[7]Canaan Banana, *Theology of Promise: The Dynamics of Self-reliance* (Harare, Zimbabwe: the College Press, 1982), p. 34.

[8]Paulo Freire, *Pedagogy of the Oppressed* (New York: Continuum, 1982), p. 33.

in formulating educational objectives to ensure cultural enrichment and diversity. Once goals are established, the curriculum is so designed that it comes into line with national purpose. This reaffirmation of the importance of cultural diversity also suggests that, for Africa, redefining cultural values as an objective of education carries an importance that cannot be taken for granted and that cannot be accomplished through the existing educational system.

This realization requires the transformation of social institutions in order to ensure the transmission of cultural values to students even though, at the primary level, they are rudimentary in nature. It is here where educational innovation plays a critical role in preparing schools to teach students early in life the indispensability of cultural tolerance and acceptance, not of division and conflict as was the case during the colonial period. Once students understand the importance of eliminating cultural prejudice, they will view all human beings as members of an embracing family with shared social values. Once this objective has been accomplished, tribal or ethnic conflict that often paralyzes national efforts toward advancement will also be eliminated.

Beyond making efforts to seek solutions to problems of human conflict, regarding cultural acceptance and diversity as a focus of educational objectives helps to extend to all students a sense of confidence both in themselves and in national leaders as they come to understand that the notion of a superior-inferior ideology has no place in the national order. This forms an essential component of national character. When education emphasizes a new national character embedded in the ideals of a plural cultural enrichment, no ethnic group feels threatened or dominated.

In this kind of sociocultural environment, the concept of equal opportunity is practiced to the fullest. The tragedy of cultural domination that exploded into bitter civil wars in Nigeria in 1967, in Liberia in 1989, and in Mali in 1991 must be avoided at all costs. Only through the search for innovation in the educational process can this national objective be achieved.

The inability of African leaders to carve a new national cultural identity or direction has also accentuated their inability to resolve conflict situations that often emerge in the question of who comes first, the individual or society. That national leaders argue that the interests of the nation must come first is a strategy they use to gain absolute loyalty of all citizens without extending to them the benefits that are often associated with a national identity.

This situation has created a scenario in which ethnic groups feel that they have been deliberately excluded from participation in the affairs of their country and so they withdraw from involvement in national programs and replace their national loyalty with loyalty to their own ethnic groups. This voluntary self-alienation has further contributing to an environment of conflict because excluded ethnic groups often feel that they are being exploited for political reasons to benefit those in positions of power.[9]

---

[9] Thompson, *Education and Development in Africa*, p. 77.

Another critical objective of education is political integration and national unity. The colonial governments did not practice democracy in Africa because they argued that the Africans were not educated enough to understand its complex process; certainly this must dictate fundamental change in both the political process and the educational system. If the colonial governments believed that the lack of education inhibited the ability of the Africans to function in a political setting, then why did they not do something to change the situation? The important thing for African nations to remember is that, just as economic development and literacy must benefit the individual before they can benefit society, the educational process must first be directed at improving the position of the individual as a political being. This is how society wi;ll benefit.

The process of becoming a supreme political being always demands education that is comprehensive enough to enable students to grasp the essential components of a political society. A. R. Thompson argued that in order to serve the needs of the people in a way it is intended to do, education must not be removed from the political interests of the individual first and then the interests of society as a whole.[10]

When Thompson continued that national governments "must recognize that the growing scale and complexity of educational planning must be met largely from the public purse and must therefore be subject to political accountability,"[11] he was actually suggesting that the educational process must be directed toward political integration and national unity. One must therefore ask the question: What do political integration and national unity mean as objectives of education?

In independent Africa, education and politics have remained as far apart as they were during the colonial period because there has been an inherent unwillingness to acknowledge their interdependence. Most African national leaders are either insensitive to or against popular participation in the political arena because they tend to associate such activity with efforts to remove them from office. Many are still victims of a thinking that prevailed during the struggle for independence: that political activity entails radical political change that would threaten the status quo.

The proper thing for African nations to do is formulate national policy that seeks to bring education and politics together in a productive manner. To accomplish this fundamental objective, change in the educational system is essential, and it requires establishment of objectives different from the past. This would enable all people to view the political process as ensuring national development.

This kind of setting creates a national environment which citizens can develop a collective political identity. Collective identity requires a clear understanding that, although they hold opposing political views and belong to different political parties as a necessary condition for sustaining democracy, citizens must sustain and strengthen national institutions and fulfill goals compatible with commonly held values. The Africans should

---

[10]Ibid., p. 47.
[11]Ibid., p. 48.

learn to view political activity in the same way as do members of the Labour Party and the Conservative Party in Great Britain or the Democratic Party and the Republican Party in the United States.

The responsibility for developing national understanding rests squarely on the shoulders of national leaders. By formulating educational objectives intended to strengthen a national character, political differences can be seen as beneficial to the country. The violence that is often associated with political activity in Africa robs the continent of the vital resources needed to build dynamic societies for the benefit of all.

These are the essential elements that constitute a definition of political integration and national unity. Upon his release from prison on February 12, 1990, Nelson Mandela put political advancement as an objective of education into proper perspective when he said: "Twenty-seven years ago when I went to prison I could not vote. Twenty-seven years later I still cannot vote. Education under apartheid is a crime against humanity."[12]

Along with formulating educational objectives to strengthen political institutions and to ensure political integration and national unity, nations of Africa must relentlessly work toward improving the economy and literacy. Formulating educational objectives is a task that must be undertaken with a clear understanding of national purpose. For African nations, this is the first step toward the process of self-rediscovery as Paulo Freire defines it.

JAPAN: SEEKING TO ENSURE THE DEVELOPMENT OF THE NEXT GENERATION

To understand educational objectives in Japan, one has to appreciate the varied features of its society and relationships the the rest of the world. The character of Japanese society manifests itself in its culture. The Japanese language began to take a modern form in 1868, the year the Rescript of Education was introduced. The Japanese language is spoken in different forms according to the demands of changing social situations.

In 1948, while Japan was still under the occupation, the Allies persuaded the Ministry of Education to formulate a program designed to simplify the system of writing in order to facilitate communication with the rest of the world. This program attempted to reduce the number of characters to 1,850 from more than 2,000. It was important for Japan to communicate with the international community under new demanding conditions.

Because, as in other countries, literature is an important part of everyday life for the Japanese people, people are encouraged to produce literature that reflects the basic Japanese cultural values. Because the Japanese have a deep love of their cultural traditions, the educational system is designed to sustain them. Realizing that culture is central to the survival of a people, the Japanese go a second mile in seeking to preserve that character by having the schools teach the young generation that abandoning cultural traditions might lead to social disintegration with severe consequences for the nation itself. It is a risk that neither the

---

[12]An address to the people of South Africa, SABC-TV, February 12, 1990.

national leadership nor the people are willing to take. This is why the Ministry of Education plays a critical role in making sure that schools understand their responsibility to the sustenance of national character. A major component of this line of thinking is the idea that if the cultural foundations were weakened, the nation's social institutional values could not be sustained. If this happened, the entire national sense of being would be lost.

Since 1945 Japan has operated under the belief that its existence would be determined by how well it makes an effort to maintain its own perspective and destiny in a hostile global environment. That it was occupied by the Allies suggested that the international community expected it to fall into line with their expectations of what it must do. For the Japanese this presented a dilemma: whether to abandon their sense of being in order to acquire a new identity expected by the international community, or to resist and face threats of foreign domination under the articles of the occupation. Japan decided to play it safe. Instead of responding to the demands of the Allies, Japan felt that placing emphasis on education would eventually meet the demands of the Allies and also satisfy its own need for development within a new international mold.

Japan formulated two basic educational objectives. The first was to place more emphasis on literacy. The second was to improve the instruction of mathematics in order to enhance its efforts toward bringing the country into line with the latest technological trends. The overall objective was "to produce a highly literate and mathematically capable population"[13] to enable the people to function in a rapidly changing environment.

To achieve this, schools were made to understand the nature and extent of their responsibility to prepare students to play an effective role in society. In order to do this they were taught to embrace discipline and cooperation as national virtues needed to build a vibrant and dynamic society on a sound foundation so that it would serve the needs of all people.

In a society that takes great pride in the value of its institutions, educational achievement and success become a major objective of the school. Achievement and success combine to "guarantee a successful career."[14] This is why, of all the students in high school in 1982, more than 65 percent decided to prepare for college, and not to take vocational courses. Because Japanese industrial and professional development demands a highly selective process, the educational system itself must aim at academic performance beyond reproach in order to allow equal opportunity to all students.

This is why the development of national industrial efficiency is considered essential. This is also why "from the time children first sit in school at the age of six, they are faced with seven hours of classes a day, two hundred days a year, and twelve years of unrelenting pressure. Twice

---

[13]*Time*, March 15, 1982.
[14]Ibid.

a year they must take examinations to get into the next grade."[15] Even the *shiken figoku*, the infamous term for examination hell, does not deter students from trying to do their very best to pass the examinations so that they are assured of climbing the educational ladder. What has been discussed here so far leads to the conclusion that Japan, like other societies, understands that education is needed to transmit skills and to ensure the value system not only for survival of the present generation but also for the development of the next.[16] In this national setting, Japan regards education as a major channel that must be utilized to shape national values and and meet the demands of emerging global settings.

This understanding of Japanese international relationships underscores the essential nature of the national economic development program to enhance trade. The educational system had to be designed with an important objective in mind: to enable students to be at their best in any educational endeavor. Teachers were made to understand that they carried a major responsibility to ensure that the students had an essential grasp of the materials they were taught to meet the demands of new technology in order to make Japan viable in a competitive world.

The Japanese, having endured the wrath of atomic power, slowly began to understand the importance of structuring an educational system to sustain a working balance between the society and the individual. In this respect the fundamental objective of education has become the realization that the character of society is a product of individual behavior and that the character of the individual emanates from the social environment. The Japanese have come to believe that the character of society cannot be separated from the character of the individual. Education in this kind of relationship has to be transformed objectives that help the system improve the role of the individual in influencing the character of society and sharpen his own perception of self.[17]

In aspiring to be a modern industrial state, Japan has steadily endeavored to maintain a working relationship between educational development and industrial development. This demands a clear understanding of educational objectives to ensure that the training of skilled labor is relevant to a broader educational purpose that suits the needs of the country. This is what the Japanese leadership believes will give the country a viable competitive edge in the world of trade.

Students and teachers are constantly reminded that the labor needs of the country and the development of manpower constitute a major objective of education to promote the economic interests of the country educational success, such as the quality of graduates from both high school and college, must demonstrate tangible benefits to the nation.

In demonstrating clear understanding of this purpose, Japan now seeks an economic and trade dominance that it has never known before. It seeks

---

[15]Ibid.

[16]Ronald Anderson, "Japanese Education," in Edward Ignas and Raymond Corsini (eds.), *Comparative Educational Systems* (Itasca, Ill: E. Peacock, 1982), p. 234.

[17]Ibid., p. 235.

an economic Montezuma's revenge to its atomic destruction in 1945. To the Western world, whose own technological development has not been able to catch up with that of Japan, Japan has come to pose problems that the Allies did not anticipate at the conclusion of the occupation in 1952.

That Japan has gone far beyond the level of expectation in designing an educational system that the Allies hoped would introduce the country to democratic values suggests the emergence of a new will, not only to survive, to assert itself in the competitive arena of international trade.

What is important in this regard is that the Japanese worker is not merely trained to function effectively on the production assembly line. He is also educated sufficiently to become a creative and innovative person with a sense of the importance of a national purpose and pride. Therefore, the production of skilled workers acquires a dimension consistent with the demands of a nation that has a vision of its future and a working knowledge of the past. This is how Japan is formulating educational objectives so that it can play its role well in a changing world.

A critical aspect of objectives of education in Japan is that individuals have an inviolable responsibility as consumers of the products of education to exercise choices in pursuing careers consistent with their interests and talents. For the school system to make it possible for students to exercise these choices constitutes a recognition that choice itself is a fundamental objective of education. Choice as an essential feature of any emerging nation manifests itself in various ways, ranging from industrial production to life-styles. The Japanese also know that choice in education, ranging from courses to career options, not only determines the role the individual will play in shaping the future of society, but also makes it possible to have a balance of careers for the benefit of society.[18]

Countering criticism from the West that the Japanese system of education is too rigid, the Japanese themselves are fully aware that one of its objectives is to ensure social change, not for the change's sake, but for the development of their society. Evidence of that change is a consciousness that a society void of values, such as equality, lacks what it needs to ensure its own advancement. That the concept of equality is a central objective of education underscores a basic consideration of what the educational process must envisage as one of its operational principles. For this reason, the barriers that existed in extending opportunity to women have steadily been broken, as Japan sees itself the context of global trends.

A critical outcome of this realization is the practice that boys and girls have equal chances in the pursuit of academic excellence. Course offerings and career counseling no longer reflect the thinking that girls are less capable of successful study of science and mathematics. Application of the concept of equality as an objective of education has a broader application to society itself. Therefore in Japan, as is the case in other countries, establishing educational objectives plays a critical role in shaping the character of society itself. Like other countries, Japan recognizes that

---

[18] "Japan's Classroom: A Budding Blackboard Jungle," in *New York Times* (March 29, 1982), p. 12.

without formulating objectives, designing an educational program would yield limited results.

THE UNITED STATES: SEEKING TO RESUSCITATE THE THROB OF THE NATION

In discussing the objectives of education in the United States one must keep two essential in mind. The first is that schools exist for the purpose of preparing citizens who are able to function within a social, democratic, economic, and political environment. The second is that each student must be given an opportunity to learn the essentials needed "to carry out the basic life tasks."[19] Although Edward Ignas concluded that practices of the American educational system are so varied that it is hard to crystallize universal objectives, one must remember that the development of objectives takes a historical route. In this section we discuss only a few examples to show that formulating objectives is a critical part of the educational process in the United States, as in other nations.

During the formative years of the colonial American society, schools were created to impart to students the religious and moral values they needed to function in a larger social order.[20] But as colonial America came to an end in 1776, the purpose of schools changed to suit new situations. The school's authoritarian principles had to give way to the principle that education had a fundamental objective of preparing the individual to function in a new social environment.

There was, by the beginning of the nineteenth century, a move to substitute the Bible as the cornerstone of the curriculum. The election of Andrew Jackson to the presidency and the release of the Yale Report, both in 1828, accentuated the need to change the objectives of education. Because American society was becoming a secular culture, the campaign for the common schools that Horace Mann initiated took on a new meaning.

When John Dewey argued in 1938 that, "the main objective of education is to prepare the young for future responsibility and for success in life,"[21] he was stressing the importance of the secular character of the American society as an outcome of implementing objectives consistent with change. The advent of modern industrial technology during the latter part of the nineteenth century ushered in the need to redirect the educational objectives in accordance with social and economic conditions. Mortimer Adler seems to sum it up when he argued, "To achieve the desired quality of democratic education"[22] students must be trained "to earn a living in an intelligent and responsible fashion, to function as intelligent and

---

[19]Edward Ignas, "The Traditions of American Education," in Ignas and Corsini, *Comparative Educational Systems* (Itasca, Ill.: F. E. Peacock Publishers, 1981), p. 2.

[20]Ibid., p. 3.

[21]John Dewey, *Experience and Education* (New York: Collier, 1964), p. 18.

[22]Adler, *The Paideia Proposal: An Educational Manifesto*(New York: Collier Books, 1982), p. 18.

responsible citizens and to enjoy as fully as possible all the goods that make human life as good as it can be."[23]

As is the case in Japan and Africa, the development of a democratic society has placed heavy demands on the need to formulate a set of objectives to give it substance. The concept of equality of opportunity, both in education and society, has constantly tarnished the American image as a nation determined to sustain this basic component. The continuation of racial discrimination and prejudice has cast a long shadow on the road to national development.

Edward Ignas argued that the problem of articulating educational objectives in an effort to bring the country to a new level of equality is often complicated by "attempts to balance the needs of the individual and those of society."[24] Those charged with this responsibility, including government officials, fail to realize that the interests of society can only be served by serving those of the individual. In the same way, the development of the country is best assured by extending genuine equality to all people. Beyond this imperative, Americans must recognize that extending equality of educational opportunity to all citizens, as an objective of education, supports the nation itself.

Efforts to define objectives of education for this century appear to have taken a new form. When the Commission on the Reorganization of Secondary Education outlined seven basic objectives in 1918, the thinking that objectives were important to the success of education took on a powerful dimension. The commission outlined these objectives as the following: to ensure good health; to enable all students to gain a functional knowledge of the fundamental processes; to enable students to demonstrate their worth as members of the family; to train students to gain the essentials of a vocation; to demonstrate good citizenship; to teach students to understand the values of leisure time and to use it for recreative and creative purposes; and to gain an essential understanding of ethical character.[25]

Twenty years later, in 1938, to underscore the importance of these objectives, the Education Policies Commission of the National Education Association (NEA) stressed the importance of establishing educational objectives in four critical areas of education: self-realization, human understanding, socioeconomic competence, and civic or community responsibility. In 1961 NEA added a new dimension in considering these objectives when it concluded: "The purpose which runs through and strengthens all other educational purposes is the development of the ability to think."[26] Recognition of the teacher's ability to inspire students to think is a fundamental objective of education and is accentuated by the knowledge that social issues are becoming far more complex than they

---

[23]Ibid., p. 19.

[24] Ignas, "The Traditional American Educational System," p. 3.

[25]Ibid., p. 3.

[26]Ibid., p. 4.

were in the past. Answers to critical questions are no longer as yes or no, but as critical appraisal of all pertinent factors.

For the United States this has been a period of applying moral values or principles within the context of applying the principle of choice. Changing conditions in the environment affect personal choice. This is what a pregnant high school girl faces as she ponders the consequences of exercising her choices--to have an abortion or not. Recent developments in the country advise her that she does not need to consult her parents to carry out her choices. The ability to think as an objective of education carries enormous practical consequences that were not part of the educational process in the past. As we have seen in the case of Japan, the ability to exercise choices can only be assured by an effective system of education. This is why many Americans argue that those who take sides on the paralyzing debate on abortion have lost the essential nature of the principle of choice.

In its decision in *Roe vs. Wade* of January 22, 1973, the U.S. Supreme Court appeared to have redefined morality by ruling that a woman has a constitutional right to terminate an unwanted pregnancy.[27] Those who argued in 1993 that abortion was wrong seemed to ignore this new definition. In this context, the best that the school can do is to redefine the objectives of education to take into account this change of definition and to structure the educational process so that it enables students to acquire the functional knowledge they need to exercise freedom of choice in a logical and informed manner. Unless there is a meeting of the minds on this critical national controversy, the task of formulating adequate educational objectives will remain unfulfilled and students will continue to endure the agony of collective indecision. Ultimately it is the American society itself that pays the price.

The mere fact that each year an increasing number of American girls get pregnant suggests two things. The first is that the definition of morality has been radically changing: Pregnancy outside of marriage no longer carries the social and moral stigma that it did in the past. The second is that American schools need a new set of objectives, not only to teach students to function in a new moral and social order, but also to impart a sense of who they are as individual human beings sufficiently trained to differentiate right from wrong for themselves as synonymous with what is right and what is wrong for society.

In a similar manner, the United States, like other countries, is facing some critical problems in national life. The disintegration of the nucleus family has eroded many traditional values. The phenomenon of the single parent has exerted tremendous pressures on women and their children. The uncontrollable surge of subcultures invariably threatens the very survival of a struggling nation. In recent years the United States has experienced serious social problems because it has encountered serious problems in education. It is important to understand that the search for solutions to

---

[27]On January 22, 1993, the twentieth anniversary of the decision, President Bill Clinton affirmed his support of it saying, "As a nation our goal should be to protect the freedom of the individual to make choices."

social problems cannot be separated from the search for solutions to educational problems.

While her efforts were a gallant demonstration of her commitment to rid the country of the scourge of the drug culture, Nancy Reagan's strategy of "Just say no" was a simplistic approach to a major national problem. The problems that the United States is now facing can effectively be addressed by redefining new objectives that seek to implant in students an ability to exercise critical thinking and judgment. Indeed, critical thinking enables students to evaluate the consequences of their action on both themselves and their society. What stands in the way of understanding the importance of exercising critical thinking is not so much an institutional inability to see its value, but a tragic collective failure to find solutions to major national problems. The concept of individuality has derailed national values.

The last example of the importance of formulating objectives of education in the United States is that education must address the question of social justice. Although Ignas concluded that "disagreement and controversy are so common that there is little chance of any new consensus,"[28] it seems that Americans understand that social justice is a sustaining theme of their society. Since the end of the war in 1945, various national organizations have tried to apply pressure on those who have political power toward eliminating poverty and promoting racial integration as national endeavors that can best be addressed by formulating a set of educational objectives.

The plight of the homeless--a bulging and disturbing new social phenomenon--is a national problem whose solution can be found in articulating new educational policy and objectives. Neal Peirce discussed the need to redefine both educational policy and objectives within the context of the need to restructure a new national character, saying: "Never before have our leaders so explicitly tied educational quality to this country's chances for survival. The danger is that school boards, under a false banner of local control, will delay or scuttle tough reforms. State governments must either force the boards to perform, or put them out of their misery. Policy and objectives are the twin pillars of national character."[29] The imperative of redefining educational objectives is itself an effort to resuscitate the failing pulse of a nation that finds itself in doubt about its values and the future.

THE SOVIET UNION: USING EDUCATIONAL OBJECTIVES TO BUILD A NEW SOCIETY

As in Africa, Japan, and the United States, educational objectives in the Soviet Union take a historical route. In 1919 the Communist Party Congress adopted a political platform that served as a preamble to the objectives of education, stating: "Schools will change from having been a

---

[28]Edward Ignas, "The Traditional American Educational System," p. 3.

[29]Neal Peirce, "Obstacles to Change in Schools," in *The Arizona Republic*: (October 16, 1989), p. A9.

weapon of class superiority of the bourgeoisie into a weapon of the complete abolition of the division of society into classes and for the rebirth of the Communist society."[30] Three years later in 1922, Lenin discussed some reasons why he thought the Communist party must formulate a new set of educational objectives, and went on to say: "The central feature of the situation now is that the vanguard of a new social order must not shirk the work of educating itself, of remodeling itself because it lacks the skills necessary to shape the direction of a new society."[31]

From that time to the time that Mikhail Gorbachev added two new terms to the world's knowledge of the Soviet Union, *glasnost* and *perestroika,* the quest for meaningful change and the endeavor to initiate change in the national character have been based on clear educational objectives as part of an essential national agenda to build a new society. The leadership of the Soviet Union, from Lenin to Gorbachev, recognized that it was not possible to build a new society without adjusting educational objectives to a national agenda. Therefore, as in the other three examples in this study, the formulation of educational objectives in the Soviet Union is a continuous process made so by changing conditions in both the nation and the world.

At the successful conclusion of the revolution in 1917, the Bolsheviks set out to reconstruct the educational system so that its main objective would be to destroy what they regarded as the negative morality that Nicholas demanded the schools teach and thus create a new socialist morality.[32] In seeking to fulfill this objective, the Bolsheviks immediately formulated another: a campaign to combat illiteracy.

This strategy was linked to the socialist principle that a literate population was the best national resource to ensure development of a socialist society. Achieving literacy has always been a central objective of education in all countries. But in the Soviet Union it acquired an added importance because of the conviction of its leaders that socialism was the best form of national development and that the country must set an example for other countries struggling for development to follow.

As soon as Joseph Stalin assumed office he recognized that the success of his five-year development plan would depend on how fast universal literacy was achieved. He therefore ordered the schools to accept a higher level of responsibility in implementing a policy based on new objectives: to eliminate illiteracy in twenty years. This was to ensure that every student got from the school process the basic skills needed to function in a world of socialism. Stalin was quite adamant in reminding schools that these

---

[30]Vitali Prokhorov, *Pages from History in the U.S.S.R.: A Time of Difficult Questions* (Moscow: Novosti Press, 1990), p. 28.

[31]Ibid., p. 33.

[32]B. P. Yesipov and N. K. Gonshorov, "For Bolshevik Character: The Principles of Moral Education", in *I Want to Be Like Lenin*, trans. G. S. Counts (London: Victor Gallanez, 1948), p. 115.

skills included literacy. This is why illiteracy increased from 8 percent in 1928 to 40 percent in 1950.[33]

But Stalin had to enslave his own people to accomplish this objective. Launching a national agenda to accomplish the objectives of a political ideology at the expense of one's people is not a correct definition of objectives to ensure national development. In spite of Stalin's objectives and national agenda, the Soviet Union had a long way to go before it could reach the 98 percent literacy that it finally accomplished by 1991.

On assuming her duties as the commissar for education at the inception of the Bolshevik administration, Nedezhda K. Krupskaya outlined the central principles underlying national efforts to redefine educational objectives for schools to fulfill their task:

> The system of education aims at developing every child's ability to engage in activity, to develop a consciousness of his personality, and to ensure his individuality. We are for all-round development of our children. We want to make them strong physically and morally. We want to teach them to be collectivists and not individualistic in the capitalist sense because it does not stress a child's personality in a collective society and does not seek to improve the quality of his education.[34]

While the objective of promoting all-round development of the individual through collective action has universal application, because every person lives in relation to other members of society, it had a special meaning to the socialist character of the Soviet Union as its leaders envisaged it. This special meaning was the objective of building an egalitarian state. Although that objective has remained elusive, it is one that the Soviet leadership was not willing to abandon, including the reformist Mikhail Gorbachev.

This is the line of thinking that V. Yelyutin, Minister of Higher Education, took into consideration in saying in 1959, under the direction of Nikita Khrushchev,"The role of Soviet education is to assist in the building up of a Communist society, in reshaping the materialist world outlook of the students, equipping them with a good grounding in different fields of knowledge and preparing them for socially useful work."[35] But one must seek to understand the general character of educational objectives during Khrushchev's tenure from a perspective of what education was intended to do.

In 1961 the powerful and influential Council of Ministers outlined the basic objectives of higher education that were to guide its development: "Higher education, like every other branch of the educational system, is organized to meet social, political, and economic needs of the Soviet

---

[33] Chapter 1 of this study has concluded that no country has achieved 100 percent literacy.

[34] N. K. Krupskaya, *On Education* (Moscow: Foreign Languages Publishing House, 1957), p. 120. This is, of course, self-contradictory.

[35] V. Yelyutin, *Higher Education in the U.S.S.R.*, Soviet Booklet No. 51 (London: 1959), p. 40.

society and to render assistance to those nations struggling for development."[36] This statement shows that Khrushchev wanted it known that the educational system in general and higher education in particular must operate under seven basic objectives. These were:

(1) to train highly qualified specialists educated in the spirit of Marxism-Leninism and well versed in the latest achievement of science and technology;

(2) to carry out research that would enable students to contribute solutions to the problems of building socialism throughout the world;

(3) to produce textbooks and other educational materials of high standard;

(4) to train teachers and education workers who would have sufficient knowledge of the objectives of the socialist philosophy;

(5) to provide advanced training for specialists with higher education working in various fields of the national economy, the arts, and social services;

(6) to train people to disseminate scientific and political knowledge among people struggling against political domination by capitalist powers;

(7) to study the problems associated with graduates and with improving the quality of their training to understand the nature of the world in which they live.[37]

There is no question that in seeking to implement these objectives Khrushchev was primarily concerned with the level and quality of industrial and agricultural production as example of the success of socialism. He concluded that if these domestic programs succeeded then, with the aid the Soviet Union would be prepared to give, there would no reason why they would not succeed elsewhere in the world.

The introduction of five-year plans, the introduction of ten-year schooling, the establishment of agricultural communes, and efforts to improve literacy were all developments that Khrushchev wanted to use to prove to a skeptical world that socialism was a more productive and egalitarian system than capitalism. During a tour of the United States in 1959, Khrushchev repeatedly argued in favor of this position. He was, in fact, trying to fulfill the ideals that Lenin had expressed in a speech to the Third All-Russia Congress in October 1920:

A builder of the Communist society must not only master the basic sciences, but must have a polytechnic education as well. Communist morality is based on the struggle for victory of Communism to improve productivity and to reject capitalist

---

[36]Council of Ministers, *Statute of Higher Education in the U.S.S.R.* (Moscow: Ministry of Education), 1961.

[37]Ibid.

morality and to instill equality. These demand the development of new goals of education.[38]

When Leonid Brezhnev succeeded Khrushchev in 1964, he was under no illusion about the extent of the problems he faced. He worked hard to formulate objectives consistent with those of his predecessors and with Soviet goals both at home and abroad. He felt that the central Communist Party must be more involved in defining educational objectives, and he gave the Ministry of Education more power to define these goals.

By 1971 Brezhnev felt that he needed to assure the party that under his leadership things had improved because during the past six years he and his administration had defined the objectives of education more clearly than had Khrushchev. During an address to the twenty-fourth Communist Party Congress in 1971, Brezhnev received wild applause when he told delegates that there had been a significant rise in the standard of living of the Soviet people because there had been better production.[39]

By the time of his death in 1982, Brezhnev could claim that he had established a set of objectives of education to improve the quality of life of the people. Among these objectives were eight that made Brezhnev's administration distinct in the history of education in the Soviet Union. These were the following:

(1) to strengthen the national ministry of education so that it would have authority to design new educational policy;
(2) to expect university students to study more science and foreign languages in order to understand the world better;
(3) to provide an environment in which students would excel in all areas of educational endeavor, including athletic competition;
(4) to ensure that there was a frequent revision of the curriculum to make sure that it was still relevant to the needs of Soviet society;
(5) to structure general education in such a way that it would produce qualified scientists well trained in the latest advancements of technology and space exploration;
(6) to institute research at institutions of higher learning;
(7) to prepare students to meet the challenges of non-socialist systems;
(8) to bring into institutions of higher learning students from the Third World and teach them how to fight against capitalist exploitation.

When Mikhail Gorbachev assumed office, he did not seek to invalidate the accomplishments of his predecessors, but to build a new national program based on what he considered positive attributes of their work. In a speech to the All-Union Student Forum in 1989, Gorbachev paid tribute to his predecessors: "We are carrying forth the past valuable demands of our education as part of our heritage. Everything heroic and of universal

---

[38]N. Kuzin and M. Kondokov, *Education in the U.S.S.R.* (Moscow: Progress Press, 1977), p. 176.

[39]Brian Holmes, "Education in the Soviet Union," in Ignas and Corsini (eds.), *Comparative Educational Systems* (Itasca, Ill.: F. E. Peacock, 1982), p. 329.

importance demands our commitment. Above all we must carry the banner of the October Revolution to ensure our advancement."[40]

Like his predecessors, Gorbachev began his term of office by outlining the objectives of his administration. *Glasnost* and *perestroika* are essential components of these objectives. Gorbachev recognized that before national programs are put in place, it is important to understand *glasnost* and *perestroika*.

Because Gorbachev wanted to improve conditions of life in the Soviet Union based on the success he believed his predecessors had accomplished, he outlined the following objective as the thrust of his own national agenda:

(1)   to ensure that education makes it possible for all citizens to see themselves as they are in relation to what they could be. This would enable them to appraise national programs and to be involved in shaping new directions;

(2)   to have education become the focus of community activity so that the people can determine how best those programs could serve their needs;

(3)   to help students understand that openness constitutes an important step toward a free society where education helps create a new climate of political, social, and economic systems in which all people are able to express their views and offer ideas in an effort to build a dynamic and vibrant nation;

(4)   to have education serve the needs of each individual so that they in turn can serve the needs of the country.[41]

In a manner that seemed a paraphrase of Lenin and mindful of his legacy, Gorbachev summed up the relationship that he saw between educational objectives, *perestroika*, and making efforts toward social reform: "Without *glasnost* and *perestroika* there is no democracy. Without democracy, there will be no primacy of reason. Without reason there is no education and science. In turn, without science, education and culture as the chief spiritual mainstay of our existence, democracy cannot be firmly established."[42]

In addition to setting new conditions for the development of education through establishing new objectives, Gorbachev was also placing his countrymen in a new environment to discover the essence of their being based on the new thought process he was putting in place. The implementation of these objectives suggests that for the Soviet Union there was no going back. Under Gorbachev, the Soviet Union was poised for an experiment in collective human enterprise that would give new meaning to

---

[40]Mikhail Gorbachev, *Channel the Energy of Youth into Perestroika*, speech given to the All-Union Student Forum, November 15, 1989 (Moscow: Novosti Press, 1989), p. 14.

[41]Ibid.

[42]Ibid.

the concept of society and national development. The collapse of the Soviet Union in 1992 brought the experiment to a sudden end.

SUMMARY AND CONCLUSION

The discussion in this chapter leads to two basic conclusions. The first is that formulating objectives of education is a critical initial step in an effort to build a viable system of education for the purpose of serving the needs of society. Without clearly defined objectives the educational process has no direction, and without direction it has no real function. After formulating a theory of education, a nation needs to state its objectives before the educational process is put into place. Objectives become the vehicle of the educational system itself; they determine the direction, the purpose, and the possible outcome of educational programs. It is quite possible that the outcomes of the educational process can also determine the outcomes of other national programs.

The second conclusion is that stating educational objectives is a collective exercise. This is far too important to be left to a single national agency. It is also a continuous process because conditions of national life continue to change. The task of making objectives relevant demands thoroughness, vision, and foresight .

Once objectives are clearly set, then developing the curriculum becomes more manageable. The task that nations face in formulating objectives is to keep in mind the needs of students, taking into consideration the nature of social change that is likely to happen in the future. This is also an important component of national character.

5

The Curriculum: An Instrument of Fulfilling National Purpose

To view the curriculum as a form of cultural politics assumes that the social dimensions are the primary categories for schooling.

Peter McLaren, 1989

The restructuring of higher and secondary education is a powerful factor promoting society's steady progress.

Mikhail Gorbachev, 1989

THE UNIVERSALITY OF THE CURRICULUM

The conclusion we reached in the last chapter--that formulating educational objectives is a continuous process because there is continuous change in the conditions that govern national life--is equally true about the curriculum. While objectives determine the character of education, the curriculum determines the outcome. In this context, the curriculum also becomes an instrument of fulfilling a larger national purpose; shaping the character of society itself.

In all societies, developed or underdeveloped, Western or non-Western, the character of education largely depends on the extent to which the curriculum seeks to fulfill objectives. This suggests a relationship between objectives and the curriculum as a universal principle of the educational process. Writing on the universality of the curriculum, John Dewey observed: "Finding the material for learning is only the first step. The next step is the progressive development of what is already experienced into a fuller, richer, and more organized form."[1]

Dewey cautioned against the danger of designing a curriculum that attempts to sustain its own interests--that is, those who design it are heavily influenced by the interests of the nation, rather than those of the

---

[1]John Dewey, *Experience and Education* (New York: Collier, 1964), p. 73.

students: "Because the studies of the traditional school consisted of subject matter that was selected and arranged on the basis of the judgment of adults as to what would be useful to the young sometime in the future, the material to be learned was settled upon outside the present life experience of the learner."[2]

What Dewey was suggesting is that the inevitable consequence of designing a curriculum that seeks to place the interests of society above those of the student is that students may lose interest in the educational process and, thus, in society. Once students lose interest in the educational process, society pays the ultimate price. Perhaps nations that are facing an increasingly high drop-out rate take this into consideration in designing their curriculum.

One way of helping students sustain their interest in the educational process is assuring them that the curriculum and the related activity are designed with their best educational interests in mind. Therefore, in designing the curriculum a nation must remain conscious of the question: How best can the curriculum serve the needs of students? The curricular structure that emerges as a result of an effort to provide an answer to this question brings to the educational process benefits that would otherwise be lost.

Education also generates a new level of interest among students because they begin to see themselves as its primary objective. It makes it possible for education to extend to all students a new sense of their individuality so essential to building diversity as a component of national character. It provides for broadly based programs that offer a unique opportunity for students to engage in various areas of study and so allow their country to meet its manpower needs. It helps students participate in various sectors of the economy and thus help strengthen it. Only a curriculum developed from this perspective embraces the essential elements of national development: the economic, social, cultural, and political dimensions.

Peter McLaren took this line of thinking when he discussed the universality of the curriculum: "To view the curriculum as a form of cultural politics assumes that the social, cultural, political and economic dimensions are the primary categories of understanding contemporary schooling."[3] This way of looking at education suggests that the curriculum creates a national climate in which students see themselves as active and indispensable political, social, and economic entities that the nation needs to build a foundation for the future.

Once this reality becomes part of the school system, both students and the community in which it is located begin to understand the curriculum not as an institutional structure created to serve the super interests of the nation, but as a sociocultural establishment with varying shades of accommodating interests that are in harmony with each other, and not on a collision course. We now examine the implications of these universal

---

[2]Ibid., p. 76.

[3]Peter McLaren, *Life in Schools: An Introduction to Critical Pedagogy*, in *The Foundations of Education* (New York: Longman, 1989), p. 185.

principles on the character of the curriculum in the four areas selected for this study.

AFRICA: SEEKING AN END TO THE AGONY OF UNDERDEVELOPMENT

To understand how critical the curriculum is in Africa to fulfilling national purpose, one needs to understand the character of education in traditional society and during the colonial period. Contrary to the belief among colonial officials, education in traditional African society--the one that existed before the intrusion of the colonial systems--was quite complete and comprehensive.

This reality was recognized even by some colonial officials. For example, in 1965, F. G. Loveridge, who was a senior education officer in colonial Zimbabwe with special responsibility for developing the curriculum for schools for Africans, recognized the comprehensive nature of education in traditional African society. Addressing the Rotary Club, Loveridge admitted:

> In his traditional society the African was given all the education that he needed to function in his culture. That education was quite complete and the subject matter was quite comprehensive and inclusive. Today, the African student has fallen away because Western education does not prepare him to function in Western cultural settings which control his life. At the same time it does not prepare him to function in his own culture because the white man tells him that it is primitive. The African who goes to school in Western cultural settings is in a socioeconomic limbo.[4]

What Loveridge suggested is that, when applied in African cultural settings, Western education had to be adjusted to suit conditions in Africa. In essence Loveridge was posing the question: What kind of curriculum must be taught in African schools to reflect the character of the colonial society? The answer would depend on the objectives that the colonial officials outlined. In 1974, during a period of intense struggle for political independence from colonial domination, an elderly African told the author why he thought the introduction of Western education to Africa disrupted the essential features of African culture:

> What was taught in schools was not based on objectives intended to serve the developmental needs of the Africans, but to suit the purposes of the colonial culture. Before the coming of the white man to our country, no aspect of life, no boy or girl was ever neglected by our educational system. Today, we are told that only so many can go to school. Why so many only and not all? Besides, why is it that what is taught in white schools is different from what is taught in African schools? We thought that because education is universal what is taught in white schools must be the same as what is taught in African schools. Besides, if education

---

[4] F. G. Loveridge, "Disturbing Reality of Western Education in Africa," address to the Rotary Club International, Harare, Zimbabwe, March 13, 1965. Courtesy of the Old Mutare Methodist Archives.

is universal, there is no need to practice racial discrimination in it. Do you fail to see the intent of the colonial government in the education of our children?[5]

During the colonial period the absence of defined educational objectives to ensure the development of the Africans led directly to the absence of an effective curriculum. This combination meant that the Africans endured the agony of underdevelopment as they made an effort to initiate a transitional process from living in their traditional cultural environment to accepting the white man's education. U. S. Methodist Bishop James Crane Hartzell, who was sent to Africa in 1896, recognized this agony when he argued in 1918: "Africa has suffered from many evils. Slave trade and exploitation by the white man have through many years preyed upon the life of the people and left them uncertain about the future. To their dismay, the Natives of Africa have realized that the white man has offered them his form of education only to enable them to function as cheap laborers."[6]

There is no question that using the curriculum to exploit the Africans economically and politically was a deliberate policy of the colonial governments. Because this was the only strategy they utilized in order to survive, the colonial governments had no alternative course of action to take with respect to the education of the Africans without putting their own interests into jeopardy. This serious situation suggests that the task before African nations is to redesign the curriculum so that it is compatible with developmental needs of the people in their efforts to ensure national development.

The only way by which this objective can be accomplished is by abandoning the thinking surrounding the curriculum of the colonial governments. Unfortunately, many African leaders have found it politically expedient to utilize the strategies of the colonial governments to ensure that they remain in power. In this manner they hurt the developmental interests of their own people and, thus, those of their nations.

The action of the colonial governments in enacting school legislation detrimental to the development of the Africans shows a clear intent to fulfill the labor needs of the country as the primary purpose of education. This legislative action became a major way to exploit the Africans. The main purpose of this legislation was to give the colonial governments a legal basis for designing a curriculum fulfilling two sets of educational objectives--one for white students and the other for black students. This was why, in colonial Southern Rhodesia, for example, the Education Ordinance of 1899 provided for financial aid of four dollars per year per white student who had met an academic standard or proficiency in English, Latin, literature, history, geography, science, music, and shorthand, and

---

[5]During an interview in Mutare, Zimbabwe, May 10, 1974. See Dickson A. Mungazi, "The Change of Black Attitudes towards Education in Rhodesia, 1900-1975," (Ph.D. diss. University of Nebraska, 1977), p. 79.

[6]James Crane Hartzell, "The Future of Africa," in *The Africa Advance* vol. 12, no. 1 (July 1918).

one dollar per year per African student who had demonstrated proficiency in manual training.[7]

By carefully calculated and deliberate intent and design, then, Section B of this ordinance made provision for African schools to receive aid grants of one dollar per year per student, provided the school offered no less than two hours per day of manual training from a total of four hours per day and provided the average daily attendance was not fewer than fifty students during the preceding school year of two hundred days.[8]

The reasoning behind the action of the colonial governments in designing the curriculum to suit the conditions of the two racial groups was the belief that "The black peril will only become a reality when the results of a misguided system of education has taken root and the veneer of European civilization struggles with the innate savage nature of the African."[9] There is no doubt that this thinking demonstrates a fear among colonial officials that if the African had the same opportunity for educational development as the whites, there would be no basis for justifying differences in the curriculum.

If the fear of the white man was that the Africans would threaten his civilization if they were educated in the same way as the whites was the main reason for the colonial governments to act in the way they did, what had happened to the argument they used in the nineteenth century that education would bring Western civilization to them and that the only reason this did not happen was that they did not want it?

What came out of the thinking among colonial officials is practice that lasted throughout the colonial period, which did not make it possible for the curriculum in African schools to develop along viable and dynamic academic lines. This is why education produced nothing more than cheap laborers out of the Africans. The euphoria with which the colonial governments designed the curriculum for white students and African students could be considered concurrent with the kind of society that they wanted to build.

The sad result of the colonial curriculum is that the liberated African governments adopted elements of colonial thinking. The rigidity that characterized education during the colonial period was now substituted by a rigidity that compelled new African national leaders to adopt a strategy of political survival. Some African countries, former colonies of Britain, simply continued the system of education just as it had been during the colonial period. In the name of maintaining standards, the curriculum was dictated to by the universities of Cambridge, Oxford, and London in a more powerful way than in the past.

Emphasis on passing public examinations associated with these universities became the sole criterion of educational success. In this manner, former British colonies in Africa entered a period of

---

[7]Southern Rhodesia, Ordinance Number 18 of 1899: The Appointment of Inspector of Education, better known as Education Ordinance of 1899.

[8]Ibid., Section B.

[9]*The Rhodesia Herald* (April 4, 1903).

neocolonialism more powerful than that of the colonial period. The agony of underdevelopment that the African nations had endured during the colonial period now acquired powerful new dimensions.

For the Africans of the age of colonialism there was no escape from the far-reaching arms of the colonial octopus. Since Africans began to struggle for political independence once the war ended in 1945, the development of an effective curriculum to suit the needs of a new era has been subjected to the political game-playing tactics of former colonial masters. The development of a good curriculum in Africa has become either a helpless or a hopeless victim of a situation the Africans cannot control.

A question must be asked: What kind of curriculum must African nations design in order to end this agony of underdevelopment? The curriculum in emerging nations of Africans must include two critical components: social sciences and physical sciences. With respect to the first, the study of history, geography, economics, and political science must, by their very nature, be related to national character. The national character manifests itself in what the leaders do to help the people understand the importance of cooperation. But they must realize that this is unlikely to happen unless they demonstrate their commitment to advancement through a dynamic curriculum that enables students to understand the critical nature of the national issues confronting their country.

One critical way in which this national objective can be accomplished is by taking ethnicity and cultural diversity into account in designing the curriculum so that no group feels threatened. Unless the curriculum is designed to enhance the richness of cultural diversity as a national asset, it offers little of lasting value to an identity that seeks to eliminate the negative legacy of the colonial period.

With respect to the second, nations of Africa must remember that the world of today operates more efficiently through technology. In Africa, more than any other region of the world, science courses must be directly related to technological advancement. Solutions to the problems of a rapidly increasing population, economic development, enhancing agricultural productivity, improving medical services, an effective system of communication and transport, and industrial productivity are all essential to national identity and character.

The inclusion of physical sciences into the curriculum can make these a viable contribution to national development efforts. Unless African nations abandon the thinking that was central to the behavior of the colonial governments toward the curriculum, they will continue to experience the scourge of underdevelopment. This situation perpetuates a climate of conflict that has handicapped their efforts to chart a course of national development. This is the challenge that African nations must meet.

African nations must come to grips with the fact that to require high school students to study the history and the geography of the British Isles simply because an examination authority in Britain demands it in the name of maintaining academic standards is to lose sight of the fact that the curriculum must become an instrument of fulfilling educational objectives that in turn fulfill national purpose. The financial aid that some countries of Africa receive from former colonial masters, and the opportunity students are given to attend educational institutions in Europe as a result of maintaining the educational standards of the colonial period, are not adequate substitutes for making genuine efforts to introduce a new system of education based on the actual needs of students as a means of meeting national needs.

JAPAN: DESIGNING A CURRICULUM FOR THE AGE OF NEW TECHNOLOGY

In Africa the curriculum is an imitation of the one in place during the colonial period with minor changes. In Japan, however, the curriculum is designed to ensure the development of technology to suit the conditions of a new age. To appreciate how Japan has designed a curriculum that has helped it acquire a new technology, one needs to understand some developments that have taken place since the end of the war in 1945.

Prior to the outbreak of the war in 1939, the national Ministry of Education had authority to design a national curriculum consistent with the demands made by the emperor that students make a viable contribution to the development of Japanese society. Therefore, emphasis was placed on religious, moral, civic, social, and technical knowledge. Students were expected to engage in the study of these values to prepare them to fit into the.

During the occupation by Allied forces from 1945 to 1952, that curriculum was abolished to minimize the impact of loyalty that the Japanese showed to their emperor, in an effort to have him regarded as human and not as a deity. The occupation authorities replaced the national curriculum developed during the rescript with one by which teachers, as in the United States, were free to proceed their own curricula without any regard to national requirements. The problem that the schools faced with this reformed format was that, because the occupation authorities failed to provide specific guidelines, the teachers could not design an effective curriculum.[10] Slowly, the educational process, that presumed hallmark of democracy as it was practiced in the West, was in a state of decline from lack of direction and meaning.

In 1958, conscious of criticism from both teachers and citizens, the legislature decided to enact laws to strengthen the curriculum and give the ministry new powers in designing it. It must be remembered that world events in 1958 played a major part in bringing a new awareness to Japan to do something dramatic to improve its education on a national level. In the same year the United States enacted the National Defense Education Act to improve its curriculum, following the launching of Sputnik in 1956.

That this legislation emphasized the teaching of science and technological development was a fact that the Japanese Diet took into account in redesigning its curriculum. Although the inclusion in the

---

[10]Ronald Anderson, "Japanese Education," in Edward Ignas and Raymond Corsini(eds.), *Comparative Educational System* (Itasca, Ill: F. E. Peacock, 1982), p. 248.

curriculum of religious and moral values was controversial,[11] the Japanese people seemed to accept the basic rationale for them, as they would give their nation a new ethical quality so critical to national character.

With this action Japan was once again ready to chart a challenging course in curriculum development. The power of the Ministry of Education to direct the course of education gave a sense of urgency. A major component of that power was to demand that schools excel in science, mathematics, technology, and language arts. In 1976 a national curriculum committee was appointed and charged with the task of recommending improvement of the curriculum.

The committee made three recommendations it thought important to curriculum development: (1) the curriculum must include more science, mathematics, modern technology, and foreign language at the primary and secondary levels (2) basic departments should be established in each primary school and high school to introduce students to computer technology, and (3) the curriculum must be revised from time to time to make sure that it is compatible with industrial production of the nation and to meet competition from other nations.[12]

With these curricular elements established, the curriculum began to take definite form. By 1978, the curriculum in the primary school consisted of the following subjects: Japanese language, elementary mathematics, science, social studies, music, arts and crafts, homemaking, physical education, and moral and religious education. That the ministry prescribed the number of weekly hours for each subject suggests the importance it attached to the curriculum. In addition to these subjects, students were required to take part in club activities, excursions, school assemblies and ceremonies, and community-related activities.

These extra curricular activities were considered important to the integration of academic courses outside the school and as an important segment of education itself. They were also considered an important means of enabling students to understand the character of their society and the nature of the contribution they were expected to make to its development. Finally, extra curricular activities were designed to generate in students an awareness of their potential so that in the course of acquiring education to meet their needs, they were also preparing themselves to meet the needs of society.[13]

An important aspect of this curriculum is the requirement that the progress of the student be measured by a system of public examinations conducted by the Ministry of Education. This meant that from the inception of formal education the students must constantly be reminded that their progress is important to the development of the nation. Both students and teachers were made to understand that their failure, either in the

---

[11]Ibid., p. 249.

[12]Japanese Ministry of Education, Science, and Culture (Tokyo 1976), p. 2.

[13]Ibid., p. 249.

examinations or in discharging their respective duties, was the failure of the nation.[14]

If the curricular elements at the primary level were meant to emphasize the importance of the development of technology to suit the demands of the new age, one must understand that they had far more importance at the high school and higher education levels. The course requirements at the high school level included Japanese language, foreign languages, social studies, physical sciences, mathematics, health science, physical education, fine arts, computer technology, and recreative arts. Extra curricular activities were far more extensive than at the primary level. Secondary students were often involved in the operations of the business community in order to learn firsthand what it takes to lead a successful enterprise. This approach to education was considered essential for a comprehensive understanding of national development.[15]

The curriculum structure at the higher education level provides an opportunity for students to learn about the dynamics of technological culture. It confronts them with assuming national responsibility in a vastly changing social order. It provides an opportunity for them to adapt to the demands of a new industrial and technological system. It helps them integrate their social responsibilities with a new knowledge of science. This means that the curriculum at the higher education level is far more extensive than at the high school level. However, it is an extension of the other two levels and still includes Japanese language, social studies, physical sciences, mathematics, foreign languages, and computer technology.

Although vocational education is provided beyond high school, it does not receive the importance that academic education does. Most students and their parents think that attending vocational school is a demonstration of failure in the pursuit of education. Although graduates of vocational schools do well in their chosen fields, they do not seem to enjoy the same social and status as do graduates of academic universities. Before 1973 special education was not readily available; in 1980 a special education curriculum was developed to meet the needs of students with special problems.

The underlying principle in initiating special education on a scale different from the past was that those students, if properly trained, can make as viable a contribution to society as other students. To give students with special learning needs an opportunity to learn a trade or undertake an educational program consistent with their needs would raise the level of their self-confidence to the extent that it would enable them to make a considerable contribution to the national agenda. But the curriculum in this kind of setting is carefully designed to meet the needs of students.

It is important to realize that all levels of education have some common curricular components. Among these are Japanese language, social studies, mathematics, and science. These are considered important to

---

[14]Japanese Ministry of Education, Science and Culture.
[15]Ibid.

instilling mental discipline[16] in the manner that Charles Eliot argued in the nineteenth century. There are three basic reasons for considering the concept of mental discipline important to the educational process in contemporary Japan. The first is that mental discipline makes it possible to be creative; this is how an individual is considered to become a productive citizen. The second is that mental discipline makes it possible to live a rich and more productive life.

The third is that mental discipline prepares students to play a unique role in society because they remind themselves constantly of its needs. To provide every student an opportunity to master the essentials of the curriculum, education up to the high school has been made compulsory. The demands placed by public examinations for academic excellence is seen as a means of enhancing the understanding of all students of their expectations of the society, both now and in the future.

An important aspect of the curriculum in Japan relative to special education is an increasing national awareness that meeting the needs of the handicapped forms part of a national thrust for development and that educating them properly demonstrates that they can be independent economically. This is why responsibility for their education has been moved from individual families to the national government. That the curriculum is as diverse as it is in the regular schools suggests the inclusive nature of special education. Another important aspect of special education in Japan is that before the curriculum is designed an assessment of needs has to be made so that the curriculum fulfills defined objectives.

Ronald Anderson concludes that this exercise focuses on three areas. The first is to identify early in the life of the student the extent and nature of the impairment. The second is to establish national centers for training and continuing research. The third is to diversify educational programs to accommodate the needs and interests of all students in special education programs and those in other segments of the educational system so that special education students do not feel isolated.[17] One can see that the curricular structure in Japan offers every student an opportunity to realize his or her goals and so prepare to play a role in shaping society .

THE UNITED STATES: USING THE CURRICULUM TO WIN VICTORY FOR HUMANITY

The question of the curriculum in the United States, like that of the other three examples in this study, has been an important one since the inception of formal education during the colonial period. An important feature of the curriculum has been the involvement of teachers in its development. In all systems of education teachers are in the forefront of the development of the curriculum because they are the ones who come into direct contact with students. Although the development of the curriculum has also involved university professors and politicians, classroom teachers

---

[16] Anderson, "Japanese Education," p. 251.

[17] Ibid., p. 252.

have played an important role in its structure.[18] Teachers have likewise been involved in developing resource materials that are needed to aid the implementation of the curriculum.

The basic thinking behind this practice is that teachers know best what the learning needs of their students are, and teachers can best prepare students for effective roles in society. William van Til observes that whereas some school systems attempt curricular uniformity, the concept of local development is still practiced[19] because the idea of control of the curriculum by any agent other than local authorities is against American traditions. This suggests that the development of the curriculum often takes into account political considerations. It has become an established and accepted practice that since the U.S. Constitution relegates education to the states, the states in turn relegate it to local school boards.

This is the setting in which teachers play a critical role in developing the curriculum. To have a clear understanding of the development of the curriculum in the United States, one needs to examine events that began to unfold during the colonial period. Because education had two primary purposes--to enable students to function and survive in the wilderness and to impart religious and moral values--the development of the curriculum was a result of cooperation between the church and the state.

By 1690 the *New England Primer* had become one of the most widely used textbooks in elementary school.[20] That the primer combined rudiments of literature and religious instruction suggests the elements of the curriculum considered essential to education at that time. The practice that emerged during the colonial period that the state could support education of a religious nature was not considered a conflict between church and state because it was believed that the state could benefit from individuals with high religious values.

During the Revolutionary War and after, individuals began to articulate new ideas about the curriculum. Among them was Thomas Jefferson, who "sought to assess the condition of education and plan the reforms needed to assure the continuing existence of the United States as a sovereign and independent nation."[21] This is why in 1779 Jefferson introduced into the Virginia legislature a "Bill for the More General Diffusion of Knowledge," based on three basic assumptions.

The first was that America could develop more rapidly as a democracy if education was available to as many people as possible; to make this possible the curriculum must be broad enough to allow for diverse interests among students. The second was that state control of education was the only viable method of ensuring a broad curriculum because the federal government was likely to exercise red tape that might stand in the

---

[18]William van Til, *Education: A Beginning* (Boston: Houghton Mifflin, 1974), p. 461.

[19]Ibid., p. 462.

[20]Gerald Gutek, *An Historical Introduction to American Education* (Prospect Heights, Ill.: Waveland Press, 1991), p. 17.

[21]Ibid., p. 23.

way of progress. The third was that the curriculum must include more social and political than religious courses because the country was slowly becoming a secular society.[22]

Benjamin Franklin (1706-1790) shared Jefferson's views on the curriculum and suggested a broad range of courses, including mathematics, English grammar, trade courses, history, geography, literature, agriculture, and Latin and Greek. Franklin felt that because the country was going through a period of transition, it was necessary to make the curriculum as broad as possible to ensure that students were properly trained. In the same way, Noah Webster (1758-1843) felt that schools must play a major role in building a developing society.

The only way in which to accomplish this objective was to make the curriculum more inclusive than it had been in the past. Webster also felt that teaching American, not British, English was important to efforts to give the nation a new direction. This is why in 1783 he published *A Grammatical Institute of the English Language*. To help schools accomplish the task of teaching, Webster worked over a period of time to produce a dictionary that is associated with his name to this day.

One can see that the curriculum as envisaged by Jefferson, Franklin, and Webster began to take on political dimensions that were important to shaping the country. Today political dimensions seem to take two forms that exert important influence on the curriculum: international events and national developments. The surprise attack on Pearl Harbor in December 1941 by Japan demanded a change in the curriculum to suit conditions imposed by the war.[23]

In the same way, launching the Sputnik on October 4, 1957, and shooting down the American U-2 plane in 1960 by the Soviet Union created an international climate that demanded a new approach to the curriculum in the United States as did the beginning of the civil rights movement in December 1955. The curriculum has always been expected to provide the kind of education that would prepare Americans to solve social problems: "Confronted by angry youths and dissenting Blacks and dismay at crime, bombings, and incipient revolution, American society turned to the school for help."[24]

Seeking to understand development of the curriculum in the United States is best done from a historical perspective. The curriculum has been designed to serve the needs of students and society in response to change in social conditions at various stages in history of the country. The classical curriculum that came into being as a result of the Yale Report of 1828 was considered important because education was intended to prepare an elite class who would run the country in various ways.

The election of Andrew Jackson to the presidency in the same year introduced a new way of thinking. Because the country would require participation of all people to progress, the curriculum must be designed so

---

[22]Ibid., p. 33.

[23]Van Til, *Education: A Beginning,* p. 463.

[24]Ibid., p. 464.

that it would afford all students an opportunity for education. This line of thinking was the beginning of questioning the classical curriculum and the role of the elite. As immigration got under way in the mid-nineteenth century, there was a need to rethink the nature of the curriculum once more.

When Horace Mann, a successful lawyer and politician, assumed the position of secretary of the Massachusetts Board of Education in 1837, he launched a campaign for the abolishment of charity schools and for the establishment of common schools in which the curriculum was a major factor. When Mann's ideas began to be realized as essential to educational development, the birth of public schools also became a reality. For this reason Mann has been regarded as the father of the public school system.

What earned Mann this distinction is not so much that his ideas of the common schools were accepted, but that the kind of curriculum he advocated was accepted as the beginning of a new era in education in America. His philosophy that the curriculum must be designed to allow every student an opportunity to fulfill his or her needs and so serve society is why he argued during a graduation address at Antioch College (of which he was president) in 1859: "Be ashamed to die until you have won some victory for mankind."[25] Mann was careful to add that the only way students could use the curriculum to win a victory for humanity was to use it first to win victory for themselves.

During the Industrial Revolution of the nineteenth century, Eliot's view of the curriculum as consisting essentially of the classics was slowly giving way to the need for a vocational training. By 1917 it had been accepted that there should be a balance between academic education and vocational training. While this was happening, educational leaders began to explore ways of using the curriculum to suit the demands of an emerging era.

John Dewey was an advocate of a curriculum that would place the industrial student at the center of the educational process. Out of this thinking came the idea of progressive education. While Eliot opposed it because he argued that the classical curriculum strengthened mental discipline, Dewey's concept of progressive education gained wide acceptance and support because it was intended to meet the needs of all students.

In 1958, responding partly to the criticism that American education was not responding to realities of the day and partly in response to the launching of the Sputnik the previous year, President Dwight Eisenhower submitted to Congress the National Defense Education Bill with wide provisions for the curriculum. When the bill became law, its major provisions included more extensive courses in science, mathematics, foreign languages, and social studies, along with more research, both in high school and in college. Because some people thought that these curricular components were introduced in response to the cold war,

---

[25]Quoted in Jonathan Messer, *Horace Mann* (New York: Alfred A. Knopf, 1972), p. 584.

skepticism over federal involvement in education continued in spite of the large sums of money the federal government committed.[26]

Development of the curriculum in the United States must also be viewed from two critical perspectives. First is the socioeconomic factor. The demand for reform of the curriculum of the 1950s emanated partly from the demand for equality. This in itself was an outcome of the civil rights movement and partly from a new approach to educational issues through research. A number of cognitive psychologists including Jerome Bruner went beyond Jean Piaget's concept of developmental stages to suggest, among other things, how children learn.

The central argument that emerged from this thinking was that, although the curriculum had changed considerably following the era of progressive education, education was still elitist in content. Educational psychologists and researchers began to argue that minority groups did more poorly in school because they lacked access to an educational environment that promoted their strengths, and that this was a result of racial discrimination. When stacked against the preponderance of statistical data obtained through research, it was difficult to refute this conclusion. America had entered a new phase in the process of thinking about race and ethnicity.

The second factor is the political factor. The decade of the 1980s produced some outstanding black athletes whose ability caused problems for people like Jim "the Greek" Schneider and Al Campanese. Both men appeared on television to make racial remarks that were considered offensive. Jesse Jackson has taken the position that if black Americans can become star athletes, then there is no reason why they cannot become academic stars. What this suggests is that the notion of black mental and intellectual inferiority has finally been laid to rest.

Affirmative action and Head Start programs were put in place as a result of the national call to end discrimination in education. Part of the effort was directed toward eliminating the effect of past discrimination in economic life. The decision of the Bush administration in December 1990 that scholarships offered exclusively to minority students might constitute reverse discrimination was a cause of great concern among members of the minority community.

However, during the height of the struggle for social equality and educational opportunity the curriculum went through a dramatic period of change. Black studies, urban studies, women's studies, multicultural studies, and bilingual education all found an important place in the curriculum of institutions of higher education. It is doubtful that, were it not for political action restructuring such a curriculum would not have come about. Minority students and women were taught to have respect for themselves and to value their potential as individuals and the contribution they were capable of making to the course of national development. Black students found in Alex Haley's *Roots* an inspiration they did not find elsewhere to learn more about their background.

---

[26]van Til, *Education: A Beginning*, p. 462.

Trips to Africa became part of the curriculum intended to enhance their understanding of themselves, both as individuals and as a people in search of an identity in a complex world. Jane Fonda, Joan Baez, and Angela Davis took center stage in promoting the concept of feminism and its contributing to national character. The American curriculum had been transformed permanently. The education that it represents is now more inclusive. More changes have been made in the educational process than Dewey's concept of progressive education ever envisaged.

The curriculum at institutions of higher learning at first developed according to disciplines, such as mathematics, social studies, science, and literature. In recent years, however, a trend has been developing toward interdisciplinary studies to allow flexibility and to eliminate rigidity in selecting areas of concentration.[27] This flexibility has not been limited to institutions of higher learning but has also characterized the curriculum in the high school, making it possible for more students to attend college.

Edward Ignas argued that this is why, for example, about 90 percent of high school graduates qualified for college entrance in 1982.[28] This development has paralleled the development of the nonacademic curriculum. In most institutions of higher learning today football or basketball scholarships have become an important part of the curriculum. In a similar manner vocational education programs, such as those offered at community colleges, have added a critical dimension to the curriculum. As a result, American education has gone through a transformation. This is how the curriculum has been used to win victory for humanity, as Horace Mann advised in 1859.

THE SOVIET UNION: USING THE CURRICULUM TO CREATE A NEW SOCIALIST SOCIETY

To appreciate the nature of the curriculum in the Soviet Union, one must understand its purpose as defined at the time of the October Revolution, 1917. Soviet author Vasily Sukhominsky concludes that because the Bolsheviks wanted to instill a sense of social and political values they decided to introduce a curriculum that would give students skills they needed to function in a new socioeconomic and political order.[29] In the early days of the Revolution, emphasis was placed on the ability to understand why socialism was important. Among the curricular components that received special attention in the early grades were "fluent, expressive, perceptive reading, rapid and correct reproduction of texts dictated by teachers, detailed observation of phenomenon from the student's environment relative to socialist values."[30]

---

[27]Edward Ignas, "Traditions of American Education," in Ignas and Corsini (eds.) *Comparative Educational Systems*, p. 19.

[28]Ibid., p. 18.

[29]Vasily Sukhomlinsky, *On Education in the Soviet Union* (Moscow: Progress Press, 1977), p. 169.

[30]Ibid., p. 170.

N. Kuzin and M. Kondokov added that all children were expected to learn proper attitudes toward work early in their education: "In a socialist society labor is not only a duty but a matter of honor for each citizen. A certain attitude toward work is instilled in children from the very first grades."[31] When Joseph Stalin assumed power in 1928, he immediately incorporated the concept of labor into the curriculum by forcing people into labor communes in which education was expected to play a decisive role. Stalin's introduction of the five-year plan in the same year was intended to integrate the curriculum into industrial production.

Under this plan Stalin tried to design a new curriculum that also included his idea of collective agricultural operations to reduce the increasing shortage of food. Stalin's demand that the curriculum include mathematics and science was a move to strengthen his idea of the relationship between education and economic production. But whatever Stalin saw as a positive outcome of his way of thinking about the curriculum, his approach to it with an iron fist diminished the results. This is why Mikhail Gorbachev has been more cautious in dealing with the economic crisis caused by his efforts to reform the system.

When Nikita Khrushchev took office in 1958 the curriculum took a more organized form from primary school through higher education. In the primary school the curriculum stressed language skills, elementary mathematics, social studies, and value systems. The main reason for this emphasis was that every student must acquire basic skills necessary for future development. As Khrushchev saw it, social studies and language skills combined to give the student the essentials of effective participation in a socialist world and ideals of equality that he believed the entire world would embrace.[32] In demanding that the curriculum stress elementary mathematics as language skills and social studies, Khrushchev recognized the critical role that children must play in shaping a new world order.

In demanding a reconstruction of the curriculum in the secondary school, Khrushchev ordered more emphasis on history, geography, economics, natural science, modern foreign languages, industrial technology, mathematics, and language skills. He believed that because the world was about to embrace socialism, schools in the Soviet Union must design a curriculum that would place the nation in a position to exert its proper influence in shaping that development.[33] By 1959 Khrushchev had become so enthusiastic about the role of the Soviet Union in shaping a new world order that he ordered a comprehensive redefinition of the curriculum at the secondary level. This ideology resulted in the ten-year curriculum of 1959. By 1965, this curriculum made the educational system in the Soviet Union the envy of many nations in the Third World. Khrushchev's legacy was the excitement that socialism was about to engulf the entire world as an ideal system designed to solve all socioeconomic and political problems.

---

[31]N. Kuzin and M. Kondokov, *Education in the U.S.S.R.* (Moscow: Progress Press, 1973), p. 41.

[32]Ibid., p. 53.

[33]Nigel Grant, *Soviet Education* (London: Longman, 1977), p. 90.

Khrushchev, a poorly educated man himself, left his mark on the quest for an ideal educational system in the curriculum of institutions of higher learning. Recognizing that higher education was to help determine the character of the Soviet Union and the world itself, he carefully designed a curriculum that he believed would bring reality to his hopes and the aspirations of his people. Because he saw the major objective of higher education as promoting science and industrial technology, Khrushchev argued that the curriculum in institutions of higher learning be designed to give the Soviet Union a leading role in influencing the direction the international community was taking.

Khrushchev's famous outburst at the UN in 1959, "We will bury you," was, indeed, an attempt to assert that leading role. Khrushchev was not speaking about Soviet military action but about how to promote socialism as the ideal socioeconomic and political system to replace capitalism throughout the world. One wonders how Khrushchev would have reacted to Gorbachev's introduction of *glasnost* and *perestroika* in 1989.

It is also important to remember that Khrushchev used his enthusiasm to promote socialism as a basis of his ideas about the curriculum in institutions of higher learning. Seeking to integrate the ten-year curriculum with higher education, he made sure that the curriculum in institutions of higher learning was strong enough to make the Soviet Union a prominent actor on the stage of world politics. Therefore, he wanted to see a more extensive curriculum at that level. To accomplish that objective, he ordered the inclusion of advanced science, world history, geography, sociology, political science, international studies, agricultural science, advanced mathematics, and physical science. These curricular components were intended to facilitate the production of food and the development of other national resources in order to improve the standard of living of struggling people all over the world.

When Leonid Brezhnev assumed office in 1964, he also sought to strengthen the curriculum in order to serve the needs of the country and to promote socialist ideals throughout the world. At that time the cold war was reaching a new level of intensity. Even the signing of the Strategic Arms Limitations Talks (SALT) by both President Richard Nixon and President Jimmy Carter did nothing to implant a sense of collective realism in Brezhnev's thinking about the need to view the problems of the world and of superpower relationships from a perspective of understanding and cooperation.

Because Brezhnev, like his predecessors from Lenin to Khrushchev, was committed to the promotion of socialism, he refused to compromise on basic terms of global security and peace unless they were based in socialist ideology. In this context Brezhnev saw the curriculum at all levels of education as a means of building a new national social system and an emerging global order.

In seeking to elevate the Soviet Union to a new level of power and global influence, Brezhnev argued that the curriculum in institutions of higher learning be reviewed from time to time to make sure that it was relevant to conditions of the times. This is why in 1975 he ordered that it include research in all important areas, including science, space exploration, technology, economics, international studies, and political theory as it related to socialist ideology.[34]

Brezhnev found Lenin's belief that, "we could not believe in teaching, training and education if they were restricted only to the schoolroom and divorced from the ferment of life"[35] quite appealing and relevant to world conditions of 1975. This suggests his conviction that the curriculum in institutions of higher learning must place the Soviet Union in a position from which it could influence the direction of global relations and development. This is also why he believed that technological and economic development must combine to give the elusive concept of social equality a distinct meaning among the masses in the Third World struggling for development.

Brezhnev was different from previous leaders of the Soviet Union in one important respect in thinking about the curriculum. He felt that on every rung on the educational ladder, the curriculum must be designed to impress on students the sociohistorical importance of the family. In this manner they could be expected to learn what they must in order to play their appropriate role in shaping the socialist ideology and political character that were destined to exert decisive influence on the social character of the world.

Brezhnev went a step further in demanding that, because extra-curricular activities were a critical component of this approach to education, athletic competition must receive special attention because it helps in promoting character and moral values, both individual and national.[36] This is why in recent years athletes from the Soviet Union have approached international competition with a sense of its importance to both national policy and education. To emphasize the importance of athletic competition as part of the curriculum, all students are expected to demonstrate their potential on which to base future development under the guidance of their teachers.

When Mikhail Gorbachev assumed office in 1984, he regarded the development of the curriculum as a central component of *glasnost* and *perestroika*. He therefore required that schools approach their responsibility from the perspective of his belief that the encouragement of openness is critical to the generation of new ideas that any society needs for its own transformation and development. Gorbachev also argued that *perestroika* is based on this line of thinking.

If the fabric of society has to be transformed to ensure progress people in it must accept the concept of active involvement, Gorbachev concluded adding, "Together with the economic and political reforms, the restructuring of higher and secondary education is a powerful factor

---

[34]Kuzin and Kondokov, *Education in the U.S.S.R.*, p. 40.

[35]Ibid., p. 41.

[36]Brian Holmes, "Education in the Soviet Union," in Ignas and Corsini (eds.), *Comparative Educational Systems*, p. 353.

promoting society's steady progress."[37] In essence Gorbachev was suggesting that the curriculum must become an instrument of fulfilling national objectives and a means of building a new society.

SUMMARY AND CONCLUSION

The discussion in this chapter leads to two basic conclusions. The first is that because the curriculum is directly related to educational objectives, the act of formulating objectives cannot be removed from the act of designing the curriculum. While it is a common tendency to think that objectives determine the character of the curriculum, the fact is that as each supplements the other. Those who formulate educational objectives must keep in mind that nations must emerge from the process stronger as a result of fulfilling the objectives and implementing the curriculum.

The combination of formulating objectives and implementing the curriculum determines the character of education, and the character of education in turn determines the character of society. But for education to determine the character of society it must envisage its steady transformation in a manner that represents social change to ensure its progress. This is what Gorbachev had in mind when he said that the curriculum must be constructed in such a way that it brings together the elements that make economic and political integration a distinct feature of social advancement.

The second conclusion is that the curriculum must not be viewed as a permanent feature of education, but must be regarded as flexible enough to reflect the changing structure of society, especially the need to improve socioeconomic and political systems. This requires that the educational system be evaluated from time to time to make sure that it is in line with what is today place in both the country and the world. This is what Gorbachev had in mind when he argued that "the reform of the school must ensure the constant development and renewal of the entire system of education in keeping with rapidly changing times."[38]

This suggests that nations have a responsibility to make sure that the curriculum meets the needs of students in order to meet those of nations. The practice that one sees in many Third World nations of placing the interests of nations--that is, the interests of politicians--above those of students leads to conflict that robs both the people and the country of the resources they need to ensure their development. Avoiding this outcome is the kind of national purpose that the curriculum must be designed to serve. Unless it does this, the curriculum does nothing else of real lasting national value.

Indeed, national values constitute a set of essential elements needed to build national character. Without national character a country loses the purpose for which it exists. Because the curriculum has an important role to play in this endeavor, those charged with the responsibility of designing

---

[37]Mikhail Gorbachev, *Channel the Energy of Youth into Perestroika*, speech given to the All-Union Student Forum, November 15, 1989 (Moscow: Novosti Press, 1989), p. 24.

[38]Ibid., p. 26.

it must not take it lightly. The future depends on how effective it is as an instrument of preparing students for their role in society.

6

Administration: The Vehicle of the Educational System

> *The government will make every effort to provide in-service training for those teachers with non-standard qualifications to assist them in fulfilling their functions more effectively.*

> Canaan Banana, State President of Zimbabwe, 1980

SOME ESSENTIAL FACTORS OF ADMINISTRATION

Chapter 5 concluded that the curriculum must be designed as an instrument to fulfill objectives, both educational and national. The relatedness of the objectives and the curriculum is that their operation depends on the administrative structure. In essence, the administrative structure is the vehicle that carries the educational system to its destination--national development. A good and effective educational system will need a sound theoretical base, a good set of objectives, and a carefully structured curriculum.[1] But without a properly designed administrative structure, the educational process that emanates from these educational components may still fail to help in accomplishing their intended purpose. This suggests that the success of any educational system depends on an effective combination of all relevant factors.

The question now is: What does it take to have an effective system of educational administration? There are three important factors that those charged with the responsibility for the administration of education must keep in mind. The first factor is that administrators must have a clearly demonstrated understanding of four essential elements of education: theory, objectives, curriculum, and problems.[2] Without a clear knowledge of them the administrative structure has little purpose.

---

[1]George Psacharopoulos and Mauren Woodhall, *Education for Development* (New York: Oxford University Press, 1985), p. 43.

[2]For the latter see Chapter 7 of this study.

Conversely, without an effective administrative system, the effect of these four elements may be elusive, and the educational process has no direction. Those who have the responsibility for designing administrative systems of education must remember that their main task is implementing objectives and the curriculum. If objectives are poorly defined, the curriculum is faulty, and if the curriculum is faulty, its implementation cannot effectively be made. This in turn poorly reflects on the administrative system.

The second factor is that the educational administrative structure must be such that implementation of the curriculum must begin to show expected results by a specified time. This will enable planners of educational programs to assess their impact on national life and the nature of the contribution students make after their education is completed.[3] If no tangible results are demonstrated, the failure may suggest two things. The first is that the objectives and the curriculum are incompatible, which demands a fresh start in evaluating both to see where dysfunction lies. The second is that there are substantial shortcomings in the administrative structure itself, especially in the implementation process. If this is the case, then the entire structure must be reexamined in accordance with specific guidelines.

The third factor is that working out an implementation instrument or plan is an essential part of the administrative structure, and this exercise cannot be taken lightly. It demands thorough knowledge of all pertinent issues and skills in the dynamics of human interactions and the responsibility that each must assume. It demands opening effective means of communication and negates dictatorial behavior so typical of bureaucratic machinery. Education is no place to play political power games.

In the process of developing an instrument of implementation, it is important to keep some questions in mind: Who must be involved in the implementation process? What level of the administrative system must take part in the implementation process? Should the responsibility for educational administration be shared between the national level and the local level? If so, what exactly is the role of each? What resources are needed to ensure an effective administrative system? What elements of cooperation and coordination must be observed? To what extent is the public involved in the administrative structure? Are objectives clearly defined so that they guide the operations of the administration? Are deadlines established by which results are expected? Is an effective system of evaluation of the administrative process in place?

The importance of keeping these questions in mind is that they make it possible for careful planning before the administrative machine begins its operations. This strategy also means that the educational process is properly organized and not run haphazardly. Of the four examples selected for this study, three--Africa, Japan, and the former Soviet Union--have a national system of administration that tends to create a bureaucratic machine that operates inefficiently. The fourth example, the United States,

---

[3]Psacharopoulos and Woodhall, *Education for Development*, p. 44.

has a local system of administration, which, while quite efficient, experiences political problems because the school board is elected every four years.

The purpose of this chapter is not to pass judgment on whether one system of administration is better than another, but to discuss the various implications that these systems have on education. In the process of doing this, comparisons will be made in the interest of determining what these systems have in common and what differences exist between them, and the extent to which these differences affect the educational process.

AFRICA: THE LEGACY OF THE COLONIAL ADMINISTRATIVE SYSTEM

The administrative system of education in Africa is rooted in its colonial past, and African nations have made little or no effort to make necessary adjustments to suit current   conditions. The concept of innovation is not a hallmark of educational vision[4] in contemporary Africa, nor was it a quality of the colonial educational system. The administrative structure of education during the colonial period entailed three stages of operations.

The first was to pass legislation that made specific provisions for direct government involvement. In passing this legislation the colonial governments were directed by both the educational objectives they had outlined in accordance with their philosophy and the kind of curriculum they wished to have in schools. The second stage was to determine the budget allocation for education. The third stage was to establish two administrative systems, one for white students and the other for African students. This means that from the initial involvement of the colonial governments in educational administration, education was segregated by race.

This line of thinking by the colonial governments was standard throughout Africa. For example, in colonial Southern Rhodesia enactment of Ordinance Number 8: Appointment of the Director of Education, in 1899, made specific provisions for the kind of curriculum it wanted. This is why it specified the curricular components in African schools as distinctly different from those in white schools.[5] To give effect to this legislation, the colonial government appointed a team of inspectors whose main function was to ensure that the schools were implementing the provisions of the law.

The intent of this legislation and its amendments in 1902, 1903, and 1907 was to administer African education differently from the way the government administered white education. This administrative character influenced the development of the curriculum and thus the educational process. The practice of racial discrimination thus created in education

---

[4]A. R. Thompson, *Education and Development in Africa* (New York: St. Martin's Press, 1982), p. 266.

[5]Southern Rhodesia: Ordinance Number 8, 1899: Appointment of Director of Education.

remained a permanent feature of education during the entire colonial period.

The administrative character of education seemed to reveal another side of colonial society itself. The colonial governments utilized the power they gave themselves through the legislative process to design sets of educational policies that totally inhibited Africans from developing along viable academic lines, so that they were forced into manual labor more than anything else.[6] In 1983, Ian Smith, the last colonial prime minister of Zimbabwe, who served from 1964 to 1979, expressed to this author views that were characteristic of colonial officials:

> Academic education is not the only form of education that helps a Third World nation develop. In fact, academic education is not for everyone. Practical education enables one to use one's head as much as academic education does. Practical education has an advantage over academic, it enables one to use one's hands in mustering the skills that one needs to have a respectable job and to earn a decent income. Academic education has nothing to offer in terms of practical value.[7]

If what Smith said was true, why did his own administration vigorously pursue the same policy as his predecessors in offering academic education to white students? However, some colonial officials recognized the adverse effect of the hidden agenda in this administrative character of the colonial governments. For example, in 1905, George Duthie, the chief administrator of education in colonial Zimbabwe, warned the colonial government, of which he was a part, of the consequences of pursuing this hidden agenda not only in education but in colonial society itself.

Duthie went on to say: "By the rough and ready plan of making the Native students learn by heart to condition them to the labor needs of the country, large numbers of Natives will have very little opportunity of learning the importance of their proper role in society. In this way innumerable misunderstandings will arise between the races."[8] Duthie was suggesting that an administrative process must be exercised in such a manner as to promote development of the Africans, not to protect the political interests of colonial government officials.

But to expect the colonial governments to heed this message would have been to question the very purpose and mode of their existence. No one, not even Duthie himself in all his liberal views, would have suggested, as his comments seem to imply, that the educational policy of the government was wrong. However, this reality did not make Duthie's message invalid or irrelevant; it simply means that at some point in the future the colonial governments would pay a price for disregarding that

---

[6]Dickson A. Mungazi, *Education and Government Control in Zimbabwe: A Study of the Commissions of Inquiry, 1908-1974.* (New York: Praeger, 1990), p. 9.

[7]For the entire interview, see Dickson A. Mungazi, *The Struggle for Social Change in Southern Africa: Visions of Liberty* (New York: Taylor and Francis, 1989), pp. 120-27.

[8]George Duthie, "Education in Rhodesia," in British South Africa Association for the Advancement of Science, vol. 4, 1905.

important message because discretion and proper judgment on critical social issues were not attributes regarded as essential for a progressive society. While the colonial officials regarded Duthie's warning as a cry in the wilderness of hopelessness and colonial idealism, its impact would be felt years later when it was too late for the colonial systems to listen to it and correct the situation.

What exactly did the administrative system during the colonial governments achieve? Throughout colonial Africa the educational administrative systems were designed to sustain the political power structure of the colonial governments themselves. To understand why this was necessary, one must understand the educational objectives and the curriculum. On the one hand, the main objective of African education was to prepare the Africans to function as laborers, so the curriculum consisted mainly of manual labor or practical training.

On the other hand, the main objective of white education was to prepare whites to exercise political and economic power, so the curriculum consisted of rigorous academic courses.[9] The function of the administrative structure was to ensure that these differences were maintained. But the colonial governments did not know that in pursuing this set of objectives and curriculum, they were putting in place a machinery for their own demise.

Therefore, while the system of administration was intended to promote the objectives of education as defined by the colonial governments through the curriculum, its side effect was to alienate white students from African students, creating a climate of conflict, because the people of the two racial groups never quite came to know each other, and the opportunity to develop mutual trust was lost forever. Instead, the whites saw the Africans as a class of people destined to serve them and the Africans saw the whites as a group of usurpers determined to perpetuate their exploitive behavior. There was nothing that anyone could have done to narrow this chasm and build bridges of human understanding for the benefit of the country. Such is the tragedy of colonial systems anywhere.

At the end of the colonial period, the advent of African governments did little to change the situation. Again, let us take Zimbabwe as an example. In 1980, following a bitter fifteen-year war of independence, the government was faced with enormous problems. Eighty percent of the schools had been destroyed, bridges in rural areas had been laid to waste: national installations had been reduced to rubble. Literacy had actually declined from 30 percent to 20 percent. Industrial productivity had come to a screeching halt. Racial bitterness had reached an unprecedented high.

As a nation, Zimbabwe was dying a violent and painful death. The destruction caused by the war had given way to the perils of building a new nation. These were the conditions that the new government of Zimbabwe took into consideration in launching its reconstruction programs. On May 14, 1980, a month after taking office, State President Canaan Banana outlined the administrative approach of his government to the enormous problems the country was facing.

---

[9]Southern Rhodesia, Education Ordinance, 1899, Section A.

Speaking on the occasion of the opening of the first session of the first parliament of independent Zimbabwe, Banana said:

> It is the intention of my government to pursue vigorously the reopening of the many schools which were closed as a result of the war. This will involve the recruitment of large numbers of teachers, many of whom will have no professional teaching qualifications. My government will therefore make every effort to provide in-service training for those teachers with non-standard qualifications to assist them in fulfilling their functions more effectively. In its determination to work strenuously towards the maintenance and raising of standards of education in Zimbabwe, my government will do all it can in its power to provide modern development in education.[10]

To make it possible for the government to carry out this enormous task, the legislature voted to spend $300 million for the coming fiscal year. But with an expected total enrollment of 1.9 million students from primary school to university by 1981, Zimbabwe had to borrow $1.8 billion from the International Monetary Fund (IMF).

In this seemingly gallant effort to rescue the country from a devastating situation, the government of Zimbabwe put in place an administrative system that only compounded the problem. Its decision to employ large numbers of untrained teachers to increase enrollment forced it to reduce the salaries of trained teachers in order to pay them all. This not only reduced the quality of education but also reduced the position of the trained teachers, setting in motion a rapidly deteriorating situation that caused a decline in the relationship between the government and the country's teachers.

By 1982 the economic position of the teachers was so weak that they were forced to go on strike, which threatened to derail the entire educational program that Zimbabwe was trying to build as a blueprint for national development in Africa. For the next eight years the government managed to sustain only an uneasy and delicate rapport with the teachers, making it hard to measure the progress that the educational process was making in building a new and vibrant nation. In 1989 Zimbabwe was once again poised for a national crisis.

While President Robert Mugabe was on a mission to find a formula for peace in Mozambique, events back home in Zimbabwe were moving toward a new level of conflict. Edgar Tekere, a leading member of the ruling ZANU-PF Party that Mugabe led, resigned in 1988 to protest the possibility of the introduction of a one-party state, which Mugabe said in 1980 he would prefer to a multiparty system. Tekere was also protesting reported widespread corruption among government officials.[11] When, on August 4, 1989, Dzingai Mutumbuka, Minister of Education and Culture, was fined $105,000 for his part in the scandal that rocked the government,

---

[10]*Government Policy Statement Number 5: Presidential Directive* (Harare, Zimbabwe: Government Printer, May 14, 1980).

[11]For details, see *The Herald*, August 4, 1989.

public confidence was eroded, bringing the country to the brink of a major national crisis.

Within a few days, events edged closer to a new national crisis as professors and students at the University of Zimbabwe issued a statement criticizing the government for "making it impossible for the institution to discharge its proper responsibilities and functions"[12] and for pursuing a general administrative policy that was having an adverse effect on education in the country. On August 9, Joshua Nkomo, Senior Government Minister, and Faye Chung, the newly appointed Minister of Education,[13] went to the university in an effort to defuse the situation.

In an impassioned appeal to the restive students, Nkomo pleaded, "We do not want confrontation with our children. We have gone gray because we have a heritage to protect and that heritage is yourselves."[14] In spite of Nkomo's appeal, relationships between the university and the government continued to deteriorate so rapidly that the government decided to close down the university for three weeks. To compound the problems of administration the government was facing, teachers went on strike, paralyzing the educational system in the country. It was only because of Mugabe's integrity that a solution to the problem was found.

The point of this discussion is that the problems that Zimbabwe was facing in its administration of education were common throughout Africa. For example, in July 1990 massive demonstrations were staged in Lusaka, Zambia, against government educational policy. In South Africa, application of the Bantu Education Act of 1953 led to the massacre at Sharpeville in 1960 and the Soweto uprising in 1976. In Mozambique and Angola, brutal civil wars have been raging since 1975 due to inefficiency in government administration policy.

The sad part of these problems is that the governments of Africa are not aware that they are caused by two basic factors. The first is that in their enthusiasm to bring about improvement in education, they adopt administrative policies and practices that have an adverse effect on the development of education. It is ironic that this policy is often a duplication of the policies that the colonial governments pursued. The colonial legacy has found a way of perpetuating itself in Africa in ways that retard progress.

The second factor is that in designing a new policy, not only in the administration of education but in other areas of national life, the African governments tend to disregard involvement of the people at all levels. The thinking that the government knows everything and that its actions are infallible erodes the confidence of the people as they begin to believe that the government is doing what it is doing not because of a sincere desire to serve their needs, but to serve its own political interests. This is why government policy often carries larger political implications beyond the

---

[12]*Parade Magazine*, August 1989.

[13]Chung became minister on August 4, 1989, when Dzingai Mutumbuka resigned after his trial and conviction on corruption charges.

[14]*The Herald*, August 11, 1989.

issue it intends to address. The people tend to feel that the government puts its own political interests above the good of the country.

This is a practice that existed during the colonial period, and somehow the African governments have strengthened it in not so subtle ways. African nations are coming to a point where they must recognize that the entire system of administration needs a complete overhaul. If this does not happen, the climate of conflict that hangs perilously over national endeavors will accentuate the colonial legacy that they have been trying to eliminate.

This is not to suggest that African nations have done nothing for the development of their people. Incredible efforts have been made in some countries, such as Botswana, Gabon, Zimbabwe, Zaire, Nigeria, Ghana, and Kenya. But the limited success that has been achieved must not be allowed to overshadow the enormous problems that have to be resolved if genuine national progress is to be made. African nations have at their disposal such organizations as the Organization of African Unity (OAU) and UNESCO from which to seek help as they put into place administrative systems directed at specific national objectives. The cooperation among members of OAU would yield enormous benefits in the form of developing new strategies of dealing with continental problems.

No country in Africa has sufficient resources to go it alone. By learning to cooperate in designing effective system of administration, the leaders of Africa can identify themselves with the aspirations of their people far beyond the level of mere cooperation. While this endeavor may not be easy, the consequences of any other course of action may be devastating. The legacy of the colonial administrative system that African nations must eliminate is the belief that every aspect of administration must rest with the central government. How long can this thinking continue without hurting the nations of Africa?

JAPAN: FUNCTIONS OF A MONOLITHIC ADMINISTRATIVE BUREAUCRACY

Like African countries, Japan has a national system of educational administration vested in the Ministry of Education, Science, and Culture. As in African nations, the functions of the ministry are defined by the legislature. As in African nations also, the operational budget is determined annually by the legislature. This means that the ministry is responsible to both the legislature and the people. The functions and responsibilities of the ministry are many and varied. It oversees the conduct of the nation's educational institutions from primary school to higher education.

In 1982 there were eighty-one national universities, thirty-one junior colleges, and fifty-four technical colleges, as well as twelve youth houses for the training of youth leaders,[15] and hundreds of primary schools and secondary school of all kinds. The ministry drafts bills on education. It allocates financial resources to various educational units in the country. It

---

[15]Ronald Anderson, "Japanese Education," in Edward Ignas and Raymond Corsini (eds.), *Comparative Educational Systems* (Itasca, Ill.: F. E. Peacock, 1982), p. 262.

designs a national syllabus consistent with national objectives. It assumes responsibility for the character and implementation of public examinations. It assumes the responsibility of initiating change in the structure and functions of the local educational boards. This suggests that, as in Africa, there are three levels of administration of education--the national, the provincial, and the local.

One can see that while the intent of this administrative structure is to ensure efficiency, the system has become too much a bureaucratic machine. The responsibility of the ministry includes the power to control other critical components of the educational process. Its composition and structure make it becomes a powerful monolithic bureaucracy. It consists of five or six members appointed by the minister of education who hold office for four years or at the pleasure of the minister. This powerful council, in turn, appoints workers who oversee operations of the educational process all over the country. These include superintendents, principals, and provincial prefectural boards.[16]

The regional rung of the educational ladder is represented by members of the prefectural boards. Their responsibilities include establishing uniform standards, recommending revisions of educational objectives and the curriculum, recommending textbooks and other instructional materials, and suggesting names of individuals to the national ministry for appointment as principals, teachers, and other personnel. The prefectural boards conduct in-service training for teachers and make annual reports on all matters pertaining to education in the region. They oversee the admission of students, and they transfer and monitor the work done by superintendents and principals.

The change of policy in 1956 from having elected members of the prefectural boards to an appointed council appears to have been made under the assumption that a strong central board, such as the national Ministry of Education, was needed for a unified approach to critical issues. But the actual effect that this change has had on education is that because they hold office at the pleasure of the minister, members of the prefectural boards have lost the independence they once exercised in carrying out their duties to serve the needs of the students and the country.

By resorting to political process that gave it more power, the national ministry alienated itself from the people it was there to serve. As a result, policy has been made, not in the educational interests of the students, but in the interest of sustaining the existing political power structure. In the same way, the change meant that, instead of becoming sensitive to the educational needs of the region, members of the prefectural boards have become increasingly motivated by the political aspirations of their superiors in Tokyo. National priorities have become confused with the political agenda.

It is clear from this that the concentration of power in the hands of bureaucrats in the national ministry has reduced the role of the regions in improving education. The complexity of operations does not allow rapid solutions to be found to problems because a bureaucratic chain of

[16]Ibid., p. 263.

command has to run its course. The question that one must ask is: Does the government of Japan not see the problems that the bureaucratic machine has been creating, both for education and the people? The answer is that, while the ministry is aware of these problems, it believes that the problems caused by bureaucracy are the lesser of two evils.

The local level of the administrative hierarchy consists of principals, teachers, and school boards. Their responsibilities include dealing with matters relating to daily school activities, such as scheduling, solving disciplinary problems, assigning duties to school personnel, and maintaining school equipment in working order.[17] They supervise the implementation of the curriculum and make sure that instruction is conducted in accordance with the requirements of the national curriculum and that students are adequately prepared to take public examinations.

The local level also involves a number of politicians, such as mayors and city officials. Their functions are similar, but less in degree, to those of regional prefectural boards. The school activities are defined in annual regulations issued by the ministry. But still, the local authorities are made to feel that they have an important role to play in a national effort to shape the character of education. Among the activities that constitute that role are conducting in-service training for teachers and school personnel--helping teachers improve the level of their professional skills, helping them work with others, helping them in every way possible in carrying out their responsibilities to their students, and monitoring teachers whose work is below the level of minimum expectation.

In spite of their lack of meaningful involvement in the administrative system of education, Japanese teachers enjoy a tradition of respect within their community and the country as a whole.[18] They know that theirs is a profession that offers them high social status because the Japanese believe teachers make a viable contribution to the development of the country. The call in 1975 for teachers to form unions invoked a mixed response. Some felt that in a world where labor conditions determine performance it was a right move in order to protect the position of teachers from any action by politicians that might hurt their interests.

Others felt that teachers belong to an exclusive professional group and must stand out by themselves to demonstrate the importance of their profession. While the arguments on both sides of the issue were quite strong and reasonable, the fact that neither side succeeded in swaying the other to its line of thinking suggests the critical nature of the controversy and the need to find an answer as part of making a national effort to improve the administrative structure of education.

An interesting aspect of the administrative structure of education in Japan is the absence of direct political implications as is the case in Africa. This may be due to two reasons. The first is that the Japanese have more faith in their government than the Africans have in theirs. Although, from time to time, the Japanese government is rocked by outbreaks of scandal,

---

[17]Ibid., p. 264.
[18]Ibid., p. 265.

their effects are more profoundly felt on the government itself than on the people. This is not the case in Africa, where when a scandal breaks out, its impact is often felt on the people because the economy is so fragile. Following the outbreak of corruption in Zimbabwe in 1989, the author listened to the anguish of a general dealer, who told him:

> You see, this is why many of us feel that the president must be limited to a term of office beyond which he cannot run. The budget presented to parliament recently shows that the government has to increase taxes in order to generate more revenue. This means I have to raise the price of goods in this store. This means fewer people will be able to afford the things they need. The government has not told us that one reason for increasing taxes is the need to make up the loss it has sustained through corruption. We the people are made to feel the effects of the government's own action. This is not right.[19]

In Japan such a direct effect is unlikely.

The second reason is that since the end of the occupation in 1952, Japan has increasingly become the leading technological giant of the twentieth century. The insistence by its national leadership that education must be directed from a national syllabus to enable every student to acquire basic technological skills has convinced students of the wisdom of accepting both a national policy and an administrative structure that give them an opportunity to be part of a rare society that demands nothing less than the best. This tends to negate the effect of political ineptitude on the people as the Japanese believe that there is more than political action to national life. This is why the Japanese see little relationship between political inadequacy and educational development.

An important effect the administrative structure of education has on students in Japan is a constant reminder that their educational success or failure is determined by how well or how poorly they do in public examinations. From the beginning of their educational career students are gripped by examination hell. The national ministry, wishing to ensure parents and the public that it is discharging its responsibility well, does not allow the students to forget that fact. The need to pass examinations determines the character of education itself.

To pass public examinations in a way that ensures admission into a university is the height of educational success. This is why the 40 percent of the students who did not do well in the public examinations of 1991 found themselves in an abyss of uncertainty about the future. Having satisfied itself that it had done all it could to ensure the success of all students, the administration sees no reason to change the system that has caused so much grief for many students.

It is quite clear that those in the administrative system in Japan understand that examination hell exists at two levels: the entrance examination and the graduating examination. As soon as students enroll in primary school they are reminded that they have to pass entrance examinations to be accepted into junior high school. Once they enroll in

---

[19]A business executive to the author in Harare, Zimbabwe, July 27, 1989.

junior high school, they are reminded that they have to pass graduating examinations to be admitted into high school; and once they are in high school they are reminded that they have to pass graduating examinations at that level to be admitted into college.

Finally, once they are enrolled in college courses, they are reminded that they have to pass graduating examinations to climb that prestigious corporate ladder. The reality of examination hell has become an important component of the institutional structure of education, and the administrative system makes sure that conditions affecting the examinations remain as stringent as they have been since 1956.

Two observations must be made regarding the administration of education in Japan. The first is that the Japanese believe that the administrative structure of education gives their country a distinctive national character that has made it what it has become in the closing decade of the twentieth century. The belief in this distinctive character has served Japan in preparing students to function in a larger technological and social sphere. The administration uses this to argue against changing the system because it has worked well so far, top government officials see no need to take risks by changing an effective system for something that is uncertain and risky. Because there is little relationship between the educational process and the political system, change in educational administration is not likely to come about any time soon.

The second observation is that the constant reminder by administration officials, not by the teaching personnel, that educators at all levels must respect regulations seems to have a positive impact on students in that they better understand the purpose of education. This brings the problems of discipline and motivation to a more manageable level, enabling teachers to accomplish their objectives. One must conclude that the administrative structure becomes the vehicle of the educational process itself. Understanding the importance of the administrative structure and the role it plays in promoting education for national development creates a national climate quite different from the one that exists in Africa.

While the administrative system in Japan is a monolithic bureaucracy, it is designed to enable the educational process to mean to the students what it is intended to mean: developing the economic interests of the country. This author does not defend the system; he is merely discussing its structure and the effect it has on a nation struggling for its proper place in the world. Who would have thought that in April 1991 Mikhail Gorbachev, the leader of a superpower, would go to Japan to beg for technological and economic assistance to rebuild the shattered political and economic systems of the Soviet Union? Rigid as it is, there must be something positive about an administrative system that carves an economic and technological giant out of a country that was destroyed by atomic might less than fifty years ago.

THE UNITED STATES: THE EFFECT OF THE
THREE ADMINISTRATIVE DIMENSIONS

Like Japan, the United States has three levels of educational administration--federal, state, and local. But their functions are different. In Japan the most influential power is at the national level, whereas in the United States it is at the local level. This does not mean, however, that the federal level in the United States has less power than the local level; it is just as powerful. Students of the American system of education quite often get confused by the concept of local control of education and by the fact that the federal government still plays a major role in the administrative system. Let us take each of these administrative levels and briefly discuss its role in contributing to the structure of the administrative vehicle of the educational process.

There are three dimensions of educational administration at the federal level. These are the executive branch, represented by the president; the legislative branch, or Congress; and the judiciary branch, or the courts. Although the president can involve himself in the administrative system through executive action, the federal courts and Congress play the decisive role even though the U.S. Constitution does not delegate education as a federal responsibility. Congress takes action in the form of legislation. Enactment of the Morrill Land Grant Act in 1862, for example, made it possible to establish the U.S. Office of Education in 1867. One of this office's major functions was to administer the dissemination of information and oversee the opening of colleges in accordance with the provisions of the act.[20]

Once the legislative role was established, it became an important part of the administrative structure. But political considerations were to play a critical role in its operations. For example, in 1945 the National Education Association (NEA) and the American Federation of Teachers (AFT) sponsored two bills providing for federal financial aid to education. After three years of debate and amendments the bill was defeated because members of Congress felt strongly that the law would violate the principle of state rights and responsibilities to conduct education in their own way. Moreover, they believed the federal courts might rule it unconstitutional if the bill came to them for arbitration. No one will ever know what the federal courts might have done if the bill had actually become law.

However, political and congressional considerations of the administrative structure of education acquired powerful dimensions when the Soviet Union successfully launched the Sputnik in October 1957, elevating the stakes of the cold war era to new heights. Suddenly national political considerations had given way to international political realities. These are the realities that President Eisenhower took into consideration in presenting to Congress the National Defense Education Bill which became law in 1958, changing the administrative character of American education forever.

---

[20]Joel Spring, *American Education: An Introduction to Social and Political Aspects* (New York: Longman, 1978), p. 40.

For the first time in the history of education in the United States Congress exercised direct administrative power by enacting legislation that made provisions for what it considered appropriate to the requirements of a new era. This is why the National Defense Education Act made some specific curriculum provisions that included content improvement in science, foreign languages, mathematics, social science, and research. Throughout the 1960s, the educational process, at both the high school and college levels, incorporated these requirements of the National Defense Education Act.

Believing that it had achieved a reasonable degree of success in responding to the critical international issues of the day, the U.S. Congress now turned its attention to seeking answers to critical national problems. The beginning of the civil rights movement in December 1955 convinced Congress that it must do something to find an answer to the problems of educational inequality resulting from racial segregation.

By 1964 it had become evident that legislative action was needed to direct the course of education to meet the needs of an emerging society. That action came in the form of the Civil Rights Act of 1964. That Title IV of this law authorized federal authorities to withhold federal funds from any educational institution that practiced discrimination on the basis of race shows the importance of two issues. The first is that federal funds were becoming increasingly important as an instrument for shaping the development of education. It was no longer possible for school districts to ignore this . The second is that Congress wanted the country to understand that educational opportunity must be open to all students on the basis of equality and without any regard to race.

Again, school districts had to take this legislative administrative directive into account in operating their schools. From now on racial discrimination in education and in society was no longer possible without paying a price.[21] One does not have to look far to reach the conclusion that with its legislative action, Congress was playing a major role in the administrative system of education. Whether the school districts wanted it or not, they had to obey the law of the land.

The thinking that equality of educational opportunity would result in equality of opportunity for economic and political development was an outcome of the belief that ending poverty, especially among minority groups, was essential to national development. This was why Congress enacted the Elementary and Secondary Education Act in 1965. Under this law the famous Head Start programs were initiated across the country to help children of deprived socioeconomic backgrounds to begin their education early to reduce the likelihood of failure in the future.[22] This legislation became a major weapon in fighting the war on poverty, the hallmark of Lyndon Johnson's presidency. The educational benefits of this legislation were felt in school districts across the country in profound ways.

---

[21]James Shields and Colin Greer, *Foundations of Education: Dissenting Views* (New York: John Wiley, 1974), p. 139.

[22]Ibid., p. 140.

Still wishing to ensure equality for all students as an operative principle of American education, Congress now turned its attention to seeking ways of ending inequality based on gender. In 1972 it passed the Higher Education Act to make sure through Title IX that: "no person in the United States shall, on the basis of sex, be excluded from participating in, be denied the benefits of, or be subjected to discrimination under any education program or activity receiving federal assistance."[23]

Enactment of this legislation represented a successful conclusion to the struggle that women in the United States had launched in 1848 to achieve social equality with men. The political victory that they won in 1920 by gaining the right to vote provided a new impetus to continue their struggle. That soon after the enactment of Title IX nearly four hundred charges of discrimination based on gender were filed suggests the strength of the new law and the determination with which women were fighting for their cause. It was a new day for American women. No longer were they excluded from advancing to the top levels of the administrative system. Many began to assume positions of responsibility in education. Women as superintendents, principals, and college presidents become a familiar sight in the decade that followed.

In 1974 the federal role in promoting and protecting the concept of equal opportunity was expanded by the Buckley Amendment.[24] The amendment, part of the Education Amendment Act of 1974, required that educational institutions allow parents access to the school records of their children or they would lose federal funding. The reason for the Buckley Amendment was that educational institutions routinely placed materials in students' files that might later prove damaging, without either the parents or the students themselves knowing about their existence. That the Buckley Amendment gave students and their parents the right to examine these files and eliminate any inaccuracies demanded a substantial change in the manner in which educational institutions kept records. This revealing administrative procedure initiated by Congress acquired a meaning that had not been understood in the past about the nature of educational administration.

Federal administrative action on education is also evident in the rulings of the courts. Since the Dred Scott case of 1857, the federal courts have played a major role in shaping the character of education in the United States. Four landmark decisions deserve a brief discussion. In 1896 the Supreme Court made a ruling that lasted half a century in *Plessy vs. Ferguson,* in which it sanctioned racial segregation. In *Brown vs. Board of Education of Topeka* of 1954, the same court reversed the decision and ordered that schools be desegregated without delay. The social agony and racial bitterness that emanated from the *Brown* decision were of such proportions that they threatened the very existence of the nation, just as emancipation had threatened to divide it a century before.

---

[23]U.S. Title IX, Amendment to Higher Education Act, 1972.

[24]Named after its author, Senator James Buckley, Republican from New York.

But the Supreme Court stood firm. There is no question that the *Brown* decision had an enormous impact on the administrative character of education. School districts were faced with the task of how to reorganize the system in order to comply with the law. Distribution of resources, redesigning the curriculum, hiring of teachers and other school personnel were all new administrative features that had to be taken into account. The administrative vehicle that the Supreme Court had built was expected to run on the highway of local cooperation and systems of operations.

The question of how to achieve equality of educational opportunity inevitably led to examination of how schools could best achieve integration. In 1971 the Supreme Court ruled in *Swann vs. Charlotte-Mecklenburg Board of Education* that busing students was a proper constitutional means of achieving equality. In reaching this decision the Supreme Court warned school districts that schools of one race in racially mixed neighborhoods could not hide under state statutes that permitted segregation.[25] This warning reminded both the states and the school districts that were inclined to show disrespect of the court's decisions that although education had been delegated a state responsibility by the U.S. Constitution, federal action had to supersede any state law. For many school districts and state legislatures, this was a bitter pill to swallow, but swallow it they had to.

The action that some politicians took--such as Governor George Wallace standing at the door of the University of Alabama to prevent the admission of black students--only intensified the determination of the federal courts to ensure that its decisions were implemented. Three years later, in 1974, the Supreme Court went further in ruling in *Oliver vs. Michigan State Board of Education* that any school district found guilty of practicing racial discrimination must submit a plan for integration to be developed with the assistance of independent experts.

From this decision one is led to the conclusion that the federal courts were assuming a major role in the administration of education in the country. It also means that the federal courts had come to recognize that to serve the country's developmental needs, educational opportunity must be readily available to all students equally. Legislative action was a call for the nation to live up to the true meaning of its constitutional mandate that all people are born with certain basic rights regardless of their racial or economic condition. This is the fundamental principle of democracy that made the American experiment unique. It was the very basis of the greatness of a nation. That the Supreme Court and Congress saw things in no other way suggests the critical nature of their approach to national issues.

The actions of Congress and the federal courts suggest that these branches of the U.S. government have assumed much power in deciding the administrative character of education. This leads to the question: What is left for the state and local authorities to do?

---

[25]Spring, *American Education: An Introduction to Social and Political Aspects*, p. 63.

The states, through their legislative process, set minimum standards for curriculum and graduation. They specify requirements for teaching, administration, and counseling certificates. They specify safety requirements for schools and educational facilities, such as libraries and food catering services. They define the length of the school day and of the academic year. They make their own financial allocations to school districts and oversee the distribution of federal funds. They ensure that teachers are properly paid and that the conditions of their service are clearly outlined. These are critical functions of the administrative structure guiding the effectiveness of the school system.

In a similar fashion, local school boards have important educational functions to fulfill. They establish a hiring policy. They determine conditions of service for teachers and administrators such as superintendents, principals, and other school officials. They set conditions of leave for teachers, including female teachers in their child-bearing years. They maintain such as buses, building, equipment, school grounds, and educational facilities. They set guidelines for teachers in dealing with various aspects of student life.

Local school boards also establish an annual budget and general policy. These are important administrative functions, but how do they compare with those of Japan and Africa? One can see that within the context of American education, both the states and the local school boards must relate their responsibility to the requirements established by the federal authorities.

In this manner they are similar to the practice in Japan and Africa. However, both the states and the local school boards enjoy a higher degree of independence than do the regional and local levels in Africa and Japan. This degree of independence has a substantial effect on the administrative conduct of education in the United States. The local level in the United States is very different from that in Japan and Africa in two critical aspects of education. The first is that the teacher has the responsibility to design a syllabus consistent with the guidelines established by the school board.

The second aspect is that the teacher also has the responsibility of determining the progress and promotion of the student. The absence of a national system of public examinations gives teachers both an opportunity to respond to the real educational needs of their students and the responsibility to develop skills that are essential in the exercise of his or her duties. These are very important differences. This practice exists in the American system of education because there is a basic assumption that the teacher knows more about the needs and progress of the student than any other person.

What this shows is that the teacher plays an important role in the administrative system of education in the United States in ways teachers in the other systems in this study do not. Altogether the system of administration of education is a shared responsibility at the federal, state, and local levels. The question now is: Does this shared responsibility improve the effectiveness of the system, or does it create problems? The reader is at liberty to express some opinions.

THE SOVIET UNION: NEW ELEMENTS OF ADMINISTRATION UNDER *GLASNOST* AND *PERESTROIKA*

As in the other three examples in this study, the administrative structure of education in the Soviet Union has three levels--national, regional, and local. Their functions are similar to those in Japan and Africa but considerably different from those of the United States. Because at the time of the Revolution in 1917 the Bolsheviks believed that restructuring education was essential to shaping the development of a new society, they decided that the central government must assume the responsibility of directing its course of development.

This is why Lenin established the People's Commissariat for Education with Anatoly Lunacharsky as its director and directly responsible to him. That one of its major functions was to design a new administrative structure that would make it possible to eliminate illiteracy underscores the critical nature of putting new elements into the administrative process to ensure the rapid social change they envisaged.[26]

The commissariat was also charged with the responsibility of establishing a national educational policy to ensure that the people were properly educated. To this day the national Ministry of Education, Science, and Culture has exercised this function. At the Eighth Congress of the Communist Party held in 1919 a resolution was adopted calling for the introduction of free general education and technical training to be administered by the central government under a nationally prescribed curriculum. An all-Russian congress on adult education held in May 1919 adopted a resolution calling for the national government to allocate funds toward combating illiteracy.[27] This is why, in December of that year, all those who were illiterate were required to attend schools.[28]

The thinking behind this requirement was that a literate society was more productive and meaningful to national endeavors. At the end of the study period the commissariat would administer an examination in accordance with national objectives and standards to determine if indeed they had been achieved. It is also for this reason that the national ministry allocates funds through an annual budget. To this day also the ministry of education has this administrative responsibility .

By 1929 industrial production had improved significantly as a result of the first five-year developmental plan that Stalin had introduced. But he considered the literacy rate of 8 percent too low to enable the country to maintain the progress he thought it was making in agriculture and industry. Therefore, at the Seventeenth Party Congress in 1934, a resolution was

---

[26]M. Zinovycv and A. Pleshokova, *How Illiteracy Was Wiped Out in the U.S.S.R.* (Moscow: Foreign Language Publishing House, 1981), p. 19.

[27]Ibid., p. 20.

[28]Brian Holmes, "Education in the Soviet Union," in Ignas and Corsini (eds.), *Comparative Educational Systems*, p. 361.

adopted urging the central government to do more to eliminate the scourge of illiteracy by introducing a set of regulations that would guide the efforts of the educational institutions in their efforts to combat it. Among the major administrative functions of the central government today are establishing a national educational policy, prescribing a national syllabus, allocating an annual budget, conducting examinations, and issuing regulations to govern the general conduct of education.

The requirement stipulated by Nikita Khrushchev in 1959 for the introduction of ten-year schooling dramatically increased the administrative role of the government in education.[29] From that time to the time that Mikhail Gorbachev assumed office in 1984 any major move made in education had to be initiated under the direction of the national Ministry of Education, whether it was seeking to implement a policy or educational programs. But it is Gorbachev himself who introduced *glasnost* and *perestroika* as the twin pillars of enhancing the administrative role of the government in the educational process.

In 1989 Gorbachev explained new elements of the administrative character of education under the influence of *glasnost* and *perestroika*, saying: "To remain loyal to Lenin's teaching means to develop its creative spirit, to enrich it with new ideas and administrative provisions. This we must do in the knowledge that man is the ultimate aim of educational development, the measure of society's progress. Administrative changes in education affect living conditions of our people, their interests, needs and views, and of the world."[30]

Here, one must ask the question: If the central government has so much power to exercise in the administrative structure of education, what is left for the regional and local authorities to do? At the Sixteenth Communist Party Congress held in 1930 a resolution was passed, which seems to answer this question. The resolution stated that because the country had achieved considerable progress due to the adoption of socialism, it was now necessary to restructure the administration of education so that the responsibility would be shared among the national, regional, and local levels. This system of administration would ensure efficiency and enhance the quality of educational programs and so serve the needs of both the students and the country.

That the congress adopted a plan of action that stipulated that the national government would assume the responsibility for designing a national policy, budgetary matters, the curriculum, examinations and promotion of students, and seeking an improvement in higher education shows how important it thought the new administrative system to be. The regional level would cooperate with the national administration to strengthen educational programs. In turn, the local level would cooperate with regional administration to make educational programs more

---

[29]Nigel Grant, *Soviet Education* (London: Penguin, 1979), p. 90.

[30]Mikhail Gorbachev, *Channel the Energy of Youth into Perestroika*, speech given to the All-Soviet Union Student Conference, November 15, 1989 (Moscow: Novosti Press, 1989), p. 15.

effective.[31] This means that the administrative machinery was well coordinated to disseminate both socialist ideology and the educational programs themselves.

From 1931 to 1933 the new administrative structure was put into effect, and the functions of the regional authority were defined to include designing a provincial educational policy consistent with the policy of the national ministry, forming educational programs consistent with curricular provisions outlined by the national ministry, ensuring that all students in the region received adequate education, coordinating financial resources allocated by the Ministry of Education, maintaining facilities and equipment, and making sure that all schools in the region complied with the regulations issued by the national ministry.

In the same way the functions of the local authorities were defined as providing adequate education to all students, consulting with regional authorities on matters of the curriculum and other educational issues, inviting parents to be involved in the education of their children, submitting reports to the national ministry through the regional authorities, and ensuring that daily school activities were properly structured.

In 1946 the central Communist Party decided that while the concept of regional authority was serving a good administrative purpose, changes in economic and social operations demanded a corresponding reform of the administrative system. Along with the change that was taking place to allow each of the fifteen republics to make political contributions to the development of the country came a change in the perception of regional authority placing more power in the hands of the republics.

This means that the republics now assumed the responsibility for the administration of education through their respective constitutional structures. The demand of the Baltic republics to secede from the Soviet Union was fostered in part by such background events. However, the republics were required to coordinate their educational activities in such a way that they were compatible with the objectives of the national government.

To accomplish this objective the republics were encouraged to form an association known as the Soviet Federative Socialist Republics, where function was to extend beyond the administration of education.[32] Under the requirements of *glasnost* and *perestroika* there was a change in the structure of this important organization. Membership to it had to be by the election of candidates nominated by the people. This meant that the association no longer represented the national government but the interests of the people. This seems to be a major positive outcome of *glasnost* and *perestroika*. The functions of the association also changed to ensure that one of its responsibilities was to make recommendations on policy reform and implementation. In December 1990, when economic and political problems were placing Gorbachev in a very difficult position, questions were being raised as to whether his entire reform program would succeed.

---

[31]Zinovycv and Pleshokova, *How Illiteracy Was Wiped Out*, p. 21.

[32]V. Strezikon, "The Soviet Union," in J. A. Lauwerys and David Scanlon (eds.), *Examinations: World Year Book of Education* (London: Evans, 1969), p. 165.

The Fundamental Law in 1977 included a clause on education, which stated that, because all citizens had a right to educational opportunity, organization and administration had to be restructured to allow authorities in the republics an opportunity to play a role. What emerged from this law is that local authorities consisted of school officials, teachers, and parents assumed responsibilities that included educational activities of an administrative nature. Among them were to ensure parental involvement in the education of their children, to make an input into the educational system as a whole, to form organizations that would help run the school, to help maintain facilities and equipment, and to suggest new policy. This leads to the conclusion that all levels of administration have an important role to play in making the educational system more effective.

These are the realities that Gorbachev took into consideration in initiating basic reform under *glasnost* and *perestroika*. The threat that came from the Baltic republics to secede raised fundamental questions as to whether Gorbachev would survive politically and whether he would be able to maintain a united nation. This forced him to seek the permission of the party to use the powers of presidential decree to achieve his purpose and sustain his dream of creating a new democratic state in which *glasnost* and *perestroika* became the central operative principles.

In this hour of national crisis Gorbachev refused to abandon the decision he had made in 1989 to allow the republics a much greater say in the administrative system of the country, even though he knew that he was highly vulnerable to criticism from aspiring politicians including Boris Yeltsin. Gorbachev knew that his entire reform program and efforts to introduce democratic principles to a nation that had never known it involved great risks, but he was prepared to take them in order to raise the country to a new level of development based on the values he believed in.

SUMMARY AND CONCLUSION

The discussion in this chapter leads to two conclusions. The first is that in all the four examples selected for this study the administrative system of education is the vehicle of the educational process itself. Without the administrative structure the educational process has no direction and its purpose and meaning are lost. Implementation of the curriculum, so crucial to educational success, lacks effect. The administrative structure makes it possible to remind schools that they must carry out their duties in accordance with their objectives, which they fulfill through the curriculum.

The administrative system also makes it possible for nations to measure the effectiveness of their system of education as a whole and to make changes to ensure improvement. These important aspects of education cannot be assumed; they must be the result of clear knowledge of the direction in which education is moving and how it will facilitate the process of social change.

The second conclusion is that while all four examples have three levels of administration, these levels have different responsibilities. These responsibilities are similar at the local level in Japan, Africa, and the former Soviet Union, but in the United States the local level seems to play a more meaningful role than in the other three. However, at the national level, the United States seems to exert more influence through the actions of the courts than is the case in the other three examples in spite of the constitutional provision designating education a state responsibility. The question now is: What effect does this difference in the role of the three levels of administration have on the character of education in these four areas? The answer is not easy to define.

One would have to say that by allowing the local level to play a more meaningful role, the interest and cooperation of the people become more active as the nation tries to find solutions to the problems it faces. This author is not suggesting that one system of administration is better than the others, but is simply stating that considerable differences do exist and that they determine the character of education. Chapter 7 discusses some of the problems that arise as these four areas struggle for educational development.

7

Problems: Detractors from the Educational Process

> *The consequent disparity between educational systems and their environment is the essence of the worldwide crisis in education.*

Philip Coombs, 1985

THE BEST OF TIMES AND THE WORST OF TIMES

Writing about conditions of late eighteenth-century life in Europe in *A Tale of Two Cities* in 1859, Charles Dickens (1812-1870) began with lines that have become a classic and universal indicator of the problems and contradictions that characterize human existence:

It was the best of times, it was the worst of times. It was the age of wisdom, it was the age of foolishness. It was the epoch of belief, it was the epoch of incredulity. It was the season of light, it was the season of darkness. It was the spring of hope, it was the winter of despair. We had everything before us, we had nothing before us. We were all going direct to heaven, we were all going direct the other way.[1]

Dickens's description of irreconcilable contradictions during the Age of Reason, or the Enlightenment, when human civilization was poised for a great leap forward, also describes the late twentieth century, the age of advanced technology when there seems to be a long shadow cast over human values.

It is clear that Dickens was advising the world about what is must do to solve the problems it was facing. Among the problems that nations must design education to solve are national and human conflicts. It is now recognized that "while conflict is part of human experience, the search for

---

[1] Quoted from William van Til, *Education: A Beginning* (Boston: Houghton Mifflin, 1974), p. 7.

solutions to it has also been its parallel development."[2] The purpose of this chapter is to discuss some problems that the four areas selected for this study are facing.

An examination of the situation that the late twentieth century faces reveals striking similarities to the contradictions that Dickens so eloquently described. The advancements made in science and technology suggest that the world enjoys an unprecedented standard of living, especially in Western nations. For those in the fortunate position to enjoy this improved standard of living, it is the best of times. But within these nations, the increasing number of homeless and destitute people reflects the worst of times.

Twentieth-century man would like to think that he is wiser than his predecessor. At the conclusion of the war in 1945 the inauguration of the UN and UNESCO ushered in a new age under the notion that collective wisdom would ensure world security. Erwin H. Goldenstein concluded, "The hopes of UNESCO's founders that education on an international scale is the essential key, *sine qua non*, to the achievement of human understanding"[3] became the basis of that collective action.

This action would imply that the best of times was now a reality of human existence. Yet, in 1991 the conflict between Iraq and the international community proved that the world was still dominated by the age of foolishness--an inability to resolve conflict by utilizing reason. Neither Iraq nor the international community was aware of the potential for massive destruction that the conflict would leave behind. Even though the allied forces claimed to have scored a victory and there were celebrations in many countries, it was a shallow victory because the bitterness and the aftermath of the war have been far more devastating than the military battle. The massive destruction of the oil fields in Kuwait, the massive suffering of the Kurds who were fleeing from Iraq, the helplessness of the same victorious allied nations, and the continuing escalation of tension between them and Iraq--all combine to suggest that the international community as a whole was moving not toward heaven but the other way .

The assumption of office by Mikhail Gorbachev in the Soviet Union in 1984 set the stage for an entirely new kind of relationship between the two superpowers. When the cold war officially came to an end in 1990, the world breathed a sigh of relief. Now the resources that were being used to wage an ideological warfare between the Soviet Union and the United States could be used to serve human needs. The weak and small nations that were the focus of the conflict no longer felt they had to play the game of international relationships according to the rules set by the United States and the Soviet Union.

Indeed, for them and the rest of the world it was a new epoch of belief that the two superpowers were allied in a well coordinated endeavor to

[2]Dickson A. Mungazi, *International Education and the Search for Human Understanding* (Center for Excellence in Education Monograph Series Flagstaff: Northern Arizona University, 1991), p. 2.

[3]Erwin H. Goldenstein, "Foreword," in Mungazi, *International Education and the Search for Human Understanding,* p. vii.

ensure a lasting peace. But the escalation of conflict between Israel and the Arab states, racial and ethnic violence in South Africa, sectarian conflict in Northern Ireland, and the scourge of poverty and economic misery among the deprived masses of the world raised the stakes of national disaster to a new level of incredulity.

In 1990 the world watched in amazement as the Berlin Wall, that infamous symbol of human conflict, was unceremoniously brought down, paving the way for reunification of Germany. The entire set of Eastern Bloc countries, once under the political control of the Soviet Union, now began to yearn for that most irrepressible of all human urges, freedom. For the people in this critical region, it was, indeed, the best of times as events ushered in the spring of hope. The people of Germany were now poised to create a society in which all its people would be free from the weight of domination from the superpowers. They stood on the verge of economic prosperity unmatched by any period in the past.

But the season of despair surged forth as people from former East Germany and West Germany faced each other in a senseless confrontation arising from the belief that each side was seeking to dominate the other. The reunited German leadership was at a loss to understand the reemergence of the hostility that characterized the relationships of the divided Germany during the height of the cold war. This new wave of conflict threatened to derail the programs of revitalization of a country that had endured the agony of division for forty-five years.

In the Soviet Union the reforms of Mikhail Gorbachev were seen by some old-timers in April 1991 as a radical socioeconomic and political intention to undo the progress that Lenin began at the beginning of the Bolshevik Revolution in 1917. Gorbachev was seen not as a legitimate successor to the framers of the ideology of socialism, but as a traitor to its most valued principles. By April 1991 serious doubts were being openly expressed as to whether Gorbachev would last more than a few more months. It is ironic that a nation that was instrumental in reuniting Germany should walk down the spiraling and slippery road of social and national disintegration.

While Gorbachev's reforms were meant to introduce democracy and free enterprise consistent with practices in Western countries, the wave of doubt about the wisdom of changing national course combined with wave of ethnic violence to force the country to take a dramatic turn for the worse with no end in sight. Gorbachev's own position and the fate of his reforms hung perilously on the cliff of national strife and disintegration. For the Soviet Union these events represented a cold winter of despair.

The founding of UNESCO, right on the heels of the inauguration of the UN marked the beginning of a new era in the struggle against illiteracy and for an environment that would make it possible for humankind to understand itself better than before ever. The effort to ensure universal literacy through universal primary schooling suggests the advent of a season of light. By the 1970s the need for "studying cultural variation as well as political and socioeconomic systems enhances the prospects of not only understanding of various people of the world, but also the importance of cooperation beyond national boundaries."[4]

Yet, by 1990 it had not been possible to eliminate illiteracy; in fact illiteracy was on the rise. Racial intolerance and violence on college campuses across the United States became a cause of great concern among members of the international community. This reality and the fact that education around the world was experiencing great difficulties, such as limited financial resources, lack of adequate management, and lack of careful planning, suggests a season of darkness.

These examples of the problems that the world was experiencing suggest two conclusions. The first is that in today's world the good and the bad, hope and despair, enlightenment and ignorance, light and darkness coexist, and all people have to deal with them all to find a new meaning for existence. Unless societies succeed in this endeavor, the place of humankind in the universe becomes perilous. In this setting humankind faces adversity of major proportions. One of the best ways to overcome this adversity is in collective action. But in order to initiate collective action, nations must agree with each other about strategies to be used to accomplish defined goals.

This is what both the UN and UNESCO have attempted to do. That they have not always succeeded has created an environment of conflict among nations. The problem does not lie so much in the nature of conditions to which people react, but in conflict within man himself. The world witnessed this in 1990 during the unfolding drama in the Persian Gulf. This is also why the problems of Northern Ireland seem to defy solutions. The best of times and the worst of times coexist in a dramatic fashion, and mankind is caught right in the middle.

The second conclusion is that nations of the world collectively and individually are facing enormous economic and political problems because they are experiencing enormous problems in education. Philip Coombs recognized the relationship that exists between the problems nations are facing in the socioeconomic and political process and those they are facing in education: "Educational systems have grown and changed more rapidly than ever before. But they have adopted all too slowly in relation to the faster pace of events around them. The consequent disparity between educational systems and the socioeconomic and political environment is the essence of the worldwide crisis in education."[5]

What Coombs seems to suggest is that the problems of education are related to the problems of national development. It is not practical for nations to seek solutions to the problems of national development without seeking those of education. The interrelatedness of the two provides a national environment in which seeking solutions to both problems constitutes an environment for creating national character. Let us now try to discuss how this is so.

---

[4] Mungazi, *International Education,* p. 11.

[5] Philip Coombs, *The World Crisis in Education: The View from the Eighties* (New York: Oxford University Press, 1985), p. 5.

AFRICA: SEEKING SOLUTIONS THROUGH A DEMOCRATIC PROCESS

One of the most serious problems that nations of Africa encounter in their education today is the legacy of the colonial influence. On granting independence to their African colonies, European nations invariably advised the new governments against introducing change into their educational systems. This means that the educational systems in independent nations of Africa have retained the characteristic features that colonial nations imposed. If African nations attempt to change the system of education, their former European colonial masters warn them that they will lose the accreditation that is essential to the admission of African students into educational institutions in European countries.

This means also that while African nations have achieved political independence, the colonial legacy continues to exert unsavory influences on the educational systems in profound ways. Because African nations do not have adequate educational facilities, they are left with no alternative but to send their students to Europe for further education. Therefore, they design educational systems at home to meet the requirements of educational institutions in Europe. This situation suggests that the educational systems of African nations are still controlled by European nations.

The problem with the perpetuation of this colonial educational system is that it does not accommodate the concept of innovation to suit the needs of students and a new society. The curriculum continues to embrace the basic objectives of the colonial society. The educational programs that schools teach continue to perpetuate the myth of the inferiority of African culture and the superiority of Western culture. The education that the Africans receive in independent nations is far less relevant than it was during the colonial period.

The financial assistance that European nations gave African nations at the inception of independence, presumably to enable them to make the transition, was often directed toward strengthening the educational status quo. This is done in the name of preserving quality. Fearing to threaten their fragile political independence, African nations were left with no choice but to acquiesce. While this was happening the educational process lost appropriate meaning. This is how neocolonialism became entrenched more in education than in any other area of national life in independent Africa.

In this setting African nations are now facing a dilemma: whether to assert their independence and design educational systems that respond to their needs and thus lose the support that European nations give them, or to continue the colonial legacy and provide their students with an irrelevant education, far removed from considerations that are central to national development.

One can understand the adverse effect of adopting colonial educational systems in Africa by examining a few facts. In October 1981, for example, the *Chicago Tribune* conducted a study of the effect of colonial education in Africa and found the results disturbing. Out of every eight teachers in the primary schools, six had completed only the ninth grade.

The irrelevance of the curriculum had forced two hundred out of every three hundred students to drop out before they reached the fourth grade, wiping out any literacy they might have acquired. Of the 430 million people in Africa as a whole[6] only 11 percent could read and write in their own language. Only 56 percent of all primary school age children actually attended school, and more than 20 percent dropped out after only three or four years of schooling. About 37 percent of primary school graduates attended high school, but only 7 percent of high school graduates attended college.[7]

This critical situation is not the full extent of the educational agony that African nations have endured in their failure to eliminate the legacy of the colonial educational system. The *Chicago Tribune* discusses other adverse effects. On the average, African nations spent $419 per student per year in 1981 compared to $612 in other countries of the Third World. This is why an average of 50 percent of the teachers failed to meet the minimum qualification criteria set by their own governments. The student:teacher ratio of 50:1 was one of the highest in the world. In Malagasy Republic, the ratio was 60:1, making it hard for teachers to discharge responsibility. Few countries in Africa provided preschools. African parents spent more money on the education of their sons than on their daughters.

The traditional thinking that it is more important to educate a son than a daughter was still very strong in 1981. As a result of negating the importance of education for girls, the dropout rate among girls was twice as high as that among boys. For the same reason girls constituted only 40 percent of the enrollment in primary school, 37 percent in high school, and 26 percent in institutions of higher learning.[8]

It is sad that to a large extent some African parents still believe that educating a girl will diminish her social status because when she acquires some Western education she loses touch with her own cultural values. This, these parents also believe, reduces her chances of a good marriage. In 1974 the author heard his aunt say, "It is useless to spend money educating a girl because she will soon get married and one sees no financial return of her education to her immediate family. The benefit of her education goes only to the family she marries into."[9]

Of all the problems that African nations are facing as a result of the colonial legacy, none is more painful and inhibiting than the policy of apartheid in South Africa. Enactment of the Bantu Education Act in 1953 left a trail of racial bitterness that has paralyzed both the educational system and the socioeconomic and political institutions. The world has never witnessed anything quite like the effect of apartheid. The massacre of sixty-nine Africans, most of them women, demonstrating against the the law, the ban of the African National Congress (ANC) and the

---

[6]*The World Almanac and Book of Facts* of 1991 reported that the population of Africa in 1990 was 470,600,000.

[7]*Chicago Tribune* (October 1, 1981).

[8]Ibid.

[9]Conversation with the author, August 10, 1974.

imprisonment of its leaders, the assassination attempt on Hendrik Verwoerd, the country's president, the exclusion of South Africa from the British Commonwealth in protest against apartheid, all in 1960, were events that had an ominous impact on the future of South Africa.

The Soweto uprising of 1976, in which a thousand students were killed by the policy in reaction to their demonstrations against the kind of education they were receiving, brought the educational process to a halt. South Africa was burning in the incinerator of apartheid, and there was nothing anyone could do to save the country from dying until F. W. de Klerk attempted what appeared to be a Herculean task in 1990.

By 1980, the effect of apartheid was felt in all the countries of Southern Africa, not just South Africa. Speaking on this topic on July 2, 1980, to the Organization of African Unity (OAU), Robert Mugabe, the president of Zimbabwe, observed,

> Apartheid is on a rampage in all of Southern Africa in immoral defence of itself. In Mozambique, it is actively sponsoring acts of sabotage. In Zambia it is deploying its troops in open attack against the people. In Angola is has been committing mass murders of civilians, financing UNITA and directing numerous acts of sabotage. In Swaziland and Lesotho it has conducted incursions. In Zimbabwe it has attempted to disrupt independence celebrations and has recruited some five thousand persons for military training to defend itself in Namibia.[10]

Indeed, with the possible exception of the Horn of Africa, no part of the continent has experienced the agony of conflict between efforts to sustain a social status quo and endeavors to change the system in order to ensure the improvement of national institutions more than Southern Africa.

There is no question that the primary cause of this conflict is rooted in the persistence of apartheid. The release of Nelson Mandela from prison on February 11, 1990, did not in itself end racial bitterness in South Africa because the strength of apartheid remained in tact. Mandela's appeal to black students to remain in school went unheeded as they took to the streets to intensify their struggle to end apartheid not only in education but in all aspects of national life. As 1991 began, South Africa entered a new phase of conflict.

Elsewhere in Southern Africa the problems of education were compounded by insoluble political problems. For example, in Mozambique and Angola, both former Portuguese colonies from 1575 to 1975, the effect of the brutal civil wars was being felt on the educational system in profound ways. As soon as Portugal granted them political independence in 1975[11] as a condition of ending a fifteen-year war of liberation, the leadership of both countries decided that as a matter of national survival their first priority was to design an educational program to lay a new

---

[10]Robert Mugabe, *Zimbabwe: An Address to the OAU*, Freetown, Sierra Leone, July 2, 1980. Courtesy Zimbabwe Ministry of Information.

[11]The attainment of independence for both Angola and Mozambique in 1975 meant that only Zimbabwe, the British colony of Southern Rhodesia, and South Africa still retained colonial status.

foundation for national development. But the excitement of independence in 1975 quickly gave way to new political conflict.

In Mozambique several political parties had merged in June 1962 to form the Front for the Liberation of Mozambique (Frelimo)[12] to coordinate their struggle. Edwardo Mondlane (1920-1969) was its president. In 1975 Portugal found it easy to hand over power to Frelimo without much political struggle among political parties. But in Angola three parties vied for power to the extent that, when the Popular Movement for the Liberation of Angola (MPLA) declared itself to be the government, there was immediate conflict as the other two parties launched a renewed struggle.

The goals that had been established for the development of education gave way to the intensity of the struggle for political power, and the resources that should have been directed at developing the country were diverted to the struggle in the form of a brutal civil war that has raged on since 1975. In this way Angola entered a new phase of political strife.

The agony of colonial oppression was immediately substituted by the agony of an unprecedented civil strife with no end in sight. With a literacy rate of 30 percent, Angola set itself on a path to self-destruction. Mozambique was doing no better. In 1980 Adolfo Dhlamini led a band of dissidents against the Frelimo government, arguing that they had not been consulted at the time of independence. Receiving military assistance from South Africa, Dhlamini and the dissidents launched a campaign of violence that destroyed Mozambique.

There are other political implications that problems of education pose for the nations of Africa. The violent demonstrations staged in Zambia in July 1990 came as a surprise to no one. When the government of Kenneth Kaunda, who has been in office since the country gained independence in October 1964, decided to raise the cost of cornmeal, the staple diet of the people, from five cents to twelve cents per pound as part of the austerity measures he introduced to hold the rapid decline of the economy, the impact was profoundly felt on education.

The people were forced to economize by not sending their children to school, creating a larger national problem. Demonstrations against the government's educational and economic policies erupted into riots causing the death of 45 persons and serious injury to 153 others.[13] This national tragedy combined with the deterioration of the quality of education to cause a massive erosion of the Zambian national character.

The political problems and the deterioration of the educational process have also been compounded by actions of the African governments themselves. On assuming power, the new governments often outlaw multiparty political systems and institute instead a one-party or one-man rule that allows for no expression of alternative ideas in the interest of national development.

---

[12]For a detailed discussion of these parties, see Dickson A. Mungazi, *To Honor the Sacred Trust of Civilization: History, Politics, and Education in Southern Africa* (Cambridge, Ma.: Schenkman, 1983), p. 88.

[13]*Time* (July 9, 1990).

One major characteristic seems to define the political behavior of African leaders--they combine some traditional paternalistic practices inherent in African culture with some colonial practices to form a new and powerful instrument with keeping themselves in office for many years. This situation creates a for social and political environment in which meaningful change becomes an illusion. Corruption by government officials becomes an accepted way of running the country.[14] Political activity is directed toward serving personal gain, rather than serving the needs of the people.

A disturbing feature of the nature of politics in Africa is that it inevitably leads to serious conflict between rural areas and urban settings. The rural people struggle against formidable economic odds, depending almost entirely on subsistence agriculture. Conditions of life, such as housing, transport, communication, and social services including health and education, are so poor that they hardly make a dent in the struggle for development. The national politicians who live in urban areas often ignore the rural population on the assumption that it has little to contribute to the development of the nation. They do not even bother to campaign there. Apart from initial budgetary allocation for salaries of teachers, the governments show no interest in real development of education in rural areas.

Because of the need to help their families survive economically, rural children often leave school at an early age, which has serious implications for the individual countries. A common practice among the Africans is to regard themselves first as members of their ethnic group, then as members of their country. This does much damage to the struggle for national development. But it is a practice that is rooted in the colonial systems, and one cannot blame the rural people for adopting this line of thinking because the national politicians do not seem to care about their plight. In this kind of environment conflict between the people and the government becomes quite likely.

The most viable means of resolving the many problems that African nations face in their system of education is through the democratic process in all its dimensions. One argument against democracy for Africans has its roots in the colonial systems and is often put forth by the African leaders-- that is, the practice of democracy requires well-educated people and is costly, in addition to which it is a practice imposed by Western nations.

Those who use this argument ignore the fact that, by putting democratic elements in place, the people can quickly learn how democracy operates; they do not need a college education to observe democracy's basic principles. Once this is understood and accepted, the next step is to introduce a two-party system to allow alternative ideas to come forward. The reason that most African leaders do not practice democracy is that they fear losing the trust of the people and so they impose their own ideas under the guise of government operations.

---

[14]Dickson A. Mungazi, *The Struggle for Social Change in Southern Africa: Visions of Liberty* (New York: Taylor and Francis, 1989), p. 86.

The sad part of the involvement of the international community in the tragedy in Somalia in 1992 is not its limited efforts to provide food to the starving masses, but its failure to initiate long-range planning by teaching the people how to feed themselves. Compounding this problem is that for years the international community has watched helplessly while the leaders of African countries have assumed dictatorial power which they have systematically used to deny their people an opportunity for development. The failure of OAU to do something to find solutions to the problems of abuse of power is one of the greatest tragedies of Africa. How can African nations hope to build dynamic societies based upon the need to uphold their national character when the foundation does not exist?

The reality that many African nations fail to take into consideration is that the search for solutions to the problems of education must be related to the political process. This requires the observation of four basic principles. The first is that the practice of democracy demands opposition in the legislature, as provided for in a constitution. In this situation the party in power must hold office as a public trust. If its members violate that trust, the people have a right to remove the government from office.

The second principle is that the national president must hold office under proper constitutional provision for a specified term. The reason for this is that no matter how good a person may be, there comes a time when power corrupts and he or she may begin to regard himself or herself as infallible or indispensable. Once a person reaches this point he or she may refuse to accept the fact that other people may be right. The action taken by Julius Nyerere[15] of Tanzania in 1985 to voluntarily retire from office is very rare in Africa.

The third principle is that any national issue must be subjected to public debate or hearing before the government submits it to the legislature for action. This allows for all sides of the issue to be considered before a law is passed. The fourth principle is that the press must have a constitutional right to cover all issues or actions of the government in order to keep the citizens fully informed.

Once these democratic principles become part of the national operations, all issues are considered from their proper perspective and solutions can be found. The reality of it all is that any individuals highly motivated in utilizing the political process can also rise above the level of mere self-interest to ensure the development of their nation.

The problems of education in Africa are so immense that everything possible must be done to create a national climate in which all people, regardless of their station in society, are given the right to participate in all matters of national interest. Illiteracy, the high cost of education, population explosion--all combine to create a set of problems that demand nothing less than complete dedication by every citizen to find solutions. Unless the African leaders recognize this fact, their countries will continue to endure the agony of underdevelopment.

---

[15] Julius Nyerere was succeeded by Ali Hassan Mwinyi in an orderly transfer of power.

JAPAN: PROBLEMS OF EDUCATION
AS PROBLEMS OF SOCIETY

Chapter 6 concluded that as a monolithic bureaucracy the Japanese system of education is designed to serve the economic interests of the country. Out of this setting, Japanese students know that, upon completion of their education, they are assured of important positions in various occupations. This is why, from the beginning of their education, Japanese students are taught to understand that discipline is an essential component of educational success.[16]

In 1968, however, university students, protesting the building of Norita International Airport and under increasing academic pressure, created a national climate of resentment, not only to economic and political events that they did not think appropriate to Japan's relations with other countries, but also to national issues that had a direct impact on their lives. These issues included the manner in which the educational system was being run. This resentment of authority spread to high schools. Therefore, "because of inordinate academic pressures, students have been emboldened to become unruly and not pay attention to the teacher."[17]

One can conclude that academic pressure itself created major disciplinary problems in Japanese education. But there is something that the world does not seem to know about the problems of education in Japan, and that is that an outcast social group, the *Burakumin*, has for many years been relegated to the fringes of society and so denied any meaningful opportunity for advancement, even in school.

The only role the *Burakumin* can play is in fulfilling menial tasks. Aware that they are discriminated against in society, they have in recent years demonstrated their resentment of the poor treatment they have traditionally received and have demanded better educational opportunity as a means of seeking improvement in the conditions of their lives. The demand for better education by the *Burakumin* has created a situation that has disrupted the educational process, and the national government has neither the interest nor the means to resolve the problem.

A critical dimension of the problems of education in Japan is an element of national policy itself. Various government departments and industries recruit employees from the universities that are considered elite. This practice creates two additional problems. The first is that students are made to understand that to secure good employment they have to attend one of these elite institutions.[18] Because entrance is highly competitive, only a limited number can be admitted, creating an impression that Japanese society is elitist. In this manner, a climate of social conflict is created.

---

[16]Ronald Anderson, "Japanese Education" in Edward Ignas and Raymond Corsini (eds.), *Comparative Educational System* (Itasca, Ill.: F. E. Peacock, 1982), p. 258.

[17]Ibid., p. 259.

[18]Ibid., p. 260.

The second problem is that students who do not qualify for entrance into these institutions have to settle for less prestigious institutions where their academic performance may be less than satisfactory. In implementing this policy, Japan instituted a system of differential treatment of both schools and students. Sooner or later the system will have an adverse effect on society itself unless it is corrected.

One other major problem of education in Japan has to do with the dichotomy between the importance placed on passing examinations and the meaning and purpose of learning itself. The rigidity of the institutions leaves little room for the candidates to exercise reasoning or individuality. They rely heavily on repeating the facts given by the teacher. This demands learning by rote or memorization. Such students are characteristically known as *ronin*, a term used to refer to "the ancient *samurai*, who used to wonder aimlessly."[19]

It is difficult for the Japanese government to advance reasons to show why the University of Tokyo has been considered the most prestigious institution of higher education in the country. Although, in 1982, the university had an enrollment of 14,000 students, the national examination system has not improved enrollment figures because a single criterion to determine success of those students in higher education has remained rigid. Problems of admission into universities of the *ronin* and the *Burakumin* have still not been resolved. Japan has to seek solutions to these problems.

The problem created by "examination hell" begins early in the educational process, and students are made to understand early in their educational pursuit that their success is determined by their performance in these examinations. Twice during the academic year students in primary school must take the examinations to determine who qualifies for admission into high school. In this kind of setting students consider passing examinations a measure of educational success.

Upon completion of their education students are confronted with problems that require the application of reason, which their education has not prepared them to do. The *juku*, the famous cram schools that prepare students to pass examinations, become irrelevant to the adjustment process the students must make in order to play their role well in society.

The problems of society demand something substantially more than just passing examinations. *Time* , in the June 15, 1982, issue, described the contradiction that exists between examinations and a lack of an ability to think critically. It quotes Steve Yamamoto, a professor of physics at Tokyo University, who served as examination proctor saying, "I asked the high-ups what to do in case of a bomb threat [during the examinations]. 'Use your head,' they told me. The examinations must go on."[20]

There is no doubt that "preoccupation with examinations leads the Japanese to emphasize memorization rather than analytical thinking."[21]

---

[19] *New York Times* (March 15, 1982).

[20] Ibid.

[21] Ibid.

This serious problem arises from the Japanese pedagogical perception that teachers must teach and students must absorb what they teach. The reality of this situation is that what teachers teach has no relationship to the learning process of critical thinking. All they are required to do is teach facts, while students are forced to memorize in order to prepare themselves to take examinations.

Placing emphasis on passing examinations rather than demonstrating understanding of essential concepts is a major problem of education in Japan. However, Japan is not the only country to have a national system of education and examinations. European nations and African countries still practice the system of public examinations as a measure of educational success, unaware that it stands in the way of progress, although Japan appears to have made more progress than any other country.

From the moment students enter school at the age of six, they are made to understand that success in education is part of their obligation to their family. Parents are directly involved in the education of their children and are expected to do everything in their power to make sure they succeed. They are also made to feel guilty if they do not, and this has an adverse effect on how children learn. By overemphasizing educational success, parents make their children feel that their real educational interests and potential are being sacrificed in favor of sustaining the social position and prestige of their parents. This is why, in addition to becoming unruly to their teachers, Japanese students have recently been alienated from their society because they feel that the pressure applied on them to pass examinations is not in the best interests of their educational development.

This alienation has had an equally adverse effect on the attitude and behavior of Japanese youth toward their society. In 1982 criminal behavior among youth increased by 12.4 percent over the previous year. In the same year, juvenile crimes accounted for nearly 5 percent of all crimes reported in Japan. During the same period, violent behavior on school grounds increased by 42 percent. That most of these crimes were committed against teachers and other school personnel shows how resentful the students are of the educational system, especially examinations.[22] This means that students were taking out their negative reaction to both society and the educational process on the schools themselves.

In January 1982 things moved close to a major national crisis. A gang of more than twenty students at Yoshikawa High School near Tokyo attacked a group of teachers, accusing them of inflicting emotional and psychological damage the kind of education they were providing. The students must have forgotten that the teachers and the schools were not responsible for their educational misery; the system itself was. Therefore any change must be initiated at the national level, not at a local school.

The pressure to succeed in both education and examinations has in recent years created another serious problem. Instead of trying to beat the odds, some students give up trying and decide to take the easy way out and commit suicide. In 1982 the suicide rate was 17.6 per hundred thousand

---

[22]Ibid.

teenagers compared with 10.9 in the United States.[23] Nearly all of the suicide cases were attributed to the inability or unwillingness of the students to face the ordeal of taking examinations.

In 1983 Prime Minister Yasuhiro Nakasone was so disturbed by the rising suicide rate among high school students that he ordered the Ministry of Education to investigate the situation and to submit its report so that corrective action would be initiated.[24] Nakasone promised his worried countrymen that "finding ways to deal with violence in schools will be one of the prescriptions of the government."[25]

By 1990, however, the government had not been able to find solutions to this serious national problem. Naidai Nagai, once minister of education, now professor of educational sociology at Saphia University, concluded in 1984 that if Japan did not change its system of education, especially the system of examinations, violence was likely to increase and the consequences for Japanese society would be severe.[26] By 1991 there was no evidence to suggest that the government had heeded the warning.

One can see that while the problems of education in Africa have political implications, national leaders in Japan cannot afford to ignore the social implications of educational problems. Although the system of examinations has generated considerable public criticism, the government of Japan has defended it, arguing that (1) Japan needs a strong system of education to sustain its competitive edge in the world of high technological innovation, (2) a strong system of examinations is essential to this national endeavor, and (3) the system cannot be abandoned without forcing the country to pay a price.

The question now is: How then, can these serious problems of education be solved? The answer is not easy to find. But in failing to find solutions to the problems of education, the problems of society will intensify with the passage of time. The best that Japan can do is to confront those problems now. What might appear to be the Japanese technological best of times could also become the worst of times.

THE UNITED STATES: PROBLEMS OF EDUCATION AND SOCIAL RESPONSIBILITY

To understand the problems of education in the United States one needs to understand their origin. When the educational reform movement initiated by Horace Mann became a reality, the central question that everyone asked was how education in the common schools would be financed. The consensus that taxation was the best form of support created a new level of controversy because, at that time, the argument that not every member of the community had children in school was a powerful

---

[23]Ibid.

[24] "Japan's Classroom: A Budding Blackboard Jungle," *New York Times* (March 29, 1983).

[25]Ibid.

[26]Ibid.

factor in the decisions. Although the practice evolved over the years to use a property tax to support public education has been accepted, it has left a trail of controversy that has not been fully resolved.

Across the United States today communities have wrestled with this problem without finding an adequate solution.[27] If at the inception of the reform movement the federal government had assumed financial responsibility for education, an equitable system could have been worked out. Today some school districts are not able to meet their financial obligations simply because the system of taxation is not totally equitable.

Since the proclamation of the Fourteenth Amendment to the U.S. Constitution on July 28, 1868, granting equal rights to former slaves, the United States has not been able to solve its racial problems. The controversy surrounding the holiday honoring Martin Luther King, Jr. in some states, especially Arizona, testifies to the degree to which race has remained a factor of American life. In 1991 a leading American professor told the author during an interview:

> It is ironic that while the United States has condemned South Africa for maintaining the notorious policy of apartheid, the United States itself has not been able to resolve its racial problems. One of these days the United States will have to seek the help and advice of F.W. de Klerk, the leader of a country whose racial policy the United States found so easy to attack. After South Africa has solved its racial problems, the United States will be the only country in the world to have a racial problem. This is a frightening reality.[28]

The *Plessy* decision seemed to underscore the thinking that even though the Fourteenth Amendment explicitly stated that equal protection of the law for all people must be an operative principle of national life, the Supreme Court's interpretation of it in *Plessy* left no doubt that it was still operating under the thinking of distributive justice.

When the court tried to function by the intent of the Fourteenth Amendment in its ruling in *Brown*, it created an entirely new racial situation that had not existed before--an intensity of white opposition to the idea of racial equality. Formation of the White Citizens Council accelerated the deterioration of a situation that was taking a heavy toll on national purpose. The crisis in Little Rock in 1957 and at the University of Alabama in 1963 showed that the United States was entering a new phase of racial conflict. The increase in racial violence among young people, an age group that is traditionally intolerant of racism, troubles many people. An American educator told the author in Florida in November 1990:

> Racial unrest in the United States has taken a more serious twist than in the past. Young people are known for their liberal political views. It is painful to see that in

---

[27] A case in point, in April 1991, local school districts in Arizona attempted to organize a discussion forum involving members of the legislature to find a formula for equitable distribution of funds to support the schools.

[28] An American professor of comparative sociology of education during an interview with the author at the University of Pittsburgh, March 15, 1991. Both were attending a comparative and international education conference.

the United Sates young people are in the front line of promoting racial intolerance. What are our schools doing? Any nation that fails to teach its young to understand their social responsibility spells it own demise. I am afraid that this seems to be the direction we are moving in as a nation. Why can't our young people take lessons from the social movements of the 1960s?[29]

Enactment of the Civil Rights Act of 1964 made it possible for the United States to see other dimensions of the race issue as a major problem in education. In the same way the Elementary and Secondary Education Act of 1965 provided funds to assist the expansion and improvement of educational programs for the benefit of all students, Title V of the same law provided funds to state departments, of education and gave them power to distribute them as they saw fit. This was done to allay fears of those who were concerned that with increased funding the federal government would have more power than it should have in controlling education.[30] The United States is the only country in this study to have such financial arrangements in education.

Two problems emanated from this federal aid to education. The first problem is that the Elementary and Secondary Education Act provided for aid in special areas such as improving educational programs. Many state departments wanted financial assistance for their total budget. By limiting financial aid to specific programs, this legislation was restrictive and so limited educational expansion. By limiting the ability of local school boards to decide how federal funds should be used, this legislation also made it possible for Congress to determine educational programs. In this context, the concept of local control of education had little application beyond basic administrative systems.

The second problem is that because the federal government and the state departments had conflicting priorities, a new form of conflict emerged in the educational process, a conflict that often takes political dimensions. While this happens, the educational process becomes subjected to political grandstanding, and both professional politicians and members of the community become experts in the art of apportioning blame and doing nothing to initiate diagnostic action to find solutions to problems.

The inflexibility of federal financial aid to schools is a situation that has "forced school districts to cheat and deny the existence of large numbers of poor students in order to get federal money to support their general educational programs."[31] This implies that even when those school districts get federal funds by questionable means, they direct them toward programs that are not intended by the federal law.

This situation suggests that the question of financial support of education has not been fully resolved in spite of the method worked out during the reform movement of the nineteenth century. This suggests also

---

[29]An American professor during a conversation with the author while attending the National Social Science Conference, Fort Lauderdale, Florida, November 1-3, 1990.

[30]Joel Spring, *American Education: An Introduction to Social and Political Aspects* (New York: Longman), p. 154.

[31]Ibid., p. 155.

that if the U.S. Constitution had designated education a federal responsibility a clear answer would have been found and the number of fraudulent incidents that has been increasing in recent years could have been reduced and the funds could have been used properly.

By 1972 the misuse of federal funds designated to specified educational programs had become a serious problem. In that year Eliot Richardson, who was Secretary of Health, Education, and Welfare, went before a congressional committee to testify that the provisions made by the Elementary and Secondary Education Act forced school districts to use the designated funds to meet other financial costs. Richardson then indicated that his office had recently requested eight states to return $6.3 million which they had misused and was soon to ask another fifteen states to return an additional $23 million.[32] It is ironic that a law that was put in place to serve the educational needs of students became a major national problem.

In recent years voters have demonstrated an unwillingness to approve propositions that urge increasing taxation to ensure adequate financial support of education. President George Bush must have taken this into consideration in announcing his educational reform package in April 1991. This is also why some states like California have turned to unconventional methods of financing education, such as using a percentage of the lottery revenue. It is equally ironic that a nation that enjoys the status of superpower should resort to questionable means of financing one of its most valued institutions. What has gone wrong?

Besides finances, education in the United States is facing other serious problems that need urgent solutions. There has been increasing concern in recent years that the quality of public education is declining because, among other reasons, schools are put into a situation in which they are unable to discharge their responsibility to their students. The inability of schools to teach the basics--the 3Rs--has eroded the value and the purpose of the school. The number of illiterate students who graduate from high school and college raises serious questions about the aim and functions of schools. As this number continues to grow, one wonders what the future holds, not only for those individuals, but also for the nation as a whole.

In recent years it has been presented that because American society has become increasingly more complex than in the past, the schools must relate to social issues. The failure of educational programs to teach students to find solutions to social problems also raises fundamental questions about their objectives. The increase in violence in schools seems to reflect an increase in violence in society, and the country cannot deal with one without dealing with the other. The increase in the use of illegal drugs has nearly paralyzed the educational process. The fact that the use of illegal drugs permeates every level of American society suggests the critical nature of the problems the nation faces and the consequences that must be accepted for failing to find adequate solutions.

Edward Ignas argued that one major problem the American system of education is facing is the manner in which the school is run. While the

---

[32]Ibid., p. 156.

country adopted a democratic constitution and American society itself embodies principles of democracy, the school has been run on an authoritarian basis that allows only minimal student involvement.[33] The local school board exercises power in accordance with the requirements of its political agenda. The school board draws up conditions of service for its employees including teachers. It determines graduating requirements for students. It outlines curricular components that have little bearing on the interests of students. This is why students have lost interest in the educational process, making this a major problem. Truancy and other disciplinary problems have led to an increasing dropout rate, raising the number of illiterate individuals who are unable to function in terms of their own needs and those of their society.

There is yet another problem that seems to plague American education in the same way it does in Africa and Japan: Education seems to be run by professional educators, those highly educated bureaucrats who seem to believe that success in education lies in the application of theory. They want to put into practice the lofty ideals they learned in the prestigious universities they attended. This author has heard the argument that these bureaucrats seem to live in an ivory tower of intellectual and theoretical speculation and so lose touch with the real problems of education. For example, the school psychologist enunciates perceptions that are often irrelevant to the needs of the students.

With all their education the bureaucrats fail to understand that students are subjected to enormous difficulties that previous generations did not go through, such as absolute peer pressure, the phenomenon of the single parent family system, and conflict between traditional values and those of subcultural groups. Neither the school psychologist nor the school principal seems to understand the importance of adjusting the educational system to new settings.

While improvement in teacher education has resulted in a corresponding improvement in the quality of teaching, the teachers themselves have lost one element of their profession so critical to the success of their mission--a personal touch and relationship with their students. This traditional practice made teachers belong to a special profession. Team coaching, supervising dining halls, library duties, and increasing numbers of classes have left teachers with little time to pay attention to the personal and individual needs of their students. Teacher evaluation of the progress made by their students has contributed to the loss of interest in education. The failure of parents to be actively involved in the education of their children has also contributed to the decline of interest in the educational process among students.[34]

Edward Ignas suggested that the first place to start the search for solutions to these problems is in solving the financial problems because the problems of education are a reflection of the problems of society, and many problems of society demand financial solutions. This requires the

---

[33]Edward Ignas, "Traditions of Education," in Ignas and Corsini (eds.), *Comparative Educational Systems*, p. 50.

[34]Ibid., p. 39.

political process. This is why reaction to President Bush's educational reform package entailed political considerations that were not favorable to his presidency. However, as long as Americans see problems of education mainly through the lenses of political ideology, they may not be able to find adequate solutions to both the problems of society and those of education.

THE SOVIET UNION: SEEKING SOLUTIONS TO PROBLEMS OF HISTORY

As in the other three examples in this study, the problems of education in the Soviet Union are rooted in its history. In their enthusiasm to chart a new course for national development, the Bolsheviks instituted a system of education that was a radical departure from that of the past. As early as 1919 the People's Commissariat on Education, conscious of the fact that literacy was low, demanded the establishment of adult education programs that combined basic instruction in literacy and ideology with industrial production.[35] By the time Joseph Stalin assumed power in 1928, the establishment of communes had become the basis for educational institutions the Communist Party was determined to employ to achieve its political and ideological agenda.

One does not have to look far to reach the conclusion that, in their determination to bring change to a troubled country, the Bolsheviks created a national environment for major problems to arise. By forcing people into communes, the Bolsheviks demanded absolute and unquestionable loyalty of the people, who began to see that they wanted them to serve their own purposes, rather than national goals designed to promote the development of the people as the most important national resources. In placing their own political interests above those of the people, the Bolsheviks forced them to feel that their education was being used as an instrument of fulfilling purposes that were contrary to their own developmental interests. Stalin's use of the purge was the climax of a system that had lost the purpose for which education had been created.

At the conclusion of the war in 1945 Stalin made a change in both educational objectives and the educational process itself. Schools were now required to turn their attention to preparing students to play an effective role in Soviet society in accordance with the goals the Bolsheviks had outlined at the conclusion of the Revolution in 1917. The introduction of educational programs to emphasize socialism and the development of technology at both the high school and higher educational levels added a new dimension to national purpose and programs. Stalin now sought to implement his outlined objective of using education to enhance national industrial production and to promote party ideology.

This change in the perception of the role of education in promoting socialism stemmed from the Bolshevik criticism voiced in 1936 that neither primary nor secondary schools were training students to promote national

---

[35]Brian Holmes, "Education in the Soviet Union," in Ignas and Corsini (eds.), *Comparative Educational Systems*, p. 362.

objectives. The reality of this development is that seeking to fulfill national objectives was in direct conflict with the real purpose of education, promoting the advancement of the people, and it created a major problem that has remained a characteristic feature of education in the Soviet Union. Stalin had no idea of the extent of the problem his philosophy and ideology had created.[36]

The successful launching of Sputnik in 1957 convinced Nikita Khrushchev that the Soviet Union was winning the technological competition in which it and the United States were engaged as part of the strategy to win the cold war. He went a step further than Stalin in seeking to make both secondary and higher education come into line with socialist ideology, further alienating students from their own educational objectives because those of the nation had to come first and there was no room for both. Their pursuit of national objectives through education was a result of their understanding of what it meant to accept a national duty.

The relationship that exists today between education that focuses on the development of the people and education to promote the development of the country was reversed to stress the importance of the development of the country in order to offer benefits to the individual. This fundamental tenet of the socialist ideology has impinged heavily on the role of the people in influencing the direction their society takes.

Mikhail Gorbachev saw Khrushchev's unwillingness and inability to make some needed adjustment to Stalin's educational policy as a major problem in contemporary Soviet education and decided that fundamental reform was needed. On the problem that he believed history had left as a legacy to new national endeavors, Gorbachev wrote in 1990: "Under the influence of the Stalin-imposed dogmatic orientation that has long survived Stalin, the searching nature of Lenin's post-Octoberist writings is underestimated. Changes in his views on the building of socialism were played down as it was alleged that they could be interpreted as his weakness. Stalin's power was based on dictatorship which disregarded the interests of the people."[37]

While Khrushchev eliminated some of the methods Stalin had used, his expansion of education to include ten-year schooling left no choice to students but to accept it as part of the national program. The introduction of compulsory education did not take into account the usual considerations that are critical to its success--the interest of students as a prior condition of serving the interests of the country.[38]

The realization that under Khrushchev education had helped create more problems than solutions is one reason the Central Committee of the Communist party removed him from office in October 1964. Enthusiastic to chart a new course, his successor, Leonid Brezhnev seemed equal to the task. Basing his own programs on traditional socialist theory and

---

[36]Ibid., p. 363.

[37]Mikhail Gorbachev, Soviet Monthly Digest, *Socialism: Theory and Practice* (Moscow: Novosti Press), April 4, 1990, p. 4.

[38]Ibid., p. 15.

assumptions, Brezhnev set out to eliminate what he considered to be the weakness that characterized education during the Khrushchev era. He demanded more science courses, social science, and space technology.

The manner in which Brezhnev introduced his programs presented a new dimension the problem that Gorbachev saw as a fundamental weakness of the socialist ideology. It ignored the interest of the student and so the learning process became a mechanical drill of dry facts. Even though Brezhnev had demanded the introduction of research as part of higher education, the lack of originality and imagination became a distinct feature of education that did not offer intellectual stimulation to students.

That Brezhnev encouraged enrollment of students from the Third World in institutions of higher education in the Soviet Union was part of his agenda to promote socialism throughout the world. This was a major component of his policy. Therefore, in his own way Brezhnev was creating a new set of problems because, like his predecessors, his main objective was to advance socialism. Also like his predecessors, Brezhnev seemed to ignore the fact that any national program that puts the interests of the state above those of the people it is there to serve is bound to have an adverse effect on the national character. In essence this shows that the philosophy of socialism has not been fully accepted by the people who are expected to be part of its advancement.

Under Brezhnev the educational process took on critical dimensions as national objectives superseded the interests of the people. Although Brezhnev was no different from other socialist leaders, his educational programs presented problems that, while seemingly related to education, were actually social, ideological, and political problems. Therefore, seeking solutions to them could have been effectively done through seeking solutions to problems of education.

This is the reality that Gorbachev took into account in launching his reform through *glasnost* and *perestroika*. As soon as he assumed office in 1984 Gorbachev was determined not to repeat the mistakes of his predecessors. The challenge that Gorbachev faced was to find solutions not only to problems of contemporary education but also to those of history.

To expand the parameters of his philosophy Gorbachev utilized the philosophy of Boris Pasternak (1890-1960),[39] who argued in 1920: "The advent of a genius promises benefits while his demise is pregnant with oppression."[40] Gorbachev was not rejecting the values of the Marxist-Leninist philosophy; he was merely rejecting the interpretation of it as given by Stalin, Khrushchev, and Brezhnev in order to chart a different course of national development. If he had been able to keep the Soviet Union together as a nation, he might have succeeded.

---

[39]The author of *Doctor Zhivago*, Pasternak criticized communism and defended the right of individuals to live as they pleased. This is the idea that Soviet leaders rejected until Gorbachev assumed leadership.

[40]Quoted in Agdas Burganov, *Perestroika and the Concept of Socialism* (Moscow: Novosti Press, 1990), p. 15.

For Gorbachev openness and reconstruction cannot be separated from efforts to place the country on the road to development based on the need to develop the individual. This approach is a radical departure from approaches of past administrations. During his term of office Gorbachev found that after seventy years of walking a slippery road to socialism, changing course, even though it is necessary, is not easy. By the end of the 1980s Gorbachev faced enormous political problems that threatened to sabotage his entire reform program. In April 1991 he offered to resign from the leadership of the party if his successor would be chosen by the democratic process that his reform had helped put into place.

Realizing the risk that the party was taking and the possibility of plunging the country into a state of chaos, the party voted to keep him in office. The problems that he encountered had to do more with the concept of change and reform than with specific programs related to his agenda. In short, Gorbachev tried to find solutions to the problems of history. He found that the task was not an easy one, but felt it was one that had to be carried out if the future was to be more meaningful than the past. Unfortunately in 1992 he gave up the struggle as the Soviet Union ceased to exist as a unified nation.

The experiment he had initiated to introduce democracy under socialist ideology came to a sudden end without giving the international community an opportunity to assess its impact on life in the country. Gorbachev became the victim of the reform program that he initiated to serve the interests of the people and the country. It remained to be seen whether the national character he was trying to create would be sustained under the new constitutional arrangements that replaced the Soviet Union. As of 1992, the Commonwealth of Independent Republics that came into being was having serious political and economic problems. Was this a question of putting new wine in old bottles?

SUMMARY AND CONCLUSION

One reaches two basic conclusions from the discussion in this chapter. The first is that every country encounters serious problems in its education in the same way it encounters problems in other areas of national development, such as political and economic areas. The difference between encountering problems of education and encountering problems in other areas is the nature of the approach to them. Searching for solutions to problems in the economy and politics cannot effectively be done without finding solutions to the problems of education.

This is why nations now realize that in order to ensure national development they have to put finding solutions to the problems of education at the top of a national agenda. Because this is a delicate and complicated exercise, many nations find it easier to try to find solutions to other problems of national development first, only to go on a wild goose chase. Nations have to realize that they have to start at the beginning, and that that beginning is education, because it is so crucial to all other aspects of national development.

The second conclusion is that one problem that all nations face is limited financial resources, not because finances for education are not available, but because many nations are still victims of two misleading notions: that military spending ensures national security and that money is not needed to find solutions to the problems of education. To find solutions to the problems of education nations need to ask themselves three questions: What exactly do we want education to do? What are the causes of these problems? How best can the nation solve them?

Until nations have learned to deal with national problems from the perspective of their relatedness to education they will continue to endure the agony of underdevelopment. In this setting both the best of times and the worst of times will exist side by side, making it hard for nations to ensure their own development.

Nations also need to realize that the best of times and the worst of times are their own creation, and that with proper education the effect of the worst of times can be minimized and the prospects of the best of times can be enhanced. It is a challenge that all nations must accept even if, as in the experiment attempted by Mikhail Gorbachev, it entails considerable risks. The thrust for educational policy to make national character possible must be initiated from this perspective.

Those national leaders who launch campaigns to improve conditions for their people who are motivated by the people's best interests are more likely to succeed than those who are motivated by their own political or personal interests. Unfortunately many national leaders fall into the latter group. This is why the author salutes Gorbachev as a national leader although the experiment he initiated failed.

8

Educational Policy and National Character: Summary, Conclusions, and Implications

An education which is differentiated in accordance with the student's individual propensities would become varied in content.

Gennadi Yagodin, Soviet Educator, 1989

Our society and its educational institutions seem to have lost sight of the basic purpose of schooling, and of the high expectations and disciplined effort needed to attain them.

The U.S. National Commission on Excellence in Education, 1983

THE PURPOSE OF THE STUDY IN PERSPECTIVE

The purpose of this study was to discuss some important dimensions of education in Africa, Japan, the United States, and the former Soviet Union relative to national character. It has attempted to examine specific features that have influenced its development as a major factor of national development, including historical background, theoretical considerations, objectives, the curriculum, administration, and problems. It has also attempted to identify differences and to discuss those aspects that all four areas have in common.

Each of these four areas has positive attributes from which the other three can benefit and weaknesses they can learn to avoid. The purpose of a comparative study is to generate perceptions and understanding that become a critical basis of self-examination for each nation .

This study has also presented a composite picture of education in a state of crisis caused by a combination of factors, among them history and the rising expectations created following the end of the Second World War. It is an accepted fact that the thrust for educational development cannot successfully be undertaken unless carefully formulated plans are worked out for its development, taking into consideration some major forces that shape its course.[1] Among these factors are the status of the world economy, political conflict, and imbalance in international trade.[2]

The reality of these factors is that they cannot be isolated from forces that influence national events. The world today is shaped by a combination of these factors and forces, and any nation that neglects them runs the risk of hurting its own development. For this reason, a comparative approach to educational studies becomes important.

However, some nations do neglect the fact that the interdependence of educational development and economic development is a critical factor for national development. Since the inception of the Industrial Revolution, when industrial production became a cornerstone of national development, nations have come to recognize that education is needed for the development of industrial technology, which in turn is needed to sustain steady national development. Conversely, industrial development is necessary for continual investment in education. The fact that today nations spend billions of dollars more on the military than on education underscores the myth of peace through military strength.

To be sure, the notion that investing in education to ensure economic development is not a modern-day invention; it goes back to the time of Adam Smith and other economists of this day who stressed the importance of economic development in order to invest in education as a condition of international peace and security.[3] The practice of using the military to attempt to resolve problems of international conflict that the United States under the Bush administration adopted seemed to run in the face of history. Why nations do not seem to learn from experiences of the past is beyond comprehension.

Since Smith's time nations have come to recognize that, if education is to play its appropriate role in influencing the course of national development, then those who are entrusted with the responsibility of directing its development must not adopt a casual attitude, because its structure is vital to the development of the individual, and the development of the individual is critical to development of the nation.[4]

Because schools today are cast into a setting of conflicting social values, nations have to evolve a formula to find harmony between the educational system and society itself. Human conflict has betrayed the claim of civilization as nation goes against nation simply because they are unable to reach agreement on issues that divide them. As Bertrand Russell, the British social reformer, would put it, the failure of nations to

---

[1]Philip Coombs, *The World Crisis in Education: The View from the Eighties* (New York: Oxford University Press, 1985), p. 9.

[2]On April 25, 1991, the United States complained that a number of Asian countries, including Japan, were not practicing fair economic and trade policies and threatened to retaliate by imposing economic sanctions. This action, if it were carried out, would not improve trade relations between the United States and those countries.

[3]George Psacharopoulos and Maureen Woodhall, *Education for Development: An Analysis of Investment Choices* (New York: Oxford University Press, 1985), p. 15.

[4]Ibid., p. 16.

understand each other largely stems from the failure of those who have the responsibility to design education so that it imparts to students "the kind of tolerance that springs from an endeavor to understand those who are different."[5]

In this final chapter we review the various aspects of education to see how they are related to the national character of the four examples we have selected for this study and the influence they may have on the educational process. It is important to remember that no single factor decides the educational process; rather, their combination gives it a distinct character that in turn influences national character. It will also be seen that no system of education is perfect, and that nations need to do what is possible under the circumstances as no ideal conditions prevail.

AFRICA: SEEKING SOLUTIONS TO THE CONFLICT BETWEEN THE PAST, THE PRESENT, AND THE FUTURE

In discussing the problems of educational development in Africa one must first understand how education has affected its culture. Indeed, European powers based their colonial adventure in Africa on the assumption that theirs was a mission to save the Africans from the degradation of their culture because they thought that it had nothing to contribute to their own development. They also seemed to ignore Margaret Mead's later conclusion that cultures have a horizontal relationship and that, while they are different, difference does not imply superior or inferior.

From Mead's perspective one can see that colonial conquest of Africa implied what Rabindranath Tagore (1861-1941), the Indian philosopher and poet, saw as cultural arrogance and irrationality which created problems in the quest for human understanding.[6] Tagore was even more graphic in discussing the adverse effect of European colonial conquest, not only in Africa but also in other parts of the world. In a letter dated September 16, 1934, addressed to Professor Albert Murray of Britain, Tagore observed: "We have seen Europe spread slavery over the face of the earth. Exploitation became easier when it was based on denying educational creativity and so generated a callous attitude toward those who were its victims."[7]

The colonization of Africa thus implied much more than a physical subjection of a people to oppressive conditions; it also meant psychological and emotional conquest and subjection. From the cradle to the grave the Africans were stripped of their entire identity; their pride and

---

[5]Quoted in William van Til, *Education: A Beginning* (Boston: Houghton Mifflin, 1974), p. 13.

[6]Dickson A. Mungazi, *International Education and the Search for Human Understanding*, Center for Excellence in Education Monograph Series No. 2 (Flagstaff: Northern Arizona University, 1991), p. 6.

[7]Rabindranath Tagore in a letter dated September 16, 1934, addressed to Professor Albert Murray (the UN, New York).

everything that made them a people with unique human attributes richly embedded in their cultural traditions and values were taken away. Once the colonial powers accomplished this task, they set out to convince the Africans that they were indeed inferior to the white man in every way.

The process of subjecting the Africans to colonial domination was as relentless as it was absolute. Nothing was left to chance. The energies of the colonial governments were evident in a rigorous program of discrimination and segregation, as well as is laws that were designed to reduce the Africans to the level of bare existence. In this scheme of action, the colonial governments were motivated by a belief arising out of social Darwinism that, once they succeeded in controlling the mind of the Africans, they would no longer worry about their actions. The game of psychological survival was put into place in profound ways.

Having established a superior-inferior relationship with the Africans, the colonial governments then turned their attention to the task of training them to serve the white man as their master. In the process, the colonial governments subjected the Africans to conditions similar to those of slavery. Albert Schweitzer (1875-1965), the famous German missionary to twentieth century Africa, described the extent of the suffering that the Africans endured at the hands of their colonial conquerors: "Who can describe the misery, the injustice, and the cruelties that the Africans have suffered at the hands of Europeans? If a record could be compiled, it would make a book containing pages that the reader would have to turn over unread because their contents would be too horrible."[8] However, the thinking that the Africans must be trained to serve the white man was the beginning of Western education in Africa.

To ensure that education did what it was designed to do, the colonial governments instituted it on a racial basis, ignoring the fact that education is universal and recognizes neither race nor color. This was why education for Africans was quite different from that of white students. The theoretical considerations underlying colonial justification for different education for the two racial groups was, as Godfrey Huggins, prime minister of colonial Zimbabwe, put it in 1939: "Education will be provided for white students. This is essential if they are expected to keep their position of influence in society. Moreover, it will prevent the creation of a poor white class. In all Native education the prime importance of manual labor should be stressed to prepare them to serve the white man."[9] The only relationship that white education and African education had in common was that they were both run by the same ministry of education until after the war in 1945, when two separate ministries were created in order to separate their objectives.

Along with an education intended to make them efficient laborers, the Africans learned on their own basic skills that later translated into a powerful instrument for fulfilling self-directed purposes and activities. The assumption that they were inferior and incapable of initiating projects to

---

[8]Albert Schweitzer in *Christian Century* (New York: Methodist Church, October 8, 1975).

[9]Godfrey Huggins, *Education Policy in Southern Rhodesia: Some Notes on Certain Features* (Salisbury: Government Printer, 1939).

ensure their own development proved to be the ultimate demise of the colonial governments. The outbreak of the war in 1939 set a new stage that enabled the Africans to launch a campaign, first for nationalism, which gave them a sharpened perception of themselves, and then for political independence. This was an outcome of the war that the colonial governments never anticipated and the one that they could not control.

While they were at the height of their power, colonial governments made sure that the Africans had no chance to threaten the political and socioeconomic status quo. To accomplish this objective, they utilized a variety of strategies that included psychological conditioning based on some theoretical arguments. Among the more surprising of these arguments was the notion that evolved during the eighteenth century, when Europeans were coming into contact with Africans in increasing numbers: "The brain of the black African looks very much like the brain of a European in its infant stage. At puberty all development in the brain of the Negro ceases and becomes more ape-like as it grows older."[10] The importance of the theoretical arguments of the colonial governments did not lie in their accuracy, because they were not accurate, but in the fact that they became a basis for justifying racial policies.

Another surprising thing about colonial theories is that they lasted into the second half of the twentieth century. For example, Godfrey Huggins, who emigrated to colonial Zimbabwe in 1911 in search of adventure and fortune, argued in 1952 during a political campaign to deny the Africans an opportunity for political advancement:

> We must reject permanently the notion that democracy consists of mere counting of heads.[11] We must unhesitatingly accept the fact that the superiority of the white man rests on the color of his skin, civilization, and heredity, and that he has a monopoly of these qualities. You can call me an imperialist of the old school if you like. It would be outrageous to give the Native a so-called political partnership when he is likely to ruin himself as a result of a lack of intelligence.[12]

It is not surprising that Huggins's protege, Ian Smith, the last colonial prime minister, plunged the country into a devastating war of independence in 1966 by attempting to preserve and pursue the same theoretical argument.

Smith, believing that he had become the custodian of colonial theories, refused to reevaluate the policies that had sustained colonial systems in the past. Instead he publicly admitted to being a racist, just as Huggins had done in 1952, and turned the country into a police state. Like his mentor, Huggins, Smith went on to argue in 1966: "We have had to resort to a

---

[10]C. H. Lyons, "The Educability of the African: British Thought and Actions, 1835- 1865," in V. M. Battle and C. H. Lyons (eds.), *Essays in the History of African Education* (New York: Columbia University Press, 1970), p. 9.

[11]In effect, this is the correct meaning and true application of democracy anywhere-- counting of heads. Therefore, because colonial governments rejected this definition of democracy, they cannot be considered to have practiced it in Africa.

[12]H. M. Bate, *Report from Rhodesia* (London: Melrose, 1953), p. 164.

certain form of detention and restriction of the African politicians without trial. When you have a primitive people such as the Africans are, it would have been completely irresponsible of the government not to have done so."[13] One does not have to search far to reach the conclusion that the education that came out of these theoretical arguments produced Africans who had a confused sense of their place in society.[14]

This study has presented the evidence to lead to the conclusion that the colonial legacy influenced the Africans who succeeded the colonial governments to adopt most of their policies, political behavior, and education. The introduction of one-party rule and president for life, along with an intolerance of opposing political views on national issues, is characteristic of the colonial systems that the African governments have adopted and which have compounded the problems that existed during the colonial period.

As the African leaders tasted the power they never had before, they decided they wanted more. In this political setting anyone who attempted to offer ideas opposing those of the government faced arbitrary arrest and imprisonment without trial and without any charges brought against him-- exactly the kind of practices the colonial governments formulated. In this context the African nations experienced the influence of history in painful ways. In essence the African leaders oppressed their own people far more severely than had the colonial governments they replaced. The values of the past were confused with those of the present. This confusion cast a long shadow of conflict on efforts to learn from mistakes of the past and to plan for the future. An irony was being born before their very eyes. This is why emerging Africa is a continent of political, social, and economic disarray.

The educational endeavors that can empower a national thrust for development have suffered a severe setback. Poverty, illiteracy, and social dysfunction are increasing at an alarming rate. Population growth is out of control, and disillusionment has gripped the minds of the masses far more strongly than it did during the colonial period leaving no alternative but to resort to violence to regain a sense of self.

The conflict between the values of the past, the reality of the present, and plans for the future is evident in Africa in two basic kinds of reaction to the colonial period. These two kinds of reaction were the outcome of the hypocrisy and arrogance of colonial officials who utilized moral and cultural myths to justify their greed for political power. The first kind of reaction was that some newly independent countries of Africa rejected the colonial influence in all its forms and urged, instead, the creation of independence that showed no respect for the colonial past.

For example, Sekou Toure of Guinea wanted his new nation to get rid of all colonial influence. He expelled all former employees of the colonial government and replaced them with Africans. Toure withdrew his country

---

[13]G. Sparrow, *Rhodesian Rebellion* (London: Brighton, 1967), p. 25.

[14]For a detailed discussion of Smith's government policy toward the Africans, see Dickson A. Mungazi, *The Struggle for Social Change in Southern Africa: Visions of Liberty* (New York: Taylor and Francis, 1989), p. 120.

from the economically powerful Banque de l'Afrique Occidental, which guaranteed funds for development of former French colonies, because he thought their conditions were detrimental to the developmental interests of Guinea. He also recognized that it was not possible to shape a new course of national development under the influence of past policies and practices.

The second kind of reaction is that Toure's neighbor, Felix Houphouet-Boigny of the Ivory Coast, who took the opposite course of action. He invited foreign investment, encouraging Western countries to invest in his country, because he believed that Africa needed the economic and technical assistance of Western nations to make a new start in their developmental effort.

These two kinds of reaction are directly related to the confusion that has arisen in Africa between the values of the past and those of the present and so combine to cast doubt about the future. Indeed, Africa is caught in the conflict between the past and the present, between the threat of traditional cultural values and emerging socioeconomic and political practices, between what is and what could be, between socialist ideology and capitalist thinking, between a traditional mode of production and emerging technology, between the tested wisdom of the cultural elders and the creative potential of a new generation.

It is an irony of history that while the action taken by the UN on December 3, 1992, to send a multinational military force to Somalia to enable relief agents to resume the distribution of food to the starving masses seems plausible, it must be recognized that it also carried a serious potential for greater conflict than was recognized. With this action Somalia became an invaded and occupied country. The UN did not consider the question of what was likely to happen if the force left in January 1993, as President Bush had indicated, before political solutions were found. This suggests that the UN's efforts should have been directed at bringing much needed education to the parties in conflict and the country as a whole.

It is evident that if the UN wanted to help Somalia, then it should have given it the educational assistance it desperately needed when it was struggling for development in 1968. With reference to U.S. involvement in Somalia, *Time* observed, "The U.S. promises to feed the hungry and restore hope in Somalia, but Bush's military operation could be the wrong way to do the right thing."[15] This is what Ted Koppel of ABC's *Nightline* had in mind when he reported on December 7, 1992, that Somalia needed education more than anything else to solve its problems.

The UN's action proved to be the ultimate illusion of using the military to resolve political and socioeconomic problems. Further, if the UN wants to adopt this strategy of dealing with national and international problems, then it must be consistently applied in all cases, such as seeking an end to the tragedy of the civil conflict in the former Yugoslavia and the continuing oppression of apartheid in South Africa.

The proper function of the multinational force should have been to bring the parties in conflict together and give them basic training running a country. In this effort the force would have had an opportunity to impress

---

[15]*Time* (December 14, 1992), p. 27.

upon the mind of all Somalians that it is in their best interest to realize that utilizing the gun to impose their will on the people is a sure recipe for national disaster. For the UN to imply that problems of human relationships can be resolved only by utilizing military force is to negate the importance of dialogue and human reason, both products of education.

The kind of informal education that the UN should have initiated would have brought the added advantage of respect for democratic principles, which often ensure that dictatorship of any kind has no place as a form of political behavior among nations of the world. If the multinational force had initiated this strategy, results of its efforts would have been more lasting and beneficial. The force would also have had an opportunity to revive the dying Organization of African Unity (OAU) and help it to play its appropriate role in Africa in accordance with the principles it established at its inception in May 1963.

By ignoring the role that OAU could play in seeking solutions to the problems of Africa, the UN was assuming a position of power that it should not have assumed. However, although the UN's action in Somalia came as a great embarrassment to OAU, that organization itself should have used it to recognize the potential that it once possessed. The recognition that its inability to find solutions to the problems of Africa has been a result of the dictatorial policies adopted by the national leaders would have helped awaken in its members a new level of consciousness needed to save the continent from political and socioeconomic disasters of major proportions.

To set a new course of development for the future, African nations need to utilize the tragedy of Somalia to rediscover themselves, to resolve conflict, to make choices, to strengthen and respect democratic principles, and to establish priorities on a national agenda for action. These important objectives can only be accomplished in a national environment of democratic behavior. Indeed, for Africa, time is running out.

JAPAN: USING EDUCATION TO END CONFLICT OF VALUES

Throughout its history Japan has utilized and enhanced both the philosophy and influence of the powerful sage Confucius in all aspects of its national life. Among the emerging nations, Japan has been one of the most successful in utilizing education to build a new and vibrant society. This study has furnished evidence to show that its ability to emerge from feudal practice in 1868 to a position in which it was able to create a new system of universal education was a rare accomplishment.

In incorporating this innovative approach into a strong system of traditions inherent in Shintoism with the philosophy espoused by Buddha and Confucius, Japan built a foundation of intellectual and educational development that would play a critical role in shaping the future of the country following the end of the occupation in 1952.[16]

---

[16]Ronald Anderson, "Education in Japan," in Edward Ignas and Raymond Corsini (eds.), *Comparative Educational Systems* (Itasca, Ill.: F. E. Peacock, 1982), p. 235.

To appreciate why Japan has put such a high premium on the development of education, one needs to appreciate the relevance of Confucius's philosophy of education. Confucius's recognition that the state needs a steady supply of properly trained labor translated into educational objectives that have enabled Japan to envisage a future different from the past. But it was Confucius's idea that the demand for education of individuals to ensure their own development as a preparation for roles in society was the real basis for setting objectives. The nature of relationships that must develop between education and the development of the individual was critical to the nature of the relationship that must emerge between the individual and society. Confucius also recognized that education is important to shaping the development of relationships between members of society.

The nature of these two types of relationships is what has given Japan the ability to build a national character different from that of other emerging countries. Although the concept of competition is implanted in students early in their educational pursuit, they are reminded that it must be carried out within the spirit of recognizing the achievement of individuals as a prerequisite of national development. It is only members of a society who recognize the delicate balance between these elements who become sensitive to both their own needs and those of their society. This, in essence, is what Japan has tried to design education to accomplish.

Confucius also expressed his view that equality of educational opportunity is a critical factor of equality in society, and that any society that does not practice equality in education cannot practice it in its social system. Although Japan has found it hard to live and operate fully by the central concept of equality, its endeavor to sustain it in various dimensions of its national life has made it possible to design an educational system that has recognized the interests of all students as they aspire to reach their own objectives and those of their nation. That Japan, unlike African nations, considers education for all an important aspect of national endeavor suggests that to this day it is still conscious of the importance of Confucius's philosophy.

A critical dimension of the Confucian philosophy that Japan has found applicable to its education today is that for the educational process to mean what is intended, it must start early in the life of the students. For this reason, the state has assumed the responsibility of financing education. Japanese thinking that early childhood education is essential to the success of education at other levels is what the United States took as a basis for its Head Start programs.

But this study has also furnished evidence to show that Japan has not been immune to the problems of ethnicity. Its inability to resolve the problems that the *ronin* and the *Burakumin* have experienced for years undercuts its efforts to provide equal educational opportunity and the effectiveness of its educational programs. In this context the principles that Confucius so well defined have been rendered less than absolute. The best that Japan can do is to continue its struggle to eliminate the negative features of its culture so that it can envisage a future unmarred by influences from the past.

If the occupation was a period during which Western powers wanted Japan to renounce resorting to military means to resolve problems of international relationships, it also gave the Japanese an opportunity to rediscover themselves as a people with shared values and potential. Instead of directing its efforts toward building military power, Japan directed its energies toward rebuilding itself economically and technologically. In this change of strategy to achieve a national purpose, the Allies never realized that they were arming Japan with a type of weapon to exert new influence in international relationships. This is the reason why, by 1991, Western nations and the Soviet Union were requesting Japan's assistance to resolve their own economic problems.[17]

The decision by the occupation powers to reduce the period of their presence from the originally envisaged twenty-five years to only six was made from the realization that Japan was going to direct its efforts toward economic development as a national endeavor and purpose. They were hardly aware that during the next forty years, Japan would pose a major economic and technological threat to the supremacy of the Western nations. This unexpected development took place because as soon as the occupation came to an end, Japan placed education at the top of its national agenda Japan's national leaders knew that a nation needs good education to ensure other forms of development.

At the conclusion of the war Japan was so impoverished that its leadership found it hard to know exactly where to start. The occupation powers were not interested in its economic development at that time, but in making sure that it did not rise up again to threaten world peace. Instead of making a choice between basic education to ensure literacy and the development of other levels of education, such as technical and vocational, Japan, despite the scourge of poverty it was enduring and a lack of adequate resources, approached the problems of education from all fronts because it considered education critical. To ensure that education did what Japan envisaged, Japan introduced a system of examinations unequal to that of any other country. Two types of examinations were considered essential, entrance and graduation.

This study has also concluded that the application of these systems of examinations created serious educational problems that students have not been able to resolve. One of these problems is increasing incidents of violence in both school and society.[18] Unfortunately the problems of education have caused social problems. Japanese educational leaders have concluded that the steadily rising postwar economic growth has led to increased affluence and urbanization. These have eroded values and have threatened the nuclear family, the backbone of the social structure of the country. In the process, the young have lost the discipline that was once

---

[17]On April 27, 1991, President George Bush, recognizing that the United States was in a recession, requested Japan's assistance in resolving the economic problems he believed it had created.

[18]*New Times* (March 29), 1983.

considered essential for building a national character.[19] This is not to suggest that Japan is the only country with problems caused by a generation gap arising from a conflict of values. The influence of the subculture has been profound on the behavior of youth in all countries.

This reality seems to suggest that the increasing contact that Japan has had with Western nations during the post war era has had some negative influence on national life. The concept of individuality, the hallmark of Western nations, seems to lose its meaning when it is applied in Japanese cultural settings. The *New York Times* observes: "Today's children, increasingly influenced by the individualistic values of the West, are more likely to rebel against a system of uniform education that stresses learning by rote."[20]

Students seem to ignore two factors that suggest why personal failure in education is considerably more tragic than in Western educational settings. The first is that failure does not affect the individual student only, but the entire family. The second is that failure in Western settings is not an educational death sentence as it is in Japan. Therefore, unless cultural practices change, students in Japan cannot hope to separate their own sense of individuality from a system that embraces collective principles in the educational process.

This situation comes into sharper focus when one examines the effect of entrance and graduation examinations. Parents are intimately involved in paying for the extra coaching needed to prepare for the examinations. With a smaller number of children than in the past and with considerably higher income, families can afford to meet the cost of their children's extra help needed to put them at the top. It is quite common for mothers to go to school and take notes from lectures when their children are not able to go. This is done in the hope that it will enhance their children's chances of doing well in the examinations. While this practice shows the weaker side of examinations, it also shows that parents are seriously concerned about educational success.

When Emperor Hirohito ascended the Japanese throne on December 25, 1926, he was considered to be so divine that children were not allowed to see him. When he died in 1989, he had established himself as a scholar and researcher, setting a new example that he thought his people should emulate. Not only has Japan succeeded in its educational endeavor, but has used it to strengthen its economy and improve its monopoly on technological advancement even though there has been a price to pay. By 1989 it was reported that Japan had replaced the United States as a leader, with $10 billion going for foreign aid.[21]

This development must be what the members of the U.S. National Commission on Excellence in Education of 1983 had in mind when they reported, "Our nation is at risk. Our once unchallenged preeminence in commerce, industry, science, and technological innovation is being

---

[19]Ibid.

[20]Ibid.

[21]*The Chronicle of Year 1989* (Mount Kisco, N.Y., 1989), p. 8.

overtaken by competitors throughout the world."[22] But with this shining moment of success came a spate of darkness that has continued to haunt Japan: an increasing number of students who commit suicide every year because they are unable to adjust to the demands of a rapidly changing society.

In 1969 the rate of suicide among teenagers had increased so much that it had become a major national concern. In Nagoya a father committed suicide because he was so embarrassed "when his son was rejected by a prominent secondary school."[23] By 1983 the figures showed that the educational system needed fundamental reform, because not only was there an increasing number of students who would not qualify for entrance into secondary schools and higher education, but there was also increasing concern over the growing conflict between education and other aspects of national life. But while the need for reform is being recognized, there have been in recent years no specific suggestions as to what form it should take. While a search for a formula of educational reform is going on, inadequacies in the educational system will continue to take their toll.

Although suicide tendencies among high school students had decreased considerably in 1990, the feeling that they could dramatically increase again is based on the thinking that H. Nakamura expressed in 1964: "The basic view of life and death among the Japanese people is neither Buddhism nor Confucian, but an absolutely new phenomenon, the attitude to accept death as natural. "[24] This is why, according to the World Health Organization (WHO) report on suicide in 1973, of twelve advanced nations Japan ranked eighth in the suicide rate. [25] If this prediction is to be avoided, then Japan must assume major responsibility for introducing a different feature into its educational system, and that is, it must train teachers to function effectively as counselors to students.

In May 1991 another national phenomenon began to worry Japanese national leaders--the Japanese women, feeling the need to exercise their right of choice, decided that they wanted to have no more than two children. Concerned that this would have a negative impact on the economy, Japanese leaders decided to provide an incentive of $3,000 for families to have more children. Again, the solution to this problem lies in teachers becoming counselors.

If this were done it would help resolve two problems. The first is that it would help teachers in offering guidance to students in planning their academic work. The second is that it would assist the school in inculcating new thinking among students about the importance and value of human

---

[22] National Commission on Excellence in Education, *A Nation at Risk: The Imperative for Educational Reform* (Washington, D. C.: Government Printer, 1983), p. 5.

[23] I. Kawasaki, *Japan Unmasked* (Rutland, Vt.: Charles E. Tuttle, 1969), p. 12.

[24] H. Nakamura, *Ways of Thinking of Eastern People: India, China, Tibet, Japan* (Honolulu: East-West Center Press, 1964), p. 67.

[25] H. Hendin, "Suicide Among the Young," in H. Hendin (ed.), *Suicide in America* (New York: W. W. Norton, 1982), p. 35.

life and to understand that, even if they fail in examinations, lives are precious. H. Hendin has found that in terms of age groups, Japan ranks fifth in suicide among students between the ages of five and fourteen and fourth among those between the ages of fifteen and twenty-four.[26]

This means that the risk of suicide among students is greater the older they get, suggesting the complexity of the adjustment to new social conditions they have to face and how they have done in examinations. That beyond the age of twenty-five the suicide tendency is considerably reduced indicates that the younger the students are, the more vulnerable they become to suicide even though their understanding of their action is less than those in an older age group.

What implications do the problems of education in Japan suggest? Among other things, they indicate that as a nation Japan has gone too far in demanding that students perform well on examinations. This demand shows that passing examinations is the only criterion needed to measure educational success. The imperative for reform is there. There must be other criteria to measure educational success and some adjustment has to be made to alleviate the pressures that students are facing. In order to keep its competitive edge, Japan has to find an alternative system of education that will not subject its young to expectations that are too high. While it is important to train students to climb the corporate ladder and to help them function in a highly technological world, those goals must not be accomplished at the cost of subjecting students to pressures they cannot bear.

In this regard African nations and Japan are facing opposite problems. In the case of the former, the decline in students' performance due to irrelevant education also diminishes their ability to play a role in shaping a future different from the past. In the case of the latter, excessive pressure exerted on students to succeed is hurting the very people the educational system is designed to serve. Both African nations and Japan should realize that there is a middle ground from which to initiate a new approach to education in order to shape the development of their societies.

This means that Japan should use the effectiveness of its educational system to end the conflict of values that is steadily making it hard for it to discharge its responsibility to all its people. It is a task that has to be undertaken in the interest of national development. If Japan could rise up from the ashes of atomic destruction with a sense of its mission to the world, common sense would suggest that it has enough strength to gather its national resources and utilize them to find solutions to one of its most persistent problems--designing an educational system that would place it on a new road to development.

Indeed, the Japanese system of education has had other profound effects on its relationships with the international community. For example, when President George Bush made a tour of Japan in January 1992 in an effort to pull the United States out of recession by persuading Japan to buy more American products, there was a heightened degree of expectations that the two countries would take advantage of creating a

---

[26]Ibid., p. 37.

climate of better understanding between them. During Bush's visit, Japanese auto companies were reported to have promised to increase their purchase of auto parts from the United States to $19 billion by 1994, but they were reluctant to lift the United States out of its recession.

In spite of differences of perceptions of the role American workers, and "despite the years of wrangling between the two nations, Japan retains a large reservoir of good feeling toward the the U.S.A."[27] But as the political season began in the United States in 1992, politicians found an easy substitute when the cold war ended; bashing Japan became a familiar theme. Bush's treatment in Japan became a target of criticism. For example, Bill Clinton, then Democratic candidate for president, observed: "When the Japanese Prime Minister said that he felt sympathy for the U.S., it made me sick. If I had been there with President Bush, I'd have thrown up, too."[28] Clinton was referring to the scare experienced in Tokyo during a reception held for Bush and his party when he collapsed. The incident was broadcast throughout the world on television. Bush explained that the collapse was caused by extreme exhaustion. On November 3, 1992, he lost the Presidential election to Clinton.

THE UNITED STATES: FACING AN EDUCATIONAL SYSTEM IN CRISIS

Writing in 1965 on the relevance of education to the transformation of American society, Paul Woodring observed: "When the rate of social change is accelerated, the responsibilities of teachers multiply. No longer is it sufficient for them to merely teach children to read and to guide them along established paths; they must introduce them to a complex world."[29] Like any society in the late twentieth century, the American school and society appear to be at a crossroads. The harmonious relationship that was intended in the reform movement of the nineteenth century has not resulted in creating a national environment marked by the absence of social conflict.

The belief that the training of teachers is essential to the success of education is a historical one. Following the implementation of the reform programs that Horace Mann and Henry Barnard led, the question of training teachers became a critical issue because schools were expected to impart to students the kind of education that would help build the kind of American society consistent with the values of the day. The reality of this situation is that teacher training, among other things, was meant to ensure that teachers imparted to their students not only the basic elements of education but also the social skills essential to living in an increasingly complex world. This indicates that the training of teachers was held as an

---

[27]Barry Hillenbrand, "America in the Mind of Japan," in *Time* (February 10, 1992).

[28]Walter Shapiro, "Japan Bashing on the Campaign Trail," in *Time* (February 10, 1992), p. 24.

[29]Paul Woodring, *Introduction to American Education* (New York: Harcourt and Brace, 1965), p. 3.

important understanding because their influence extended to areas of life beyond the classroom.

As the character of American society began to change, however, the task of teachers became more complex, because by the late nineteenth century new social systems came into being and the structure of the family began to change. Teachers were caught between the expectations placed on the school system and the changing character of society. This means that teachers were not responsible for the change that was taking place in both society and school, they were still expected to impart to their students what the community wanted them to learn. This contradiction did not make their task any easier.

By the beginning of the twentieth century Americans began to believe that basic methods of teaching and child psychology were sufficient to prepare teachers to function fully. The entire curriculum for the preparation of teachers was considered a major component of their training.[30] Building a strong academic base for teacher preparation was considered incidental to methods and principles of teaching. This created a conflict between the educational process and society.

Throughout human history the school has been considered a major factor in shaping social attitudes and behavior compatible with the expectations of society. Among those expectations was an ability to adopt to moral norms. Moral behavior became the criterion of determining an individual's level of educational attainment. The concept of moral behavior is also a major component of national character. But in the United States the concept of individuality superseded any moral considerations. In this setting the definition of educational success as a product of the combination of moral values and instruction was understood within the context of individual interpretation.

As the United States moved into the late twentieth century, the definitions of morality and education became harder to formulate than in the past. Moral values were no longer universally accepted because they meant different things to different people. Life-styles were seen in terms of what the individual was and preferred to do. This is why the preparation of teachers today no longer emphasizes morality, because the teaching of moral values is now considered a family responsibility, even though few families exercise it.

During the late nineteenth century the school had an important social function to fulfill. With increasing migration from rural areas to urban areas the need to socialize the worker was felt more profoundly on the school grounds than in other social settings.[31] The importance of socialization was evident in the kind of relationships it helped develop in the pursuit of vocational education. As the United States became more industrialized, the importance of acquiring an ability to interact positively with other people manifested itself in the kind of attitudes adopted toward

---

[30]Gerald Gutek, *An Historical Introduction to American Education* (Prospect Heights, Ill.: Waveland Press, 1991), p. 203.

[31]Joel Spring, *American Education: An Introduction to Social and Political Aspects* (New York: Longman, 1985), p. 18.

classmates and later toward workmates. This determined an ability to cooperate and to be creative in order to enrich the social environment in which one lived and worked.[32]

But the reality of social adjustment had to take into account the concept of individuality in such a way that it was not quite possible to put collective social values into the context of human behavior that is universally accepted. When the National Commission on Excellence in Education released its report, *A Nation at Risk: The Imperative for Educational Reform* in 1983, it sounded an alarm of crisis:

> If an unfriendly foreign power had attempted to impose on America the mediocre educational performance that exists today, we might have viewed it as an act of war. As it stands, we have allowed this to happen to ourselves. We have even squandered the gains in student achievement made in the wake of the Sputnik challenge. Moreover, we have dismantled essential support systems which helped make those gains possible. We have, in effect, been committing an act of unthinking, unilateral educational disarmament. Our society and its educational institutions seem to have lost sight of the basic purpose of schooling, and of the high expectations and disciplined effort needed to attain them.[33]

The full extent of the problems that American education was facing was now known. But the knowledge that they existed did not translate into a set of actions designed to find solutions. In many respects solutions to the problems that education in the United States is facing have still not been found.

The elusive nature of these problems has compounded the problems of society. Illiteracy has been increasing. Laura Cavazos, secretary of education in the Reagan administration, concluded in 1988 that there were twenty-seven million illiterate adults in the United Sates and that the dropout rate from high school would cost the nation $240 billion over their lifetime in lost income and productivity. Although Cavazos suggested that the $22 billion proposed in federal spending for education for fiscal year 1989 be directed toward disadvantaged students, she was not optimistic that this action constituted a workable solution.

However, Cavazos neglected to address the question of the rapidly rising numbers of disadvantaged students caused by increasing poverty, unemployment, disintegration of the nuclear family, continuing racial disparity, the widespread use of illegal drugs, and, in 1991, the crisis in the Persian Gulf, which was partly responsible for the recession. Indeed, a nation at risk that the National Commission on Excellence in Education saw in 1983 had, by 1991, become a nation in crisis.

A nagging problem that American education has experienced over an extended period of time is the question of the curriculum. Since the days of the Yale Report of 1828 and the election of Andrew Jackson to the office of president in the same year, the question of what must be taught in schools has remained a controversial educational issue. The frightening

---

[32]Ibid., p. 19.

[33]National Commission on Excellence in Education, *A Nation at Risk*, p. 5.

aspect of this controversy is that the curriculum determines which students will succeed and which will fail.

The debate between Charles Eliot and John Dewey and their respective supporters did not leave clear answers to the question of the curriculum. Dewey's *Child of the Curriculum*, which he wrote nearly twenty years before he left the University of Chicago[34] over disagreement with the president about the curriculum, was the most definitive statement on what the curriculum should be in order to provide students an education that would serve their interests as a measure of its value to the community.[35]

Dewey left his strongest imprint on the question of the curriculum in his *Democracy and Education* (1916) in which he approached the issue from the perspective of his belief that the value of education cannot be forced on a student, and that its intended meaning is best understood in the the contribution of the student to its content and structure. This was Dewey's definition of how democracy must operate in education. The general principle operating in this line of thinking is that the human being is likely to reject anything, no matter how good, if it is imposed.

The reality of the educational process is that various levels of school authority, including the local school board in the United States, assume that they know better than the students themselves what must be taught in school. This dictatorial approach to education has caused a serious decline in student interest in education. The increasing dropout rate is partly the result of this action by school authorities.

Recognition that the curriculum determines the success or failure of the educational process has promoted efforts to improve the situation. The National Defense Education Act of 1958, the Civil Rights Act of 1964, the Elementary and Secondary Education Act of 1965, and the Education and Consolidation and Employment Act of 1981 all represent an effort to rejuvenate the declining interest in education among students. By the beginning of 1971 the United States was emerging from social traumas of the 1960s and wanted education to help reset a national agenda and priorities. In the wake of *Roe vs. Wade,* Title IX of the Higher Education Act of 1972 added a new level of conflict with its response to the emerging curriculum.

Edward Ignas concluded that by 1965, while these developments had a positive side in that nearly 90 percent of high school graduates qualified for college entrance, their performance on standard achievement tests was steadily declining.[36] The ethnic group that was hit most by this decline was black. It is ironic that in spite of the *Brown* decision of 1954 and the Civil Rights Act of 1964, affirmative action, and Head Start programs--all intended to erase past discriminatory practices--they have not had the

---

[34]Dewey was at the University of Chicago from 1894 to 1904, when he was head of the department of philosophy and education. From 1904 to 1930 he was at Columbia University, where he did most of his work on theory of education.

[35]Herbert Kliebard, *The Struggle for the American Curriculum, 1893-1958* (New York: Routledge and Kegan Paul, 1987), p. 83.

[36]Edward Ignas, "The Traditional American Education," in Ignas and Corsini (eds.), *Comparative Educational Systems*, p. 19.

impact they were intended to have on improving the educational performance of minority students. This suggests that there are still problems that have not yet been resolved. By 1991 the pursuit of educational goals had given way to gang warfare and drug-related violence on a large scale especially among black and Hispanic youth.

The grim reality of this tragedy is that in recent years it has been recognized that nearly 25 percent of black young men between the ages of 19 and 25 have been in trouble with the law. Teenage pregnancy, the phenomenon of the single parent family that Vice President Dan Quayle focused on during the presidential election campaign of 1992, a dramatic shift in social values, and the meaninglessness of schooling have taken a heavier toll on black people than on any other ethnic group, and the United States has not been able to discover the basic causes of this tragic development.

It is equally tragic that the black community itself has not been united in designing strategies for seeking solutions to the critical problems it faces and whose impact is far more serious than on any other group. Neither the federal government nor such predominantly black organizations as the Urban League and the NAACP have made a concerted effort to focus on this crisis. Although a few seminars have been held on the general topic of the black male, the results have been less than satisfactory. Moreover, the position of black Americans is rapidly deteriorating to a point worse than during emancipation. Yes, there have been a number of black elected officials at the local level and a governor of Virginia.

But as long as institutions in which they operate are under the control of the majority, it is not likely that these officials will make a significant difference in the lives of black people. The oppression of slavery has suddenly given way to a more powerful social oppression, the disintegration of the black identity. This is not a problem for black Americans, but for the nation. Where does the United States go from here?

There is another dimension to this national crisis. Those black individuals who have attained a level of success, such as mayors, other civic leaders, and businesspeople, have not addressed the problem of their collective national identity primarily because they want to remain on the good side of the vast white majority who have been part of their success. This is the tragedy of America today.

American education, like education in Africa, Japan, and the former Soviet Union, would need a major commitment at all levels to face a system in crisis and to initiate basic reform. It sounds ironic that Gorbachev's efforts to initiate such a reform program resulted in his demise and the collapse of the Soviet Union. Perhaps what America needs today is a Horace Mann, a Henry Barnard, or an Andrew Jackson to chart a fresh course to national development.

The declaration by President George Bush, at the beginning of his administration in 1989, that he wanted to be known as an education president yielded little to substantiate his claim. Bush's inability to live by his own expectations to realize the aspirations of the people contributed to his defeat by Bill Clinton. As Clinton prepared to assume office in January

1993, he was acutely aware of the serious nature of the problem the country faced.

State and local education authorities, faced with enormous budgetary problems, have given up the struggle because the task is too heavy. In June 1991 the controversy between President Bush and Congress over the Civil Rights Bill combined with the trauma that many servicemen and women were facing on their return from the Persian Gulf and with the recession to create formidable socioeconomic problems. If President Bush was not able to solve these problems, how, then, was he going to create the new global order that he said was going to result from the defeat of Iraq?

During a graduate class on December 3, 1992, J. Otto Berg, professor of adult education at Northern Arizona University, put the problems of education in the United States within the context of a search for a new national character, saying, "America faces a dilemma of choice: Either to have low levels of education and low wages and unemployment, or to have high skills and high wages brought by America being competitive in the global economic marketplace. Only then will the standard of living rise once again for a high percentage of the American population."[37]

Participating in the Clinton economic conference held in Little Rock in December 1992, John Scully discussed the same dilemma when he rhetorically asked, "Do we want high skills or do we want low wages? High skills and high paying jobs will come from a better school system."[38] In 1989 Scully, a Republican, was disappointed to see that President Bush ignored his suggestions to improve U.S. education. This is why he endorsed Bill Clinton for President in 1992. What both Berg and Scully were suggesting is that a strong national character can only come from an effective educational policy.

One is led to the conclusion that, while American education has served the needs of the people at various stages of its development, it is going through a major crisis that has to be resolved if the future is to be more meaningful than the past. With the recession having a serious impact on the U.S. economy in 1992, confidence in President Bush rapidly deteriorated to the extent that he lost the election to Bill Clinton. The crisis in Los Angeles in May 1992, caused by the trial and acquittal of four white police officers accused of using excessive force against Rodney King, a black motorist, accentuated the extent of the problems the United States was facing.

President Bush's pardon on December 24, 1992, of Caspar Weinberger and five other top officials in the Reagan administration involved in the Iran-Contra scandal raised new questions about his understanding of the need to restructure an emerging national character based upon an effective educational policy. In discussing its reasons for selecting Bill Clinton as its choice for man of the year for 1992, *Time* of

---

[37]J. Otto Berg, "America Faces a Choice," lecture given to a graduate class at Northern Arizona University, December 3, 1992.

[38]John Scully, "America's Choice," in *USA Today* (December 15, 1992).

January 4, 1993, portrayed Bush as a national leader who did not seem to understand the elements of character of the nation he was leading.[39]

The wish that Bush expressed at the beginning of his administration to be regarded as the education president became a victim of his elusive grand plan to build a new global order sustained by the military might of the United States. This is what gave *Time* reason to paint a picture of Bush leading an administration in disarray.[40] Bush's failure to define an educational policy to sustain the national character of the United States at a critical period in its development compounded the problems that the Reagan administration had created from 1981 to 1988.

THE SOVIET UNION: EFFORTS TO ELIMINATE THE AGONY OF A DYSFUNCTIONAL SYSTEM

A study of education in the former Soviet Union, like that of any other country, must, of necessity, be done from a historical perspective in order to understand all its implications. When Peter the Great returned from a visit to Britain in 1700 he brought back a vision of transforming society by transforming the educational system. Peter then established a school that emphasized the arts, navigation, and mathematics along the lines that Henry the Navigator (1394-1460) had done in Portugal in 1440. But Peter went a step further in introducing more educational reform than the system he saw in Britain. He attempted to structure a utilitarian system that he envisaged as seeking to alleviate the difficulties that the masses were enduring.[41] The concept of the enlightened despot, so characteristic of the times, was also at work in Russia.

By the end of the eighteenth century the thinking that education must be available to as many people as possible demanded a radical change in curriculum from stressing classical education to adopting a utilitarian curriculum along the lines that Peter had defined. The war between Russia and Napoleon accentuated the need to restructure the educational system so that it would enable the people to respond to the needs of the country. Soon after ascending to the throne in 1801, Alexander I refused to accept foreign influences into the educational system as Peter had done, preferring to include Russian traditions.

By the time that Nicholas II ascended the throne in 1894, the need to sustain Russian traditions in education had the effect of retarding the reform movement that Peter had initiated. By 1905 the oppression of the masses had intensified, setting in motion events that led to the revolution in 1917, from which the Bolsheviks came to power.[42]

---

[39]"Bill Clinton, Man of the Year: The Torch Is Passed," *Time* (January 4, 1993), p. 21.

[40]Ibid.

[41]Brian Holmes, "Education in the Soviet Union," in Ignas and Corsini (eds.), *Comparative Educational Systems*, p. 331.

[42]N. Kuzin and M. Kondokov, *Education in the U.S.S.R.* (Moscow: Progress Press, 1977), p. 7.

The knowledge that education under Nicholas had become an elitist bureaucracy and embraced powerful elements of oppression led the Bolsheviks to initiate a radical approach to education. Two considerations were critical to this approach. The first consideration was that education must assist in the reconstruction of society to suit the needs of a new industrial and social order. The second consideration was that utilitarian dimensions made it imperative to provide it on an equal basis. These are the elements that are central to the socialist philosophy of education, and the Bolsheviks fully embraced them as a starting point on their national journey to a social transformation of society.[43]

The Bolsheviks saw the development of modern industry as leading to an emergence of a modern society as a product of education. Since the emergence of modern industry depends on mass participation, the Bolsheviks concluded that mass education was essential to its success. A denial of equal educational opportunity would translate into a denial for the opportunity for national development.

However, the introduction of a socialist ideology had a negative side as it was applied by the Bolsheviks; they wanted it to place the importance of serving the needs of the state over the needs of the students as a prior condition of serving the needs of society. From 1918 to 1984 this adverse side of the educational process continued to take a heavy toll on the Soviet Union. Because major industries were under the control of the state, production, a major objective of education, and distribution have always been a problem. Over the years the competitive superiority that the Soviet leaders thought socialist programs would provide was replaced by mediocrity, especially during the tenure of Joseph Stalin and Nikita Khrushchev.

Both leaders resorted to unorthodox methods to force the people to face the issue. Although the Soviet Union utilized education to excel in technological development and space exploration, the level of production was still inadequate. This is why for many years the Soviet Union was forced to import grain from the West. This is also why, by the end of 1990, the Soviet Union experienced substantial shortages in food supplies, a situation that almost derailed Gorbachev's reform programs.

Until Mikhail Gorbachev assumed office in 1984, the principles of national control of education, economics, and all other aspects of life were central to socialist ideology, and the educational process was expected to promote these programs. This was based on the assumption that the security of the state was essential to the welfare of the individual.[44] In their study *Education in the U.S.S.R.*, N. Kuzin and M. Kondokov argued in 1972 that this perspective brings a much better social coherence than a capitalist system, which they say causes so much social conflict. Kuzin and Kondokov added:

---

[43]Ibid., p. 9.

[44]In this study, evidence has been presented to show that the relationship between the individual and society is different in the Western democratic form of government and in the socialist form. In the case of the former the individual comes first, but in the case of the latter the state comes first.

In the United States the Supreme Court as early as 1954 came out in favor of school integration. But to date only a small fraction of black children have received the opportunity of studying together with white children. Every year the press brings new evidence of recurring outbreaks of racial hostilities in U. S. schools. In October, 1974 in Boston a racial storm broke out. Local racists joined by KKK and storm troopers from the local organizations incited major disorders in the city to prevent the instruction of black children together with white children. Blacks have twice as great a probability of being unemployed. The capitalist system is at the center of this serious social conflict.[45]

While there is substance to the observation of these two Soviet authors about the problems of education in the United States, one has to conclude that their views provide no solace to the agony of economic and social dysfunction that the Soviet Union has endured for nearly seven decades doe to unrelenting pursuit of socialist ideology. This is why Gorbachev decided to chart a new course. But the process of change from a socialist economy to one entailing elements of free enterprise involves the painful pangs of frustration.

The decision to initiate fundamental change in the system from socialist to free enterprise created enormous problems for both the Soviet Union and Gorbachev. Opposition was intense. On April 29, 1991, President Bush, recognizing the precarious nature of Gorbachev's position and the uncertainty of the reform programs he had initiated, declined to extend to the Soviet Union a line of credit that would continue to enable it to buy grain from the United Sates. The resignation of Soviet Foreign Minister Eduard Shevardnadze[46] in December 1990, caused primarily by opposition from hard-liners, compounded the problems that Gorbachev was trying to solve under *glasnost* and *perestroika*. The nuclear disaster at Chernobyl in 1986 convinced Gorbachev that the Soviet Union would no longer conduct national business under the veil of secrecy behind the Iron Curtain.

An important aspect of Gorbachev's reform effort is important to understand here, and that is it was based on his theoretical premise that when political and economic change is initiated, corresponding reform must be introduced in the educational system to shape the development of a new national character. Indeed, because Gorbachev recognized that there was no benefit to be accrued from dysfunctional educational and economic systems, he initiated a painful process of reform, fully aware of the implications of his efforts both in the short and long terms. At that time, Shevardnadze feared that if opposition to Gorbachev's reform program succeeded a more powerful dictatorship would emerge[47] and the Soviet

---

[45]Kuzin and Kondokov, *Education in the U.S.S.R.*, p. 18.

[46]In a documentary entitled *Shevardnadze Rediscovered* aired on TV on January 18, 1993, John Palmer presented evidence to show that Shevardnadze oppressed his own people in the republic of Georgia.

[47]*Time* (December 31, 1990).

Union might very well go back to a form of dictatorship similar to that of the period of the Bolsheviks.

That in 1992 the Soviet Union was replaced, but not by a dictatorship of the kind Shevardnadze had feared. The Commonwealth of Independent Republics offered a consolation to a man who was seriously concerned about the future of his country.

Recognizing the imperative for reform, Gorbachev put the case for it during an address to the All-Union Student Forum in November 1989:

> If we are to carry through the reform program, we must change ourselves. In order to change ourselves we must take an active part in all the processes and be active in carrying out *glasnost* and *perestroika*. We must all proceed from the firm belief that the administrative system and related forms of the organization of society are in fact no longer adequate and cannot provide the inner incentives for accomplishment of the task of the country's socialist renewal.[48]

These sound words of a national leader who was committed to the transformation of his society would suggest that it was in the best interest of the country to give him the opportunity to do so. Gennadi Yogodin added an educational dimension to this unusual adventure in *perestroika*. An education which is differentiated in accordance with the student's individual propensities will become varied in content. This approach makes it possible to take into account and combine in the educational process both the requirements of society and the need to ensure the maximum development of every student.[49]

Such a clearly defined national objective no doubt becomes fulfilled only if its essential elements are in place, among them an effective leadership structured on a clear knowledge of the past with an agenda for action to give it a new meaning. This is what it takes to launch a national endeavor to salvage a country from dysfunctional practices of the past and set it on a road to new endeavors. Even Boris Yeltsin would agree. This is why he came to Gorbachev's rescue in April 1991 when he was under attack by the radicals and conservatives.

It is clear that in his efforts to reform the system of education Gorbachev was trying to eliminate the effects of a dysfunctional system that had been in place for seven decades. This is also why, speaking in Oslo in June 1991 during the ceremonies at which he received the Nobel Peace Prize for 1990, Gorbachev said that both *glasnost* and *perestroika* would remain the pillars of his reform campaign and suggested that all nations needed reform. He was unaware that within a few years the bold experiment that he initiated would cause his own demise and the collapse of the Soviet Union.

---

[48]Mikhail Gorbachev, *Channel the Energy of Youth into Perestroika*, speech given to the All-Union Student Forum, November 15, 1989 (Moscow: Novosti Press, 1989), p. 20.

[49]Gennadi Yogodin, *Towards Higher Standards in Education through Its Humanization and Democratization* (Moscow: Novosti Press, 1989), p. 7.

Three Days of Crisis in Moscow:
Threat to *Glasnost* and *Perestroika*

The political demise of Mikhail Gorbachev and the collapse of his educational reform program must be seen within the context of political events that began to unfold in a dramatic fashion beginning in August 1991. When Western nations woke up the morning of August 19, 1991, they were shocked to learn that a coup led by military generals was under way to remove Mikhail Gorbachev from office and to replace him with his vice president, the conservative hard-liner, Gennadi Yanayev. Other leaders of the coup included Vladimir Kruychkov, Dmitri Yazov, and Boris Pugo.

While the West recognized Gorbachev as a champion of democracy in the Soviet Union under *glasnost* and *perestroika*, the military establishment saw him as a traitor to the philosophy and ideals that Lenin had put in place at the beginning of the Bolshevik administration in 1918. Was there something that had gone wrong with that philosophy that Gorbachev become an agent of the West? How could a man born and raised under a system billed as a model of social development turn his back on it?

What irritated the military establishment more than anything else about Gorbachev's reforms was that for six years they had watched him create the type of history that they considered contrary to their view of the meaning of socialism. They had watched him introduce the Soviet Union to the decadence they equated with Western-type capitalism, which for seventy years the people of the Soviet Union had been told was exploitive. They had watched him grant people the kind of freedom they believed they were not prepared to exercise. They had watched him bring the country to the brink of disintegration and claimed that he did nothing to stop it.

Indeed, the generals watched the Baltic states boldly demand independence and take action to give it effect, and he was unable to use military force to stop it and so keep the country together. They watched Boris Yeltsin steadily bring the country to the edge of anarchy. They watched his form of *demokratizatsiya* tilter toward chaos and his apparent inability to stop it. Finally, the generals watched Gorbachev introduce a reform program they considered a radical departure from the socialist philosophy of state responsibility to the people.

The usual explanation given by the coup leaders that Gorbachev had been removed from office because he was sick was not substantiated by the dramatic turn of events. By August 21, due to differences within the ranks of the military establishment, the coup that was designed to turn the course of history and events around proved to be a failure. As Gorbachev flew back to Moscow from his Crimean resort where he had been placed under house arrest, he was at a loss for words to explain the dramatic turn of events that almost cost him his life. But on arriving at Moscow airport, Gorbachev was moved to admit: "These are the people I have trusted. They have turned out to be not only the participants against the President, but also against the Constitution, against the people, against democracy. I do not think that I have done anything in my life that my motherland can hold against me."[50]

One must view this abortive coup within the context of developments that began to unfold earlier. According to British intelligence, in February 1991 dissident elements of the Soviet army and the KGB rehearsed the coup to remove Gorbachev from office and replace him with a conservative military elite and a few civilians loyal to Stalinist ideology.

In July these conservative Stalinists appealed to "those who recognize the terrible plight in which our country has fallen"[51] to come forward and support an action to bring what they characterized as a malaise to an end and to restore the country to its proper Marxist-Leninist footing. That Gorbachev had set aside August 20 as the date for the signing of a new Soviet treaty giving the republics more power to run their own affairs further angered the military elite who thought this action would be a final act to cause national disarray and therefore should be stopped before it was implemented.

As this three-day drama seemed to lose both its direction and support, other actors began to appear on the stage as massive anti-coup demonstrations took place. Leading officials who had gone into hiding began to appear to direct the course of events that would restore Gorbachev to his position. Among these was Boris Yeltsin, the popular but somewhat emotional president of the Russian republic.

When he thought coup leaders were divided and that conditions were right for him, and sensing the need to play a leadership role in the direction the demonstrators wanted events to move, Yeltsin quickly jumped on stage to take control of things. He denounced the coup attempt as he assumed the role of spokesman of a group of people who had been left without a leader.

Yeltsin might have taken advantage of the coup to denounce Gorbachev for expelling him from the Communist Party for suggesting that the reform was moving too slowly. But if he had done that he would have undermined his own position. However, Yeltsin decided to use his role to claim that he had foiled the coup that was already failing to bolster his own position and force Gorbachev to make major political concessions. By the end of the week Gorbachev did just that by announcing that he was resigning from the Communist Party but was retaining his position as president of the Soviet Union.

When both men appeared together at a press conference, Gorbachev announced that he was requesting the resignation of Foreign Minister Alexander Bessmertnykh because he did nothing to stop the coup. When Gorbachev concluded that some of the ministers did not go along with the coup conspirators, Yeltsin quickly interjected and handed him the minutes of a ministerial meeting of the Russian republic which he, as president, chaired and asked him to read it. This was like a state governor in the United States ordering the president to read the minutes of a meeting held at the state level.

---

[50]*Time* (September 2, 1991), p. 50.

[51]Ibid., p. 33.

Apparently confused by the fast pace of events he did not understand, Gorbachev "read aloud that all but two of some 20 ministers had backed the junta or did not oppose it."[52] This situation did not reflect well the political truce between Gorbachev and Yeltsin. However, for the time being, the crisis over the cup that both men were to drink from had passed. The net result of this crisis is that the coup had failed, but it left a trail of bitterness that was bound to take years to heal.

In a broader context, the results of the coup can also be measured in terms of the national conditions it had created. The already fragile economy was devastated. Gorbachev's image of national leader had been seriously damaged, putting many of his reform programs on hold while he tried to recover from this serious threat. The Communist Party had been vanquished. Government operations came to a halt. The national programs that Gorbachev had initiated under *glasnost* and *perestroika* had lost much of their momentum. Gorbachev and Yeltsin were as far apart on national issues and policy as they had been at the time Gorbachev introduced his reform program.

A graduate student at Northern Arizona University who had been following this drama observed in August 1991 that: "Boris Yeltsin appeals to popular emotion while Gorbachev appeals to reason and rationality. How would Yeltsin solve the problems of the shattered economy, political and social reconstruction and educational reform if he continues to use emotion to elevate himself to the position of power?"[53]

This observation seems to be the question the people of the former Soviet Union must answer as they seek new directions for the various countries they have created in its place. The answer is not an easy one to find, but it is certain that the best solution lies in education. Perhaps the people of the former Soviet Union also need to consider other factors about Gorbachev. He is the man who broke with the debilitating past to chart a new course for the development of his country. Were it not for Gorbachev, Boris Yeltsin would never have had a chance to become president of the Russian republic.

In his enthusiasm for rapid and radical change, Yeltsin would be well advised to remember lessons from the past and that any miscalculation on his part could plunge the country into chaos. The best interests of the country, not his political ambition, should come first. The thinking that Gorbachev might have initiated the coup to improve his popularity is not substantiated by any evidence. The challenge before the republics is to go beyond the reform program that Gorbachev initiated and to design educational programs to sustain the underlying principles that he was operating under. In this manner the spirit of democracy he introduced can prevail.

When Gorbachev thought the crisis caused by the coup attempt was over, two critical events occurred on September 2, 1991, that had a profound impact not only on his reform program, but also on the future of

---

[52]Ibid., p. 27.

[53]Conversation with the author (August 26, 1991).

the Soviet Union. The first event was that President George Bush followed the example of other Western nations in extending official recognition to the Baltic republics of Estonia, Latvia, and Lithuania.

Since these republics were incorporated into the Soviet Union by the action of Adolf Hitler and Joseph Stalin in 1940, Western nations had always claimed that they did not recognize them as part of the Soviet Union. The second event was that Gorbachev himself proposed a radical reform to extend independence to the ten republics that decided to remain part of the union in deciding their own programs including the military. Only time will tell if these events constituted progress for the country.

The constructive involvement of Mikhail Gorbachev in the peace conference that opened in Madrid on October 29, 1991, between Israel and its Arab neighbors testifies to the degree to which the Soviet Union under Gorbachev saw its global role in a very different light from that of the past. Indeed, the era of the cold war was over and the new era of international cooperation had begun, although it was only for a short period of time because the era of the Soviet Union was coming to a close. But with Yeltsin's decision not to seek a second term of office as president of Russia, the question of future leadership not only of Russia, and the other republics posed serious implications.

The End of the Era of the Hammer and Sickle

The bold experiment that Mikhail Gorbachev introduced in 1986 under *glasnost* and *perestroika* led, by 1992, not to the strengthening of the Soviet Union as he had envisaged, but to its end. Beginning with the coup attempt of August 1991, events in the Soviet Union had "been writhing in a last agony that, in the words of Russian President Boris Yeltsin, seemed to drag on 'through some sort of sick eternity.'"[54] On December 7, 1991, leaders of several republics met in the city of Brest to map out a strategy for responding to events that were moving fast in the country. The logical conclusive agreement they reached was that the coup attempt had inflicted mortal political wounds on both Gorbachev and the Soviet Union.

The following week, on December 13, Yeltsin assumed the leadership void created by the inaction of the fatally wounded Gorbachev and, along with leaders of the other republics, signed a declaration that stated: "The Union of Soviet Socialist Republics, as a subject of international law and geopolitical reality, is ceasing its existence."[55] The signatories to the declaration then formed what became known as the Commonwealth of Independent Republics to take effect in January 1992.

Although Gorbachev reacted, "They have no right to declare the Soviet Union nonexistent,"[56] he was unable and unwilling to use military force to preserve the Soviet Union as it had existed since 1917. He therefore accepted his fate and went into retirement. These events brought to an end

---

[54]*Time* (December 23, 1991).
[55]Ibid.
[56]Ibid.

the era of the hammer and sickle. The republics then began to introduce into the economy features of Western-type free enterprise that plunged them into economic chaos due to lack of experience.

By 1992 it was clear that the republics had to deal with the rapidly deteriorating economy. Gorbachev's satisfaction was in the knowledge that the efforts he directed toward introducing democracy were now the basis of the efforts made by the republics to make a new start in an enormous undertaking. *Glasnost* and *perestroika* had yielded tangible benefits for the people they were intended to serve.

While accepting these developments as being in line with democratic behavior, the United States expressed serious concern over who would control the nuclear arsenal previously controlled by Gorbachev. This was why in February 1992 James Baker, United States Secretary of State, flew to Moscow to hold discussions with Yeltsin in an effort to resolve the issue. These events brought to an end the era of hammer and sickle and the untimely death of an experiment that Gorbachev had initiated under *glasnost* and *perestroika*.

The treaty that Yeltsin and Bush signed on January 3, 1993, to reduce the threat of nuclear weapons seemed to mark the starting point in new relationships between Russia and the United States. However, the glaring weakness of the treaty was the absence of a clause addressing the need for cooperation between the two countries to develop education to strengthen their respective national characters. While both Bush and Yeltsin understood how critical this was to their people's understanding of human issues in both countries, they failed to address the importance of this aspect of their national endeavors.

IMPLICATIONS

This study has attempted to discuss major developments, both historical and contemporary, in education in four selected areas of the world. It has concluded that there are five critical areas of education that all nations have in common. These are theory, objectives, the curriculum, administration, and problems. What one learns from the effect of these factors is that effective education cannot develop if it does not take these into account. The study has also identified four critical areas of national life that the development of education must reflect if it is intended to serve the purpose for which it is instituted. These are social values, administrative character, finance, and reform. Let us briefly discuss the implications that each has not only on the educational process, but also on society itself.

In many respects education is the process of adjusting to social values. It is highly sensitive to operative social norms and changes, and the values of society itself must be reflected in the educational process or the education that students receive has little or no meaning to their role in society. Students who are educated to play a role in a society that operates under a different set of values are miseducated and may find it hard to adjust to its institutional functions.

This study has furnished evidence to show that all the functions of education must come into play to enable students to prepare themselves fully for that role. It has also discussed evidence to suggest that the rapid pace of social change in Africa, Japan, the United States, and the former Soviet Union has not been reflected in the educational system. This is why students have found it hard to bear the social pressures that society imposes on them. It is the function of both society and the school to ensure that students are properly educated so that they adjust to society without experiencing any difficulties. None of the four nations in this study has worked out an adequate process of accomplishing this objective.

The study has also presented evidence to show that Africa, Japan, and the former Soviet Union have a central system of educational administration and that the United States is different in that both the federal level and the local level share administrative responsibilities. But each system encounters serious problems. In the case of the first three examples, the administrative character entails bureaucratic red tape that handicaps the development of education. The manner in which funds are distributed, the implementation of a national curriculum, public examinations, the setting of regulations--all are carried out in a fashion detrimental to the educational interests of students.

In the case of the United States, involvement by the courts Congress leaves local authorities confused as to what they must do. When things go wrong, as they often do, the federal authorities and the local authorities blame each other. This suggests that the constitutional arrangements which responsibility for education is left to the local level need to be reevaluated in light of the problems that education is facing, which the framers of the U.S. Constitution did not foresee.

In all four examples the educational process is based on theoretical considerations and historical background because both have a direct bearing on its development. Both have a profound impact on the character of education. In Africa theoretical considerations are heavily influenced by the need to eliminate the colonial legacy. While African leaders espouse theories of national unity as a desirable endeavor, the lack of basic knowledge of what exactly is involved handicaps actual development. Instead of developing programs to ensure progress, they impose on their people a false sense of national identity. This creates conflict situations that may not be resolved.

In the case of the former Soviet Union socialist ideology has been an overriding consideration. Even Mikhail Gorbachev sought to reform, not to abandon, socialist theory. When cast into the setting of contemporary world conditions this creates problems that even the application of *glasnost* and *perestroika* may not be able to solve. In the case of the United States and Japan the conflict that emerges between the position of the individual and that of society casts a shadow over the thrust for new theoretical considerations.

All four examples in this study have encountered serious financial problems in their education. In the United States in 1991, the combination of military spending and the recession adversely affected the educational process more than any other item on the national budget. Even in the new era of cooperation between the United States and the former Soviet Union, as evidenced by their activity in the conflict in the Persian Gulf, these nations still found it expedient to spend billions of dollars on the military budget and so were forced to spend less on education. For example, it was estimated at the beginning of 1991 that the United States spent $30 billion in sending armed forces to Saudi Arabia following Iraq's invasion of Kuwait in August 1990.[57] The outcome of this action was diminishing the much needed spending for education.

No matter how much military action against Iraq may be justified, it shows that nations do not make a serious effort to resolve problems through negotiations because they want to rely on military action to have their own position prevail. Most nations seem to neglect the fact that it is education, not the military, that ensures long-term national security. The problem arises in general because many countries do little or ineffective planning for education.

Of the four examples in this study, only the Soviet Union under Gorbachev attempted to initiate a fundamental reform of the educational system. After nearly seven decades of sporadic development shrouded in secrecy, the Soviet Union was not making real progress. This is why Gorbachev recognized that any society that operates in secrecy cannot initiate the basic reform needed to ensure development of the country. Both *glasnost* and *perestroika* have their origins in this line of thinking. This is the context in which the aim of education shifted from focusing on serving the needs of the state to serving those of the students. This is what Gennadi Yogodin took into account when he said, "Every educational establishment and every teacher may choose their own path and move along it at their own pace. The main thing is to move toward our common goal. This can best be done by meeting the needs of the students as a condition of meeting those of society."[58]

Gorbachev's threats to resign from the presidency soon after the coup attempt would soon derail the course he had charted for both reform and the development of the country. The inauguration of the Commonwealth of Independent Republics in January 1992 was no substitute for the bold experiment he had initiated for the development of education and the country. His legacy to them is that they should not betray the democratic principles he put in place.

The other three examples have found the task of reform too difficult to try, so they let existing inadequacies continue to take a heavy toll on the educational process. The system of public examinations has produced severe traumas for students, and yet some nations continue to use them. The sooner those nations face up to the reality of the problems they create, the better will be their educational system. But along with the need to modify the system of public examinations must be recognized the need to initiate fundamental reform in education in its entirety.

To Africa, Japan, and the United States this task remains unfulfilled and demands the effort of all involved to demonstrate beyond political rhetoric that unless it is done the future is invariably imperiled. In 1992 Bill

---

[57]This amount did not include the cost of the actual military operation to force Iraq out of Kuwait.

[58]Gennadi Yogodin, *Towards Higher Standards in Education,* p. 3.

Clinton described the extent of the crisis that education in America faced, saying: "Washington shows little concern as people pay more and get less for what matters to them: educating their children. Test scores went down while violence in the schools went up. College tuition and living costs skyrocketed."[59]

Clinton's assessment suggests that for the crisis that exists in education in Africa, Japan, and the United States, time is running out, although not to the same extent that it did for the Soviet Union. The resumption of hostilities between Iraq and the Western coalition forces on January 13, 1993--one week before President Bush left office--created a national crisis for Bill Clinton that required a delicate balancing act and presented him with a critical choice: to focus on foreign policy to find solutions to international conflict, or to direct his efforts at designing a domestic policy and developing an educational policy in order to structure a national character consistent with the requirements of a new world order made possible by the end of the communist era. It was not an easy task for Clinton.

The CBS News report of November 28, 1992, that the Commonwealth of Independent Republics was facing serious socioeconomic problems that included homelessness must compel one to raise serious questions about the wisdom of dissolving the Soviet Union. The motion made by the opposition in the Russian parliament on December 1 to impeach Boris Yeltsin for his poor handling of the economy indicated new problems for the future of the republics. When the Russian parliament voted on March 13, 1993 to reduce Yeltsin's presidential power, the former Soviet Union took a step closer to an unprecedented crisis. In this regard, therefore, one must conclude that as of the beginning of 1993 all four examples selected for this study were experiencing serious problems in the efforts of their leaders to shape a new national character because of their inability to resolve the problems they were encountering in their educational policy.

---

[59]Bill Clinton, *Putting People First: A National Economic Strategy for America* (Little Rock: Bill Clinton for President Committee, 1992), p. 14.

Selected Bibliography

AFRICA

Abdurrahman, M., and Canham, P. *The Ink of the Scholar: The Islamic Traditions of Education in Nigeria.* London: Macmillan, 1978.

Abernathy, D. B. *The Political Dilemma of Popular Education: An African Case.* Stanford, Calif.: Stanford University Press, 1966.

Ahmed, M. *The Economics of Non-formal Education in Africa.* New York: Praeger, 1975.

Albright, David (ed.). *Africa and International Communism.* London: Macmillan, 1980.

Alexander, H. T. *African Tightrope.* London: Pall Mall Press, 1965.

Allen, Charles. *Tales from the Darkness.* London: Deutsche, 1979.

Amin, Samir. *Neocolonialism in West Africa.*: London: Penguin, 1973.

Andermichael, Rerhanghun. *The OAU and the UN*: New York: Kegan Paul/Africa Publishing Company, 1976.

Anderson, C. A. *The Social Context of Educational Planning in Africa.* Paris: UNESCO, 1967.

Andreski, S. *The Africa Predicament: A Study of the Pathology of Modernization.* London: Apter, 1968.

Anglin et. al.(eds.). *Conflict and Change in Southern Africa.* Washington, D.C.: UPA, 1978.

Anstey, Roger. *King Leopold's Legacy: The Congo under Belgian Rule, 1908-1960.* London: Oxford University Press, 1966.

Austin, Dennis. *Politics of Ghana, 1946-1960*. London: Oxford University Press, 1964.

Banana, Canaan. *Theology of Promise: The Dynamics of Self-Reliance*. Harare, Zimbabwe: College Press, 1982.

Bangbose, A. (ed.). *Mother Tongue in Education: The African Experience*. London: Heinemann, 1976.

Barber, James. *Rhodesia: The Road to Rebellion*. London: Oxford University Press, 1967.

Barnett, Dan, and Harvey, Ray. *The Revolution in Angola*. Indianapolis: Bobbs-Merrill, 1972.

Barnett, D. L., and Karari, Njima. *Mau-Mau from Within*. London: Macmillan and Kee, 1966.

Battle, V. M. and Lyons, C. H. (eds.), *Essays in the History of African Education*. New York: Teachers College Press, 1970.

Bender, G. J. *Angola under the Portuguese: The Myth and the Reality*. London: Heinemann, 1978.

Berman, E. G. (ed.). *African Reaction to Missionary Education*. New York: Teachers College Press, 1975.

Bernstein, H. (ed.). *Underdevelopment and Development: The Third World Today*. Harmonsworth, Great Britain: Penguin, 1973.

Blaug, M. *Education and the Employment Problems in Developing Countries*. Geneva: ILO, 1973.

Blaug, M. *Political Geography of Africa*. London: Cambridge University Press, 1979.

Blundell, Michael. *So Rough a Wind*. London: Weidenfield and Nickleson, 1964.

Bourret, F. M. *Ghana: The Road to Independence, 1919-1957*. London: Oxford University Press, 1960.

Brockway, Fenner. *African Journeys*. London: Gallant, 1955.

Brookfield, H. C. *Interdependence and Development*. London: Methuen, 1975.

Brown, G., and Hiskett, M. (eds.). *Conflict and Harmony in Education in Tropical Africa*. London: Allen and Unwin, 1975.

Bunting, Brian. *The Rise of the South African Reich*. Baltimore: Penguin, 1975.

Cante, David. *Under the Skin: The Death of White Rhodesia*. London: Allen Lane, 1984.

Carter, Gwendolen M., and O'Meara, Patrick (eds.). *Southern Africa: The Continuing Crisis*. Bloomington: Indiana University Press, 1982.

Castle, E. B. *Education for Self-help: New Strategy for Developing Countries*. London: Oxford University Press, 1972.

Chambers, R. *Managing Rural Development: Ideas and Experience from East Africa*. Almquist: Wiksell, International, 1974.

Chidzero, Bernard. *Tanganyika and the International Trusteeship*. London: Oxford University Press, 1961.

Coles, E. K. *Adult Education in Developing Countries*. Oxford: Pergamon, 1977.

Cook, Allen. *South Africa: An Imprisoned Society*. London: International Defense Aid Publication.

Coombs, Philip. *World Crisis in Education: The View from the Eighties*. New York: Oxford University Press, 1985.

Cowan, L., et al. *Education and Nationalism in Africa*. New York: Praeger, 1965.

Cox, Courtland. *African Liberation*. New York: Negro Education Press, 1974.

Curle, Adam. *Educational Strategy for Developing Societies: A Study of Educational Social Factors in Relation to Economic Growth*. London: Tavistock, 1963.

Curle, Adam. *Education for Liberation*. New York: John Wiley and Sons, 1973.

Dale, Richard, and Mantholm, C. *Southern Africa in Perspective*. New York: Free Press, 1972.

Damachi, U. (ed.). *Development Paths in Africa and China*. London: Macmillan, 1976.

Davidson, Basil. *The African Awakening*. London: Cape, 1965.

Davidson, Basil. *In the Eye of the Storm: Angola's People*. London: Longman, 1972.

Davidson, Basil. *Africa in Modern History*. London: Allen Lane, 1978.

Davidson, Basil. *No Fist is Big Enough to Hide the Sky*. London: Zed Press, 1981.

Delf, George. *Jomo Kenyatta*. London: Gallant, 1949.

Desmond, Cosmos. *The Discarded People*. Baltimore: Penguin, 1971.

Dodd, W. H. *Primary School Inspection in New Countries*. London: OUP, 1968.

Dore, R. *The Diploma Disease: Education Qualifications and Development*. London: Allen and Unwin, 1976.

Duffy, James. *Portuguese Africa*. London: Penguin, 1962.

Dunn, John (ed.). *West African States: Failure and Promise*. London: Cambridge University Press, 1978.

Duthie, George. "Education in Rhodesia,"*British South Africa Association for the Advancement of Science*, Vol. 4, 1905.

Emmerson, D. K. *Students and Politics in Developing Nations*. London: Pall Mall, 1968.

Farson, Negles. *Last Chance in Africa*. London. Gallant, 1949.

Faure, E. et al. *Learning To Be: The World of Education Today and Tomorrow*. Paris: UNESCO, 1972.

First, Ruth. *The Berrel of a Gun: Political Power in Africa and Coup d'Etat*. London: Allen and Unwin, 1970.

Franklin, Harry. *Unholy Wedlock: The Failure of the Central African Federation*. London: Allen and Unwin, 1963.

Fraser, Donald. *The Future of Africa*. London: British Missionary Society, 1911.

Freire, Paulo. *Pedagogy of the Oppressed*. New York: Continuum, 1983.

Gann, L. H. *Burden of Empire: An Appraisal of Western Civilization South of the Sahara*. Stanford, Calf.: Hoover Institute Press, 1977.

Gardener, R. (ed.). *Teacher Education in Developing Countries: Prospects for the Eighties*. London: University of London Institute of Education, 1979.

Geertz, C. (ed.). *The Quest for Modernity in Asia and Africa*. New York: Free Press, 1962.

Gifford, Prosser, and Loomis, William Roger (eds.). *The Transfer of Power in Africa: Decolonization, 1940 - 1960*. New Haven: Yale University Press, 1982.

Gray, J. H., and Cole, M. *The Cultural Context of Learning and Thinking*. London: Methuen, 1971.

Griffiths, W. F. *The Military in Africa*. London: Methuen, 1969.

Guason, Arthur. *Crisis in Africa: Battleground of East and West*. London: Penguin, 1981.

Hailey, W. M. *An African Survey: A Study of Problems Arising in Africa South of the Sahara*. London: Oxford University Press, 1957.

Hansen, J. W., and Brembeck, C. S. (eds.). *Education and the Development of Nations*. New York: Holt, Rinehart, and Winston, 1960.

Hapgood, David. *Africa in Today's World Focus*. New York: Gunn, 1971.

Harbison, F. H. *Human Resources Approach to the Development of Africa*. Washington, D. C.: American Council of Education, (n.d.).

Harden, Blaine. *Africa: Dispatches from a Fragile Continent*. New York: Norton, 1990.

Hargraves, John. *The End of the Colonial Rule in West Africa*. London: Macmillan, 1979.

Harztell, Joseph Crane. "The Future of Africa," *The African Advance* 12, no. 1 (July 1918).

Hawes, H. R. *Lifelong Education: Schools and the Curriculum in Developing Countries*. Hamburg: UNESCO, 1975.

Henderson, Lawrence. *Angola: Five Centuries of Conflict*. Ithaca N.Y.: Cornell University Press, 1979.

Huggins, Godfrey. *Education Policy in Southern Rhodesia: Some Notes on Certain Features*. Salisbury, Southern Rhodesia: Government Printer, 1939.

Ibingra, Grace. *African Upheavals Since Independence: January, 1960 - December, 1961*. Boulder, Colo. : Westview Press, 1980.

Irvine, S. H., and Sanders, J. L. (eds.). *Cultural Adaptation Within Modern Africa.*. New York: Teachers College Press, 1972.

Jollie, Ethel Towse . Speech in *Rhodesia: Parliamentary Debate*, 1927.

Jolly, R. (ed.). *Education in Africa: Research and Action*. Nairobi: East African Publishing House, 1969.

Jones, Trevor. *Ghana's First Republic, 1960-1966*. London: Methuen, 1976.

Joseph, David. *Ghana in Transition*. Princeton, N.J.: Princeton University Press, 1972.

July, Robert. *A History of the African People*. New York: Scribner, 1974.

Kabwasa, A., and Kaunda, M. (eds.). *Correspondence Education in Africa*. London: Routledge, 1973.

Kamarek, A. M. *The Economics of African Development*. New York: Praeger, 1973.

Kanza. Thomas. The Rise and Fall of Patrice Lumumba. London: Collins, 1978.

Kaunda, Kenneth. *Humanism in Zambia*. Lusaka: Zambia Information Services, 1967.

Kenyatta, Jomo. *Facing Mount Kenya*. London: Merverg Books, 1961.

La Guma, Alex (ed.). *Apartheid: A Collection of Writings of South Africa by South Africans* . New York: International Publishers, 1978.

Lewis, L.J. *Educational Policy and Practice in British Tropical Areas*. London: Nelson, 1954.

Livingstone, David. "Missionary Travels in Southern Africa, 1857-70," in the Zimbabwe National Archives.

Lloyd, P. C. (ed.). *The New Elite in Tropical Africa*. London: Oxford University Press, 1966.

Long, N. *An Introduction to the Sociology of Rural Development*. London: Tavistock, 1971.

Marquard, Leo. *The Peoples and Policies of South Africa*. New York: Oxford University Press, 1969.

Mason, Philip. *Year of Decision: Rhodesia and Nyasaland in 1960*. London: Oxford University Press, 1960.

Mazrui, Ali. *The African Condition*. London: Hinemann, 1980.

Meredith, Martin. *The First Dance of Freedom: Black Africa in the Post War Era*. New York: Harper and Row, 1984.

Mitchell, Philip. *African Afterthought*. London: Hutchinson, 1954.

Morris, James. *Farewell to Trumpets: An Imperial Retreat*. London: Faber, 1978.

Moumouni, A. *Education in Africa*. London: Deutsch, 1968.

Mugabe, Robert. Address to the Organization of African Unity. Freetown, Sierra Leone, July 2, 1980.

Mungazi, Dickson A. "Perceptions of Culture: The Basis of Human Understanding," Paper presented at the Black School Educators Conference, Las Vegas, Nevada, March 4-6, 1993.

Mungazi, Dickson A. "Crisis in Literacy in the World after the Second World War," Paper presented at the Literacy Volunteers of Coconino County Conference, Flagstaff, Arizona, October 23-24, 1992.

Mungazi, Dickson A. "Educational Innovation and National Development in Southern Africa: Defining Purpose to Shape New Directions," Paper presented at the National Social Science Conference, Orlando, Florida, November 12-14, 1992.

Mungazi, Dickson A. "Robert July, *A History of the African People*, 4th Edition: A Review," in *The International Journal of African Historical Studies*: Boston University, (26, 1B, 1993).

Mungazi, Dickson A. Janet Vaillant, *Black, French, and African: A Life of Leopold Sadar Senghor*. A Review in *Annals: The American Academy of Political and Social Science*, 524, November 1992.

Mungazi, Dickson A. "Africa in the Context of the Columbus Controversy," a documentary film, ref. NAU/CEE, Flagstaff: Northern Arizona University, September, 1992.

Mungazi, Dickson A. *Blaine Harden. Africa: Dispatches from a Fragile Continent:* A Review" in *Annals: The American Academy of Political and Social Science.* 522 (July, 1992).

Mungazi, Dickson A. "Problems of Education in Africa: Past, Present and Future," a documentary film, African Educators Institute, Ref. NAU/CEE,Flagstaff: Northern Arizona University, 1992.

Mungazi, Dickson. *International Education and the Search for Human Understanding.* Flagstaff, Center for Excellence in Education Monograph Series, No. 2. Northern Arizona University, 1991.

Mungazi, Dickson A. *The Cross Between Rhodesia and Zimbabwe: Racial Conflict in Rhodesia, 1962-1979.* New York: Vantage, 1981.

Mungazi, Dickson A. *The Underdevelopment of African Education: A Black Zimbabwean Perspective.* Washington, D.C.: UPA, 1982.

Mungazi, Dickson A. *To Honor the Sacred Trust of Civilization: History, Politics, and Education in Southern Africa.* Cambridge Ma.: Schenkman, 1983.

Mungazi, Dickson A. "Educational Innovation in Zimbabwe: Possibilities and Problems," in *The Journal of Negro Education,* 54, no. 2 (1985).

Mungazi, Dickson A. *The Struggle for Social Change in Southern Africa: Visions of Liberty.* New York: Taylor and Francis, 1989.

Mungazi, Dickson A. *Education and Government Control in Zimbabwe: A Study of the Commissions of Inquiry, 1908-1974.* New York: Praeger, 1990.

Mungazi, Dickson A. *Colonial Education for Africans: George Stark's Policy in Zimbabwe.* Westport, Conn.: Greenwood, 1991.

Mungazi, Dickson A. *Colonial Policy and Conflict in Zimbabwe: A Study of Cultures in Collision.* Washington, D.C: Taylor and Francis, 1991.

Mutumbuka, Dzingai, "Zimbabwe's Educational Challenge," Speech given at the World Universities Conference: London, 1979.

Oldham, James. *White and Black in Africa.* London: Longman, 1930.

Rhodesia Herald, June 28, 1912.

Scanlon, David. *Traditions of African Education.* New York: Teachers College Press, 1964.

SECO. *Educational Problems in Developing Countries.* Groningen: Walters Noordhoff, 1969.

Smith, William E. *Nyerere of Tanzania.* Harare: Zimbabwe Publishing House, 1982.

Southern Rhodesia. *Annual Report of the Chief Native Commissioner,* 1905.

Southern Rhodesia. Ordinance Number 18, 1899: The Appointment of Inspector of Education, 1899.

Spoulding, S. *Teacher Education: What Next ?* Paris: UNESCO 1970.

Thompson, A. R. *Education and Development in Africa.* New York: St. Martin's Press, 1982.

Wood, A. *Informal Education and Development in Africa.* The Hague: Mouton, 1974.

Young, Crawford. *Ideology and Development in Africa.* New Haven: Yale University Press, 1982.

JAPAN

Akio, Watanabe. *Government and Politics in Modern Japan.* Tokyo: University of Tokyo Press, 1985.

Allied Forces. *Post-war Development in Japanese Education.* Tokyo, 1952.

Asahi, Shimban, *The Japan Interpreter.* Tokyo: Shimba, 1974.

Berrien, F. K. *Selected Readings on Modern Japanese Society.* Berkeley: McCutchan Publishing Corporation, 1971.

Fukahama, M. "Students Expectations on Counseling: A Gross Cultural Study," in *Japanese Psychological Research* 15 (1973).

Hayashi, C. "Changes in Japanese Thought in the Past Twenty Years," in *Changing Japanese Values.* Tokyo: Institute of Statistics, 1970.

Hillenbrand, Barry. "America in the Mind of Japan," in *Time* (February 10, 1992).

Hurwitz, Nina. "Training the Japanese Teacher," in *The Japanese Times,* March 1969. International Society of Education. *Facts About Japan: Educational System.* Tokyo: Educational Information, 1989.

Japanese Ministry of Education. *Basic Guidelines for Reforming Education: Report of the Psychological Council for Education*. Tokyo: 1972.

Japanese Ministry of Education. *Case Studies in Lower Secondary Schools in Japan*. Tokyo, 1976.

Japanese Ministry of Foreign Affairs. Diplomatic Bluebook. Tokyo, 1989.

Japanese Ministry of Foreign Affairs. *Facts and Figures About Japan*. Tokyo, 1989.

"Japan's Classroom: Budding Blackboard Jungle," in *The New York Times* (March 13, 1982).

Kawasaki, I. *Japan Unasked*. Rutland: C. E. Tuttle, 1960.

Kazuo, Ishizaka. *School Education in Japan*. Tokyo: Dai-ichi Hoki, 1980.

Masahide, Bito, and Watanabe, Akio. *A Chronological Outline of Japanese History*. Tokyo: University of Tokyo Press, 1984.

Nakamura, H. *Ways of Thinking of Eastern People: Indian, China, Tibert, Japan*. Honolulu: East-West Press Center, 1964.

Negai, M. "Higher Education in a Free Society," in *Japanese Quarterly*, 24 (1975).

Neumeyer, C. "High School Counseling in Japan," in *Personnel and Guidance Journal*. 96 (1976).

Sabirou, I. Bymnastic *Lessons in the German Democratic Republic and Japan*. 46 (1974).

Sakamoto, Y. *A Study of Japanese National Character*. Tokyo: Institute of Statistics, 1977.

Shigehiko, Masukawa. *Supply and Demand for Energy in Japan*. Tokyo: Dentsu, 1986.

Singulo, J. *Nichu: A Japanese School*. New York: Holt, Rinehart and Winston, 1967.

Sizuki, T. "A Study of the Japanese National," in *Annuals of the Institute of Statistical Mathematics*. Tokyo: Institute of Statistics, 1970.

Takafusa, Nakamura. *Economic Development of Modern Japan*. Tokyo: Ministry of Foreign Affairs, 1985.

Takeshi, Hiromatsu. *Japan's Economic Development*. Tokyo: International Educational Information, 1989.

"The Test Must Go On," in *Time* (March 12, 1982).

Tsujimura, A. "Gendai Shakai: Ronin," in *Gakukoza*. Tokyo: Tokyo University Press, 1971.

UNESCO *Courses of Study in Elementary Schools in Japan*. Paris: 1976.

UNESCO, *Education and Cultural Exchange*. Paris, 1976.

Yamamura, K., and Manley, S. "Echihimeni: Toros Educational Aspirations and the Decline of Fertility in Post-war Japan," in *The Journal of Japanese Studies*. 2 (1975).

Yutaka, Tazawa. Japan's *Cultural History: A Perspective*. Tokyo: Ministry of Foreign Affairs, 1990.

UNITED STATES

Adler, Mortimer J. (ed.). *The Paideia Proposal: An Educational Manifesto*. New York: Collier Macmillan, 1982.

Anderson, Ronald. "Japanese Education," in Ignas, Edward, and Corsini, Raymond (eds.). *Comparative Educational Systems*. Itasca, Ill.: F. E. Peacock, 1982.

Bayh, B. *Challenge for the Third Century: Education in a Safe Environment: Final Report on the Nature and Presentation of School Violence and Vandalism*. Washington, D.C.: U.S. Government Printing Office, 1977.

Berg, J. Otto. "America Faces a Choice." Lecture to a graduate class in education at Northern Arizona University, December 3, 1992.

Bill Clinton, Man of the Year: The Torch Is Passed in *Time* (January 4, 1993.

Bloom, B. *Human Characteristics and Learning in School*. New York: McGraw-Hill, 1976.

Bruner, J. S. *The Process of Education*. Cambridge, Ma.: Harvard University Press, 1960.

Clark, C. B. "Why Educational Technology Is Failing," in *Educational Technology* (1979).

Clinton, Bill. *Putting People First: A National Economic Strategy for America*. Little Rock.: Clinton for President Committee, 1992.

Coleman, J. S. *Equality of Educational Opportunity*. Washington, D.C.: U.S. Office of Education, 1966.

Corsini, Raymond, and Ignas, Edward. *Alternatives to Educational Systems*. Itasca, Ill.: F. E. Peacock, 1979.

Corsini, Raymond and Edward Ignas (eds.). *Comparative Educational Systems*. Itasca, Ill.: F. E. Peacock, 1982.

Cubberley, E. P. *Changing Concepts of Education*. Boston: Houghton Mifflin, 1909.

Dewey, John. *Experience and Education*, New York: Collier, 1964.

Fantini, M. D. *Alternative Education*. Garden City, New York: Doubleday, 1976.

Feinberg, Walter, and Soltis, Jonas. *School and Society*. New York: Teachers College Press, 1985.

Grayson, K."Human Life vs. Science," in Thomas Weaver (ed.). *To See Ourselves: Anthropology and Modern Social Issues*. Glenville, Ill.: Scott and Foresman, 1973.

Gutek, Gerald. *American Education in a Global Society: Internationalizing Teacher Education*. New York: Longman, 1993.

Gutek, Gerald. *An Historical Introduction to American Education*. Prospect Heights, Ill.: Waveland Press, 1991.

Jarolimek, John. *The Schools in Contemporary Society: An Analysis of Social Currents Issues and Focus*. New York: Macmillan, 1981.

Keyes, R. *Is There Life After High School?* New York: Warner Books, 1976.

Kliebard, Herbert. *The Struggle for the American Curriculum, 1893-1958*. New York: Routledge and Kegan Paul, 1987.

Luria, A. R. *Cognitive Development: Its Cultural and Social Foundations*. New York: Longman, 1989.

McLaren, Peter. *Life in Schools: An Introduction to Critical Pedagogy in the Foundations of Education*. New York: Longman, 1989.

Mungazi, Dickson A. "Crisis in Literacy in the World after the Second World War." (Paper presented at the Literacy Volunteers of Coconino County, Flagstaff, Arizona, October 23-24, 1992.

Mungazi, Dickson A. "The March to the Promised Land: The Progress of Black Education in the U.S., 1875-1975." Paper written for graduate class: University of Nebraska, 1975.

Mungazi, Dickson A. "Education and the Quest for Human Completion: The African and Afro-American Perspectives Compared," in *ERIC Clearinghouse for Social Studies and Social Science Education.* ref. Ed 292/713/MF01/PCO2. Bloomington: Indiana University, 1987.

Nasaw, David. *Schooled to Order: A Social History of Public Schooling in the United States.* New York: Oxford University Press, 1979.

National Commission on Excellence in Education. *A Nation at Risk: The Imperative for Educational Reform.* Washington, D.C.: Government Printing Office, 1983.

Peirce, Neal. "Obstacles to Change in Schools," in *The Arizona Republic*: (October 16, 1989).

Perkinson, Henry. *The Imperfect Panacea: American Faith in Education.* New York: Random House, 1979.

Pulliman, John D. *History of Education in America.* New York: Macmillan, 1991.

Scully, John. "America's Choice," in *USA Today* (December 15, 1992).

Shane, H. G. *Curriculum Change: Toward the 21st Century.* Washington, D.C.: National Education Association, 1977.

Shields, James, and Greer, Colin. *Foundations of Education: Dissenting Views.* New York: Wiley, 1974.

Spring, Joel. *American Education: An Introduction to Social and Political Aspects.* New York: Longman, 1985.

Til, William van. *Education: A Beginning.* Boston: Houghton Mifflin Company, 1974.

Ulich, Robert (ed.). *Education and the Idea of Mankind.* Chicago: University of Chicago Press, 1964.

Woodring, Paul. *Introduction to American Education.* New York: Harcourt, Brace, 1965.

SOVIET UNION

Azarov, Yuri. *Teaching: Calling and Skills*. Moscow: Progress Press, 1988.

Beleya, Larisa. *They Will Live in the 21st Century*. Moscow: Novosti Press, 1989.

Brezhnev, Leonid. *Following Lenin's Course*. Moscow: CPU, 1972.

Burganov, Agdas. *Perestroika and the Concept of Socialism*. Moscow: Novosti Press, 1990.

Communist Party. *The Country and its People*. Moscow: Novosti Press, 1989.

Communist Party. *A Look into the Future*. Moscow: Novosti Press, 1989.

Communist Party. *The Honor of the Uniform or the Honor of the Army: The October Revolutionary Perestroika*. Moscow: Novosti Press, 1990.

Communist Party. *On Perestroika*. Moscow: Novosti Press, 1990.

Communist Party. *Pages of History: A Time of Difficult Questions*. Moscow: Novosti Press, 1990.U. S. R. R. *Perestroika*. Moscow: Novosti Press, 1990.

Communist Party. *The Renewal of the Party Is the Key to the Success of Perestroika*. Moscow: Novosti Press, 1990.

Communist Party. *Socialism: Theory and Practice*. Moscow: Novosti Press, 1990.

Communist Party Conference. *Through the Eyes of Its Delegates*. Moscow: Novosti Press, 1988.

Gorbachev, Mikhail. *Channel the Energy of Youth into Perestroika*. Speech delivered to the All-Union Student Forum, November 15, 1989, Moscow: Novosti, 1989.

Gorbachev, Mikhail. *Towards a Humane and Democratic Socialist Society*. Moscow. Novosti Press, 1990.

Gorbachev, Mikhail. *Political Report of the Central Committee to the 28th SPSU Congress and the Party's Tasks*. Moscow: Novosti Press, 1990.

Gorbachev, Mikhail. *Report to the Congress of the People's Deputies of the U.S.S.R.* Moscow: Novosti Press, 1989.

Gorbachev, Mikhail. *Speech to the People's Deputies,* March, 1990.

"Gorbachev's Darkest Hour," in *Time*, December 31, 1990.

Grant, Nigel. *Soviet Education.* London: Penguin, 1979.

Hasbulatov, Ruslan. *Perestroika as Seen by an Economist.* Moscow: Novosti Press, 1989.

Holmes, Brian. "Education in the U.S.S.R.," in Igans, Edward, and Corsini, Raymond (eds.). *Comparative Educational Systems.* Itasca, Ill.: F. E. Peacock, 1982.

Isayev, I. *National Language in the U.S.S.R.: problems and Solutions.* Moscow: Progress Press, 1979.

Kamentsev, Vladimir. *Economic Ties: A Prerequisite of Lasting Peace.* Moscow: Novosti Press, 1988.

Krupskaya, N., K. *Education.* Moscow: Foreign Language Publishing House, 1957.

Kuzin, N. and Kondokov, M. *Education in the U.S.S.R.* Moscow: Progress Press, 1977.

Lenin, Vladimir. *Articles on Tolstoy.* Moscow: Foreign Language Publishing House, 1959.

Lisichkin, Gennadi. *Socialism: An Appraisal of Prospects.* Moscow: Novosti press, 1989.

Maiseyev, Nikita. *Perestroika as Seen by a Mathematician.* Moscow: Novosti Press, 1989.

McLevush, John. *Soviet Psychology: History, Theory, and Content.* London: Methuen, 1975.

"The New Russia: The Winter of Discontent," *Time* (December 7), 1992.

Pearson, London. *Children of Glasnost: Growing up Soviet.* Seattle: University of Washington Press, 1990.

Second Congress of the People's Deputies. *On the Politics and Legal Assessment of the Soviet-German Non-Aggression Treaty of 1939.* Moscow: Novosti Press, 1990.

Sobolev, Leonid. *The Law Will Become the Arbitor*. Moscow: Novosti Press, 1990.

Soviet Monthly Digest. *Socialism: Theory and Practice*. Moscow: Novosti Press, 1990.

Strelikov, Vladimir. *The Judge and the Court: Guarantees of Interference*. Moscow: Novosti Press, 1989.

Strezikon, V. "The Soviet Union," in Lauwerys, J. A., and Scanlon, David. *Examinations: World Year Book of Education*. London: Evans, 1969.

Sukhomlinsky, Vasily. *On Education*. Moscow: Progress Press, 1977.

Tikhonov, Vladimir. *Perestroika Through the Eyes of a Cooperator*. Moscow: Novosti Press, 1990.

Yagodin, Gennadi. *Towards Higher Standards in Education Through Its Humanization and Democratization*. Moscow: Novosti Press, 1989.

Yakovlev, Alexander. *Development of Democracies Is Imperative for the Renewal of Society*. Moscow: Novosti Press, 1989.

Yakovlev, Alexander. *The Events of 1939: Looking Back after Fifty Years*. Moscow: Novosti Press, 1989.

Yesipov, B. P., and Gonoshorov, N. K."For Bolshevik Character: The Principles of Moral Education," in *I Want to Be Like Lenin*. London: Victor Gallant, 1984.

Zinovyev, M., and Pleshokova, A. *How Illiteracy Was Wiped Out in the U.S.S.R.* Moscow: Language Publishing House, 1981.

Name Index

Subject Index

About the Author

DICKSON A. MUNGAZI is Professor of Educational Foundations and History of Southern Africa at Northern Arizona University in Flagstaff.